Accounting for Anyone

Wayne S. Boutell

PRENTICE-HALL, INC. / Englewood Cliffs, New Jersey 07632

Library of Congress Cataloging in Publication Data

Boutell, Wayne S.
Accounting for everyone.

Includes index.
1. Accounting. I. Title.
HF5635.B78115 657 81-22737
ISBN 0-13-001602-0 AACR2

Printed in the United States of America

10 9 8 7 6 5 4

ISBN 0-13-001602-0

Prentice-Hall International, Inc., *London*
Prentice-Hall of Australia Pty. Limited, *Sydney*
Prentice-Hall of Canada, Ltd., *Toronto*
Prentice-Hall of India Private Limited, *New Delhi*
Prentice-Hall of Japan, Inc., *Tokyo*
Prentice-Hall of Southeast Asia Pte. Ltd., *Singapore*
Whitehall Books Limited, *Wellington, New Zealand*

This book is dedicated to:

Dante, Tai, Julianna and Nicole Boutell,
members of our next generation who also
will need to understand financial statements.

Contents

Preface

This is a guide to financial statements as seen from the users' point of view. In fact, anyone who uses financial information may find this book useful: business owners and managers, financial professionals, investors, suppliers, creditors, members of the federal and state governments, unions, conservationists, and the public at large. Anyone may benefit who has a vital interest in the information flowing from our business firms in the form of published annual reports, press releases to the news media, and quarterly reports of operations.

Despite their vital interest in financial information, many users are frankly unaware of the accounting process and of the resultant output in the form of published financial statements. Even in the more sophisticated journals and newspapers, misleading statements often create erroneous impressions and lead to incorrect financial decisions.

Familiarity with the accounting process can help you to avoid such pitfalls, and perhaps even provide you with a sound foundation for a career, whatever it might turn out to be. After working your way through the exercises in this book, you will have a better understanding of financial statements and their interpretation. Although the objective is not to make an accountant out of you, you may feel that, after completing this material, you would like to pursue an accounting career. In such a case, you have many alternate paths available to you, including taking courses or additional study on your own.

Just to familiarize you at first, however, we start with the concept of financial statements in their most general sense. We then explore the various aspects of the accounting model in some detail, returning to the concept of financial statements and how to interpret them from a user's point of view.

This book is unique in several ways. It is the only book of its kind to include actual examples from published financial statements.

* It features extensive, substantive problem material, along with three Progress Tests to test comprehension of the basic materials.
* It is up-to-date and includes a comprehensive coverage of the latest pronouncements of the Financial Accounting Standards Board with respect to constant dollar accounting (inflation accounting).
* It also includes a comprehensive glossary of 200 words relating to financial statements.
* Complete solutions, detailing the answers to every problem, follow each chapter or Progress Test.

Although the book is designed for self-study, it can also be used as a supplement to more advanced accounting texts, such as Horngren's *Introduction to Financial Accounting*. It is written in a straightforward manner, easily understandable even by someone who has never seen an accounting textbook. This book fills a gap in the accounting literature that has existed for some time.

The original idea for this book was based on a need perceived by the Student Learning Center at the campus of the University of California, Berkeley, for basic accounting material required by students struggling with a very fast-moving course in financial accounting. The result was the development of an accounting study manual funded by a University of California Student Learning Center Faculty Mento Program Grant. The Student Learning Center, responsible for academic skills development programs for Berkeley's undergraduates, used the accounting study manual in Learning Center workshops designed to give students, enrolled in Business Administration 1 (Introduction to Financial Accounting), extra practice in working accounting problems. Tutors and students gave valuable suggestions for additions to the manual.

The author wishes to thank the tutors: Hugh Wesley Goodwin, Monica Renee Lee, Raymond Change Lee, David Rosenberg, John Strittmatter, and Philip K. Yu for their help and especially their supervisor, Ms. Rainy Rust, who coordinated the entire effort.

Particular thanks and recognition goes to George Perko, one of our doctoral candidates in accounting, for his writing of Chapter 20 on "Time and Money." Andy Goldsmith, another, doctoral candidate in accounting, provided, a portion of the problem material. William P. Enderlein, Dean of the Graduate School of Golden Gate University, rendered invaluable assistance in reviewing and critiquing the original manuscript. Finally, recognition must be given to all those students, faced with their first course in financial accounting, who raised the question that I have attempted to answer in this book. Any errors or omissions are those of the author alone.

Wayne S. Boutell

Berkeley, California

1
The Balance Sheet

What is a balance sheet? It is a couple of things. For one, it is a "snapshot" of a business' financial situation at a *particular moment of time,* usually as of the close of business on the last business day of the month. All entities, whether for profit or not-for-profit, prepare balance sheets at the end of their fiscal (or accounting) year. Accordingly, a balance sheet always carries a *single date,* such as "December 31, 1981." A balance sheet is also an inventory of Assets (which you typically find on the left-hand side of the balance sheet) and an enumeration of the claims against those assets (on the right-hand side). The total of Assets on the left-hand side must always equal the total of claims on the right-hand side. (See Figure 1-1.)

So a balance sheet always "balances." Here's why. The list of assets on the left represents what the business entity owns. On the right-hand side, all those Assets are offset either by Liabilities or by Owners' equity. If the asset has been mortgaged or pledged as a loan guarantee, then the lender has a legitimate claim on that asset. Such a claim is called a *Liability.* On the other hand, if

FIGURE 1-1

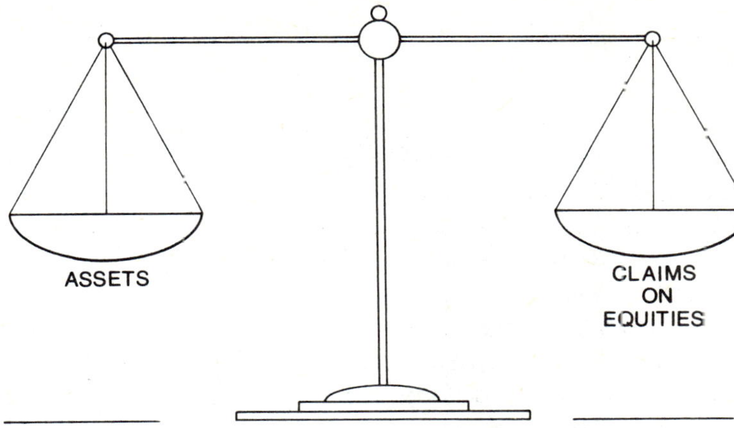

the asset has no claim against it, then it is considered the property of the business entity's owners—or *Owners' equity.* To put it another way, the owners have an equity interest in the business equal to the total of these "free-and-clear" assets. So owners' equity is the concept of *residual equity*, that is, whatever portion of the assets are left over after deducting the claims of the creditors. We can characterize this relationship by the following equation, which is called the *balance sheet equation*:

(1) Assets − Liabilities = Owners' equity

Notice also the equation 1 can also be rearranged algebraically to read:

(2) Assets = Liabilities + Owners' equity

This form of the equation is the most useful one in visualizing a balance sheet, because it is identical to the diagram in Figure 1-1.

EXERCISE 1-1*

Part of the balance sheet that was given to you by your roommate was obliterated because you spilled coffee on it. You can just barely make out that the total amount of assets is $760, and that the amount of the shareholder's (owner's) equity is $460. What is the total amount of the liabilities on the balance sheet?

$ 300

To better understand the balance sheet, let's define those basic terms a little more clearly:

**Note*: Answers to all exercises may be found at the ends of their respective chapters. For example, the answer to this exercise is on page 11.

* assets,
* liabilities, and
* owners' equity.

An *asset* is an economic resource of a business entity (a) that is expected to benefit future activities and (b) that is *measurable.* Take, for example, a business' delivery van. Such a vehicle meets both tests of an asset: (1) It is an economic resource that is expected to benefit future activities; and (b) it is measurable in the sense that it can be listed in the inventory of assets at the cost for which it was originally acquired. But now let's suppose that we have built up a thriving business based on the reputation for prompt service and top-quality merchandise. Let's call that business, "Wayne's Trains." That reputation meets one test of an asset, because it is an economic resource that should benefit future operations. But it fails the other test because it is *not measurable.* So it would not be listed as an *asset.*

EXERCISE 1-2

Circle any of all the items that would be considered assets according to our definition:

Amounts payable to banks	**Amounts due from customers**
Owner's equity	**Unpaid telephone bill**
Cash	**Wages paid to employees**
Mortgage on home	**Rent paid in advance**
Items purchased for resale	**Insurance premium paid in advance**
Delivery truck	**This book**

Now let's focus on your personal balance sheet. If you, as a student, were listing your assets, you might have: cash in your pocket, $25 (an asset); some jogging shoes, $35 (an asset); a stereo system, $350 (an asset); some textbooks, $75 (an asset); some evidence of your good grades, say, a transcript from the registrar (not an asset). On the right-hand side of your balance sheet you must first list the claims of creditors against your assets—or your *liabilities.* If you paid only **$50** in cash for the stereo system and placed the balance of **$300** on your credit card, you have created a liability of **$300.** So your personal balance sheet equation would look like this:

(1a) Assets ($25 + $35 + $350 + $75) – Liabilities ($300) = Onwers' equity ($185)

Or equivalently:

(2a) $\$25 + \$35 + \$350 + \$75 = \$300 + \$185$

This simple calculation appears in balance sheet form in Figure 1-2. Now try making up the balance sheet in Exercise 1-3.

FIGURE 1-2. A student's balance sheet

Owners Equity is equal to net Worth.

An Accounting Student
BALANCE SHEET
Today's Date

Asset		*Liabilities and Owner's Equity*	
Cash	$ 25	Liability	
Books	75	Due to Credit Card Co.	$300
Stereo	350		
Shoes	35	Owner's Equity:	
		An accounting student	185
Total assets	$485	Total equitites	$485

EXERCISE 1-3

In the space provided below, prepare a classified balance sheet from the following information for your friend as of January 31, 19XX:

Cash	$ 70
Bicycle	$ 90
Due to finance company	$ 60
Books	$ 25
Proprietorship	$150
Dress shoes	$ 25

A Friend
BALANCE SHEET
January 31, 19XX

Assets			*Liabilities and Owner's Equity*	
Current Assets:			Current Liabilities:	
Cash		$ 70	Due to Finance Company	$ 60
Property, Plant, and Equipment:			Owner's Equity:	
Bicycle	$ 90		A friend	150
Books	25			
Shoes	25	$ 140		
Total		$ 210	Total	$ 210

One further point: on the balance sheet, assets are usually listed from the most current to the least current. So cash would be listed first. On the balance sheet presented in Figure 1-2, cash should be listed first, which it is. Books are listed next, due to their trade-in value at the end of the school term. Although the stereo has a resale value, you do not intend to trade it in but to enjoy it. So it is less current than the books, which certainly will be converted into cash in less than six months. Finally, we list the jogging shoes because they have the least possibility of ever being turned into cash; they will simply be used until they wear out. Correspondly, we characteristically list the claims to assets (the Liabilities) in order of payment, that is, according to when they are due. The most immediate are listed first. Finally, the residual equity, the last group of items on the right-hand side, include the Owner's equity items.

EXERCISE 1-4

Here are some more difficult items to use in constructing a balance sheet as of June 30, 19XX for the Green Eye Shade Company:

Owner's equity	$7,500
Bank overdraft	$ 200
Amounts due from customers	$ 950
Warehouse and office building	$6,000
Prepaid insurance	$ 150
Items purchased for resale	$ 900
Accounts payable	$ 300

Green Eye Shade Company
BALANCE SHEET
June 30, 19XX

Assets			*Liabilities and Owner's Equity*		
Current Assets:			**Current Liabilities:**		
Accounts receivable	$ 950		Bank overdraft	$ 200	
Items purchased for resale	900		Accounts payable	300	$ 500
Prepaid insurance	150	$ 2000			
Property, Plant, and Equipment:			**Owner's Equity:**		
Warehouse and office Building		6000	Owner's equity (No detail provided in the problem)		7500
		$ 8000			$ 8000

To give you a little better idea of how an actual balance sheet looks, Figure 1-3 presents the balance sheet of The Institute of

FIGURE 1-3. A representative balance sheet

The Institute of Internal Auditors, Inc.

Balance Sheets
May 31, 1980 and 1979

ASSETS

	1980	1979
CURRENT ASSETS:		
Cash, including savings deposits of $55,759 in 1980 and $140,472 in 1979	$ 398,262	$ 242,659
Certificates of deposit and U.S. Government securities, at cost which approximates market (Note 4)	1,305,156	795,012
Accounts receivable, less allowance of $21,500 in 1980 and $55,000 in 1979 for doubtful accounts	189,881	163,019
Prepaid expenses and advances	39,876	30,022
Publication inventory (Note 1)	124,598	121,260
Total current assets	2,057,773	1,351,972
DEFERRED PROJECTS (Note 1)	42,174	40,385
PROPERTY AND EQUIPMENT, at cost (Note 1):		
Land	197,125	197,125
Buildings and improvements	962,368	956,739
Furniture and equipment	290,908	281,943
	1,450,401	1,435,807
Less — Accumulated depreciation	(270,814)	(196,609)
	1,179,587	1,239,198
	$3,279,534	$2,631,555

LIABILITIES AND MEMBERSHIP EQUITY

	1980	1979
CURRENT LIABILITIES:		
Current portion of mortgage note payable	$ 8,945	$ 8,178
Accounts payable and accrued expenses (Notes 2 and 3)	680,643	483,629
Deferred income (Note 1)	579,371	415,758
Total current liabilities	1,268,959	907,565
9% MORTGAGE NOTE PAYABLE, due in monthly installments of $3,073 through 1996, less current portion, collateralized by land, buildings and improvements	305,397	314,342
MEMBERSHIP EQUITY	1,705,178	1,409,648
	$3,279,534	$2,631,555

The accompanying notes are an integral part of these balance sheets.

Internal Auditors, Inc., the national organization of internal auditors. Note that, on the left-hand side, this balance sheet follows the general classification rule in that Current assets (that is, items to be converted into cash during one year) are listed first. Then comes the Deferred projects classification, which represents funds invested in research projects that will result in publications to be sold to members in the future. Finally, Property and equipment is similar to our stereo equipment in Figure 1-2.

On the right-hand side of this balance sheet, Current liabilities—those liabilities that must be paid within the coming twelve months—are listed first. Next is the mortgage, which will be paid off completely in 1996. And, finally, Membership equity represents the arithmetic difference between the total of all the assets listed less the totals of all the liabilities.

The information contained in balance sheets may be interpreted in many ways. If you just can't wait to find out how balance sheets can be used, you might want to go now to Chapter 18 before continuing with the balance sheet exercises.

Note: At the end of each chapter we present Additional Exercises, which you should complete before proceeding to the next topic. Their solutions to be found immediately after these exercises, so you can compare your results with those provided by the author. Accounting is a problem-oriented discipline, and you must work the problems to fully understand the concepts presented. So work *all* the exercises!

ADDITIONAL EXERCISES

1-5. Complete the following balance sheet:

Saturday Night Fever, Inc.
BALANCE SHEET
September 30, 19XX

Assets		*Liabilities and Stockholders' + Equities*	
Current Assets:		**Current Liabilities:**	
Cash	$ 800	Notes payable to banks	$4,000
Amounts due from customers	900	Wages payable	3,000
Items purchased for resale	1,500	Taxes payable	1,500
Prepaid Insurance	300	Total current liabilities	$8500
Total current assets	$3500		
Equipment:		Stockholders' Equity:	$4500
Machinery	$8,000		
Automobile	1,500		
Total equipment	$9500		
Total assets	$13000	Total equities	$13000

1-6. Listed in random order on the right below are the titles of *assets* from the preceding five exercises. Rank these assets in the order they would normally appear on the balance sheet, using the answer blanks on the left. The most current asset would be on line a, and the least current asset on the last line. Indicate also the classification:

CA = Current asset
PPE = Property, plant, and equipment
O = Other asset

a. Cash CA	Warehouse building
b. Amount due from Custo. CA	Shoes
c. Item held for resale CA	Amount due from customer
d. Prepaid insurance CA	Bicycle
e. Perpaid rent CA	Books
O	f. Books	Automobile
O	g. This Book	Prepaid insurance
PPE	h. Bicycle	Prepaid rent
O	i. Shoes	Delivery truck
PPE	j. Automobile	This book
PPE	k. Delivery truck	Cash
PPE	l. Ware House Build.	Items held for resale

1-7. Review the following list of asset, liability, and shareholders' accounts:

Note order of arrangement.

Assets

a. Current assets
b. Property, plant, and equipment
c. Other assets

Liabilities

d. Current liabilities
e. Noncurrent liabilities

Stockholders' Equity

f. Contributed capital
g. Retained earnings

Now classify the following balance sheet items by placing the category letter ("a" for Current assets, and so on) in the answer blanks provided:

____ Capital stock

____ Inventories (items purchased for resale)

____ Accounts receivable (amounts due from customers)

____ Notes payable to banks (6-month maturity)

____ Furniture and fixtures

____ Earnings retained in the business

____ Mortgage payable

____ Patents

____ Cash (earmarked for future construction of building)

____ Accrued royalties payable

1-8. On a separate piece of lined paper, prepare a classified balance sheet for the Bay Shore Corporation from the following information as of September 30, 19XX:

Cash	$10,000
Capital stock	$50,000
Notes payable (long-term)	$ 5,000
Accounts receivable	$15,000
Inventories	$25,000
Gas pumps	$30,000
Gas storage tanks	$50,000
Franchise from Glutted Oil, Inc.	$ 5,000
Wages payable	$ 5,000
Francise fees payable	$10,000
Accounts payable	$25,000
Retained earnings	$40,000

1-9. For the balance sheet of the Bay Shore Corporation developed in Exercise 1-8, derive the following ratios:

Current ratio $= \frac{\text{Current assets}}{\text{Current liabilities}} =$ ____

Long-term debt to equity ratio $= \frac{\text{Noncurrent liabilities}}{\text{Stockholders' equities}} =$ ____

Quick asset ratio $= \frac{\text{Cash + Accounts receivable}}{\text{Current liabilities}} =$ ____

1-10. Complete the following balance sheet. Note that brackets indicate a deduction.

Quiet Disco, Inc.
BALANCE SHEET
August 31, 19XX

Assets		*Liabilities and Stockholders' Equity*		
Current Assets:		*Current Liabilities:*		
Cash	$ 4000	Due to irate customers		$ 7,000
Records for sale	10,000	Ticket refunds requested		8,000
Prepaid insurance	5,000	Wages payable		4,000
Earplugs for sale	1,000	Royalties payable		9,000
	20,000			$28,000
Operational Assets:		Noncurrent Liabilities:		
Record player equipment (5 watts output)	$10,000	Mortgage on stereo equipment		$10,000
Other Assets:		Stockholders' Equity:		
Patent on low-volume speakers	5,000	Capital Stock	$1,000	
		Retained earnings (deficit)	($4,000)	($3,000)
Total assets	$ 35000	Total liabilities and stockholders' equity		$ 35000

SOLUTIONS

1-1. $760 – $460 = $300

1-2. Cash, Items purchased for resale, Delivery truck, Amounts due from customers, Rent paid in advance, Insurance premium paid in advance, This book

1.3.

A Friend
BALANCE SHEET
January 31, 19XX

Assets			*Liabilities and Owner's Equity*	
Current Assets:			Current Liabilities:	
Cash		$ 70	Due to Finance Company	$ 60
Property, Plant, and Equipment:			Owner's Equity:	
Bicycle	$90		A friend	150
Books	25			
Shoes	25	$140		
		$210		$210

1-4.

Green Eye Shade Company
BALANCE SHEET
June 30, 19XX

Assets			*Liabilities and Owners' Equity*		
Current Assets:			Current Liabilities:		
Accounts receivable	$950		Bank overdraft	$200	
Items purchased for resale	900		Accounts payable	300	$ 500
Prepaid insurance	150	$2,000			
Property, Plant, and Equipment:			Owner's Equity:		
Warehouse and office building		6,000	Owner's equity (No detail provided in the problem)		7,500
		$8,000			$8,000

1-5.

Total current assets	$ 3,500	Total current liabilities	$ 8,500
Equipment	$ 9,500	*Stockholders' equity*	$ 4,500
Total assets	$13,000	Total equities	$13,000

1-6. a. Cash (CA)
b. Amount due from customer (CA)
c. Items held for resale (CA)
d. This book (CA, hopefully)
e. Prepaid rent (CA)
f. Prepaid insurance (CA)
g. Bicycle (PPE)
h. Automobile (PPE)
~~i. Machinery (PPE)~~
j. Warehouse building (PPE)
k. Delivery truck (PPE)
l. Books (O)
m. Shoes (O)

In g through i, other rankings are possible.

1-7. *F* Capital stock
A Inventories (items purchased for resale)
A Accounts receivable (amounts due from customers)
D Notes payable to banks (6-month maturity)
B Furniture and fixtures
G Earnings retained in business
E Mortgage payable
C Patents
B Cash (as restricted)
D Accrued royalties payable

1-8.

Bay Shore Corporation
BALANCE SHEET
September 30, 19XX

Assets			*Liabilities and Stockholders' Equity*		
Current Assets:			Current Liabilities:		
Cash	$10,000		Wages payable	$ 5,000	
Accounts receivable	15,000		Franchise payable	10,000	
Inventories	25,000	$ 50,000	Accounts payable	25,000	$ 40,000
Property, Plant, and Equipment:			Noncurrent Liabilities:		
Gas pumps	30,000		Notes payable		5,000
Gas storage tanks	50,000				
Franchise	5,000	$ 85,000	Stockholders' Equity:		
			Capital stock	50,000	
			Retained earnings	40,000	90,000
		$135,000			$135,000

1-9. Current ratio = $50,000/$40,000 = 1.25/1

Long-term debt to equity ratio = $5,000/$90,000 = 0.06/1

Quick asset ratio = ($10,000 + $15,000)/$40,000 = 0.63/1

1-10. Cash $ 4,000
Total assets $35,000 Total liabilities and equity $35,000

2
The Income Statement

You have heard the expression, "The bottom line is ———." Or you have been asked the question, "What's the bottom line?" Of course, this expression refers simply to the last line on the income statement, which has many aliases, such as:

* the statement of income,
* the earnings statement,
* the statement of earnings, or
* the profit and loss statement.

All these titles mean the same thing. But for the sake of convenience, we will refer simply to the "income statement."

What is an income statement? First of all, *unlike* a balance sheet, it is *not* a "snapshot" of a business entity at one moment of time. Rather it depicts the results of revenue received over a given time, along with the expenses related to that revenue over the same period. The comparison of the revenues and expenses yields the amount of net income the business made over the period covered by the statement. Essentially, the income statement is summed up by the following equation:

Net income (The bottom line) = Revenues – Expenses

The revenue realized over a year is quite obviously different from the revenue realized over just one month. So it is extremely important that the period covered by the income statement is clearly stated, such as, "For the year ended September 30, 19XX or "August 1, 19X0 through September 30, 19X1." The income statement for a single month would have a heading something like:

A Company
INCOME STATEMENT
For the Month of November, 19X1

A second convention of the income statement is that its entries are usually divided into classifications to make it easier to understand (Figure 2-1). Major classifications would include:

Revenues	Revenues (or Sales) less
Less: Expenses	Cost of goods sold less Gross margin less Operating expenses equals Operating income (or Profit) less Income taxes equals
Equal: Net income	Net income (The bottom line)

A Lawyer
INCOME STATEMENT
Year Ended August 31, 19XX

Fees received from clients		$47,000
Operating Expenses:		
Office rental	$6,000	
Stationery	500	
Car expense	1,500	
Insurance expense	800	
Miscellaneous	200	9,000
Net Income		$38,000

FIGURE 2-1. An income statement.

First fill in the prepared income statement in Exercise 2-1. Then try your hand at drafting an income statement using your own format from the data given in Exercise 2-2.

EXERCISE 2-1

Prepare an income statement for the BusAdOne Corp. from the following data for the calendar year 19XX: Sales of old exams, $75; Sales of typed lecture notes, $85; Cost of reproductions of lecture notes and exams, $20; Cost of renting typewriter, $10; Advertising costs, $30; Bad debts, $5; Miscellaneous expenses, $15; Income taxes paid, $25.

BusAdOne Corp.
INCOME STATEMENT
Year Ended December 31, 19XX

Sales:		$______
Cost of Goods Sold:		______
Gross margin		______
Operating expenses:		
Typewriter rental	$______	
Advertising	______	
Bad debts and miscellaneous	______	______
Operating income		______
Income Taxes:		______
Net income		$______

EXERCISE 2-2

Complete the following income statement from the information taken from the books of Goody Wuthrie, Inc. for the fiscal year ended September 30, 19XX:

Sales of sheet music and records	$130,000
Returns of unsold records	$ 10,000
Administrative expenses	$ 15,000
Selling expenses	$ 25,000
Cost of sheet music sold	$ 30,000
Cost of records sold	$ 20,000
Income taxes paid	$ 5,000
Cost of shipping records	$ 1,000

A fairly common practice is to relate the various components of the income statement not in absolute but rather in relative terms. But "relative" to what? When we say we are running at a "40-percent Gross margin" or "20-percent Operating expenses," these items must represent percentages of some one constant amount. In other words, there must be a common denominator for expressing all these relationships, and that common denominator is *Net sales.*

Net sales may be defined as Gross sales less all returns, allowances, and discount. So a 40-percent Gross margin implies the following simple calculation:

$$\frac{\text{Gross margin (\$)}}{\text{Net sales (\$)}} = \text{Gross margin (\%)}$$

Or 20-percent Operating expenses then means:

$$\frac{\text{Operating expenses (\$)}}{\text{Net sales (\$)}} = \text{Operating expense (\%)}$$

Expressing income statement relationships in percentages has an additional advantage: you can compare income statement items from one firm to another, even though the sales volumes may be different. Succinctly, percentages make the income statement a "common-size" statement. Try out your understanding of these relationships by completing Exercise 2-3.

EXERCISE 2-3

	Dollar Amount	*Percentage to Net Sales*
Net Sales	$______	100%
Cost of Sales	______	60
Gross margin	______	40
Operating Expenses	______	15
Operating income	______	25
Income Taxes	______	15
Net Income	**$100,000**	10

In a retail store, the income statement's percentage relationships are important in establishing the amount of *markup* on merchandise. Markup is the gross margin percentage that a retailer wishes to make on merchandise. The income statement also helps in estimating the profitability of various business enterprises. Exercise 2-4 will help you to understand some of the more common relationships.

EXERCISE 2-4

Answer the following short questions relating to the income statement (assume sales are always $250,000) and consider each question independently:

a. If Sales are $250,000 and the Gross margin percentage is 40 percent, the Cost of goods sold is $____________.

b. If the Operating income is $50,000, the percentage of Operating income to Sales is ____________%.

c. If the Gross margin percentage is equal to the Cost of goods sold percentage, then the Gross margin is $____________.

d. If the Income tax *rate* (for all Operating income) is 50 percent and if Net income is $25,000, then Income taxes are $____________.

e. If Operating expenses total $75,000, and if the Gross margin percentage is 40 percent, then Operating income is $________.

Figure 2-2 presents the actual income statement of BankAmerica Corporation for the years ended December 31, 1978, 1979, and 1980 in their Annual Report for 1980. The statement is called "Consolidated Statements of Income." Its principal subdivisions are:

1. Revenue (divided between Net interest revenue and Noninterest revenue),
2. Expense (divided between Personnel expenses and Noninterest expense),
3. Income taxes, and
4. Securities transactions.

Reading further, we find that the principal source of revenue was "Interest on loans" and that the second largest source of revenue was "Interest on deposits." As you would expect, the largest expense is interest paid to depositors ($7,487,452,000). The "bottom line" for 1980—that is, Net income of $643,443,000—is somewhat meaningless to a small investor. So all annual reports express the Net income as a number called *Earnings per share* (EPS), which is obtained with the following calculation:

$$\frac{\text{Net income}}{\text{Number of shares of outstanding Common stock}} = \text{Earnings per share}$$

For BankAmerica, this figure amounts to $4.38 per share for 1980.

Figure 2-3 shows another income statement taken from a manufacturing corporation, Tandem Computers Incorporated and Subsidiaries, entitled "Consolidated Statement of Income for the Years Ended September 30, 1980 and 1979." Although we find different categories of Costs and Expenses from those in Figure 2-2, and despite the fact that the income statements come from widely diverse business enterprises, their many similarities enable a reader of the two financial statements to make some meaningful comparisons. For example, we find that the Net income per common share for Tandem Computers for the year ended September 30, 1980 is $1.06 per share, as opposed to $4.38 for BankAmerica. Chapter 18 shows the various ways of comparing different business entities, as well as how the common financial measures and ratios are applicable to all types of firms.

One last point: If the balance sheet and income statement are the two most important statements in accounting, how do they relate with each other? The balance sheet is given as of one moment of time, whereas the income statement covers a specified period. Look at it this way: The income statement is a link between two balance sheets. To explain this point of view more fully, let's examine the Owner's equity section of the balance sheet in more detail. First of all, in the case of a corporation Owner's equity becomes Shareholders' or Stockholders' equity, since this title more specifically describes the residual equity of the shareholders. Secondly, we distinguish between the monies paid in by the shareholders *(Contributed capital)* and the earnings retained in the business from past operations *(Retained earnings)*. So in the case of the corporation:

Owners' equity = Shareholders' equity
= Contributed capital + Retained earnings

Finally, we define *Retained earnings* as:

Retained earnings (beginning of the accounting year)
plus
Net income for the year
less
Distributions *(dividends)* paid to shareholders
equals
Retained earnings (end of the accounting year)

Now complete the exercises for this chapter.

FIGURE 2-2. Example of an income statement

BankAmerica Corporation
Consolidated Statements of Income

(Dollar amounts in thousands)	Year Ended December 31,		
	1980	1979	1978
Interest on loans	**$ 8,044,379**	$6,220,247	$4,499,389
Loan fees	**284,618**	223,621	194,282
Interest and dividends on investment securities:			
Taxable interest and dividend revenue	**481,320**	496,195	372,352
Nontaxable interest revenue	**83,930**	124,958	148,672
Interest on trading account securities	**42,967**	33,264	25,529
Interest on deposits	**2,110,046**	1,405,514	886,645
Interest on funds sold	**148,194**	289,339	235,047
Net leasing revenue	**80,785**	70,664	84,753
Total interest revenue	**11,276,239**	8,863,802	6,446,669
Interest on deposit liabilities	**7,487,452**	5,328,812	3,597,075
Interest on short-term borrowings	**920,063**	854,050	465,363
Interest on intermediate-term debt	**31,548**	—	—
Interest on long-term debt	**56,402**	91,775	96,415
Total interest expense	**8,495,465**	6,274,637	4,158,853
Net interest revenue	**2,780,774**	2,589,165	2,287,816
Provision for loan losses	**241,501**	226,177	176,692
Net interest revenue after loan loss provision	**2,539,273**	2,362,988	2,111,124
Trading account securities profit and commissions	**13,126**	5,187	13,521
Profit on foreign exchange activities	**99,100**	89,459	69,904
Service charges on deposit accounts	**93,387**	70,727	66,589
Fiduciary activity fees	**60,520**	54,482	49,319
Business services fees	**59,925**	52,805	42,960
Other revenue	**472,243**	313,311	274,666
Total noninterest revenue	**798,301**	585,971	516,959
Salaries	**1,111,886**	951,247	839,099
Pension and other employee benefits	**224,952**	200,754	174,128
Total personnel expense	**1,336,838**	1,152,001	1,013,227
Net occupancy expense—premises	**208,541**	182,188	166,350
Equipment—rentals, depreciation, maintenance	**152,589**	121,306	113,864
Other expense	**614,778**	545,658	490,441
Other noninterest expense	**975,908**	849,152	770,655
Income before income taxes and securities transactions	**1,024,828**	947,806	844,201
Applicable income taxes	**379,825**	347,651	329,983
Income before Securities Transactions	**645,003**	600,155	514,218
Net profit (loss) on securities transactions—after related income tax effect: **1980—$(1,773);** 1979—$11; 1978—$(16,325)	**(1,560)**	48	(16,298)
Net Income	**$ 643,443**	$ 600,203	$ 497,920
Average number of shares outstanding	**146,953,842**	146,359,597	145,874,232
Per share:			
Income before securities transactions	**$4.39**	$4.10	$3.53
Net income	**$4.38**	$4.10	$3.41
Dividends paid	**$1.41**	$1.265	$1.02

See notes to financial statements.

FIGURE 2-3. Another example of an income statement

VI TANDEM COMPUTERS INCORPORATED AND SUBSIDIARIES

CONSOLIDATED STATEMENT OF INCOME

For the Years Ended September 30, 1980 and 1979

(In Thousands Except Per Share Amounts)

	1980	1979
REVENUES (Notes 1 and 8)	$108,989	$55,974
COSTS AND EXPENSES:		
Cost of revenues	40,831	20,786
Product development	8,786	4,654
Marketing, general and administrative	40,049	20,828
Interest expense	293	84
Interest income	(2,052)	(482)
	87,907	45,870
INCOME BEFORE INCOME TAXES	21,082	10,104
Provision for Income Taxes (Note 2)	10,395	5,184
NET INCOME	$ 10,687	$ 4,920
INCOME PER COMMON SHARE* (Note 7)	$ 1.06	$ .59

*Adjusted for a two-for-one stock split in June, 1980.

The accompanying notes are an integral part of this statement.

Reprinted with the permission of Tandem Computers, Inc.

ADDITIONAL EXERCISES

2-5. Now that you understand the basic definitions for Assets, Liabilities, Stockholders' equity, Revenues, and Expenses, indicate in the spaces provided which category each item falls into. In some cases the description of the item is incomplete, and so it cannot be classified. If this is true, so indicate.

a. Wages payable ______________________

b. Taxes ______________________

c. Rent paid ______________________

d. Cost of goods sold ______________________

e. Prepaid insurance ______________________

f. Automobiles and trucks ______________________

g. Interest earned ______________________

h. Amounts due from customers ____________________

i. Amounts due to suppliers ____________________

j. Capital stock ____________________

k. Sales of merchandise ____________________

l. Accrued royalties payable ____________________

m. Retained earnings ____________________

n. Bad debts ____________________

o. Advertising ____________________

p. Merchandise held for resale ____________________

q. Repairs and maintenance ____________________

r. Travel and entertainment ____________________

s. Royalties ____________________

t. Land ____________________

2.6. Complete the following algebraic expressions:

a. Assets = Liabilities + ____________________

b. Retained Earnings (end of year) = Net income – dividends + ____________________

c. Stockholders' equity = Contributed capital + __________

d. Sales – Cost of goods sold = ____________________

e. Operating income – Income taxes = ____________________

f. Gross margin – Operating expenses = ____________________

g. Revenues – All expenses = ____________________

h. Assets – Liabilities = Retained earnings + ____________________

i. Revenues – Cost of goods sold – Operating expenses = ____________________

j. Gross margin — Operating expenses — Income taxes =

____

2-7. Indicate whether each of the following transactions is recorded as a Revenue (R), an Expense (E), or neither (N):

a. ______ An insurance policy covering manufacturing machinery is purchased.

b. ______ Proceeds of a loan are received from a bank.

c. ______ The California Department of Intercollegiate Athletics sold a season football ticket for next year.

d. ______ Merchandise is sold, but the buyer is to pick it up next week.

e. ______ A salesperson who is compensated on a straight salary basis puts in a day's work without making a sale.

f. ______ An airline ticket is purchased.

g. ______ Collection of a debt owed by a customer for goods that we sold him last month.

h. ______ A customer makes a deposit on a TV set that is to be shipped to her summer home next month.

2-8. Compute the relevant percentages (expressed as percentages of Net sales) for the following income statement:

Frisbee Spinners, Inc.
INCOME STATEMENT
Month of August, 19XX

	Amount	*Percentage to Net Sales*
Net Sales:		
Gross sales	$105,000	a. ______
Sales returns and allowances	5,000	b. ______
	100,000	c. ______

Cost of Goods Sold:	55,000	d. ______
Gross margin	45,000	e. ______
Operating Expenses:		
Warehouse expenses	10,000	f. ______
Selling expenses	15,000	g. ______
Administrative expenses	5,000	h. ______
	30,000	i. ______
Income before taxes on income	15,000	j. ______
Taxes on Income:	5,000	k. ______
Net income	$ 10,000	l. ______

2-9. Given the following information, determine the answers to the answers to the questions a through d.

General and administrative expenses	$ 196,000
Gross sales revenue	$3,920,000
Cost of goods sold	$2,416,000
Selling expenses	$ 660,000
Interest expense	$ 43,000
Sales returns and allowances	5,000
Net income (after income taxes)	$ 300,000
Shares of capital stock outstanding	100,000 shares

a. What is the Operating income ? $______________

b. What is the total of taxes on income? $______________

c. What is the Gross margin percentage $______________

d. What are the Earnings per share (EPS)? $______________

2-10. Complete the following unrelated income statements, which were started by your instructor but left unfinished:

	(a)	(b)	(c)
Sales	$100,000	$______	$50,000
Cost of sales	60,000	60,000	______
Gross margin	______	______	______
Operating expenses	10,000	11,000	5,000
Operating income	______	______	______
Other income	______	1,000	4,000
Net income (before income taxes)	55,000	______	______

Taxes on income	______	1,000	2,000
Net income	40,000	______	8,000
Shares of stock outstanding	______	6,000	2,000
Earnings per share (EPS)	50¢	$1.50	______

SOLUTIONS

2-1.

BusAdOne Corp.
INCOME STATEMENT
Year ended December 31, 19XX

Sales		$160
Cost of Goods Sold:		20
Gross Margin		140
Operating Expenses:		
Typewriter rental	$10	
Advertising	30	
Bad debts and Miscellaneous	20	60
Operating income		80
Income Taxes:		25
Net income		$ 55

2-2.

Goody Wuthrie, Inc.
INCOME STATEMENT
Year Ended September 30, 19XX

Revenues:		
Sheet music sales	$130,000	
Less: Sales returns	10,000	$120,000
Cost of Goods Sold:		
Sheet music	30,000	
Records	20,000	50,000
Gross margin		70,000
Operating Expenses:		
Administrative	15,000	
Selling	25,000	
Shipping	1,000	41,000
Income from operations		29,000
Income Taxes:		5,000
Net income		$ 24,000

2-3.

Net sales	$1,000,000
Cost of sales	600,000
Gross margin	400,000
Operating expenses	150,000
Operating income	250,000
Income taxes	150,000
Net income	$ 100,000

2-4. a. $150,000
b. 20%
c. $125,000
d. $25,000
e. $25,000

2-5. a. Wages payable—Liability
b. Taxes—Can't tell
c. Rent paid—Expense
d. Cost of goods sold—Expense
e. Prepaid insurance—Asset
f. Automobiles and trucks—Assets
g. Interest earned—Revenue
h. Amounts due from customers—Asset
i. Amounts due to suppliers—Liability
j. Capital stock—Shareholder's equity (Owner's equity)
k. Sales of merchandise—Revenue
l. Accrued royalties payable—Liability
m. Retained earnings—Shareholder's equity (Owner's equity)
n. Bad debts—Expense
o. Advertising—Can't tell
p. Merchandise held for resale—Asset
q. Repairs and maintenance—Expense
r. Travel and entertainment—Expense
s. Royalties—Can't tell
t. Land—Asset

2-6. a. Owner's equity (Shareholder's equity)
b. Retained earnings (Beginning of the year)
c. Retained earnings (End of the year)
d. Gross margin
e. Net income
f. Income from operations
g. Net income
h. Contributed capital
i. Operating income (or Income from operations)
j. Net income

2-7. a. N
b. N
c. N
d. R
e. E
f. N
g. N
h. N

2-8. a. 105%
b. 5%
c. 100%
d. 55%
e. 45%
f. 10%
g. 15%
h. 5%
i. 30%
j. 15%
k. 5%
l. 10%

2-9. a. $643,000
b. $300,000
c. $1,499/$3,915 = 38.3 percent
d. $3.00/share

2-10. (Reading down the columns)
a. $40,000, 30,000, 25,000, 15,000, 80,000 shares.
b. $80,000, 20,000, 9,000, 10,000, 9,000.
c. $39,000, 11,000, 6,000, 10,000, $4.00.

3

The Accounting Model

As you can tell from the first two chapters, there is an underlying structure to financial accounting, an analytical framework. To describe this framework, we can use various approaches. One way is by example, which was the method in the first two chapters; we used examples and illustrations of financial statements. Another way is by depicting this framework is diagrammatic form; let's see how the approach works.

First let's consider the flow of information through the accounting system. Figure 3-1 is a diagram that is composed primarily of symbols representing various books and records used by accountants. Follow along in this figure as we go over it step by step:

1. Transactions between the business entity and the outside world are captured in source documents (sales invoices, bank checks, purchase orders, and the like).
2. These source documents are entered into various journals classified according to types. For example, the *Sales Journal*

becomes a chronological listing of all the sales that occurred during the accounting period (usually summarized by months). Similarly, all checks written are recorded in the *Cash Journal,* and all purchase invoices received are recorded in the *Purchase Journal.* In the *General Journal* accountants record all transactions that do not fit into the categories of cash, sales, or purchases.

3. The transactions for an accounting period, usually one month, are summarized in these various journals and then *posted* to another accounting record, which is called a *General Ledger.* This General Ledger has a separate page for each type of account. One page would contain all the cash transactions, both receipts and disbursements, and would be labeled "Cash." Another page, labeled "Accounts receivable," would include a listing of all sales made on credit, along with a listing, or at least summary totals, of all payments by customers on their accounts.
4. The final step in the accounting process is to take the balances in the separate accounts in the General Ledger and prepare the balance sheet, income statement, and statement of retained earnings.

Still another way to present the accounting system is *algebraically.* The diagram in Figure 3-1 showed us where the statement of retained earnings comes from, but it did not tell us what is consists of.

What, specifically, is the statement of retained earnings? Perhaps the easiest way to explain this statement is to show how it ties in with the other two statements algebraically. Let's borrow

FIGURE 3-1. The traditional accounting model

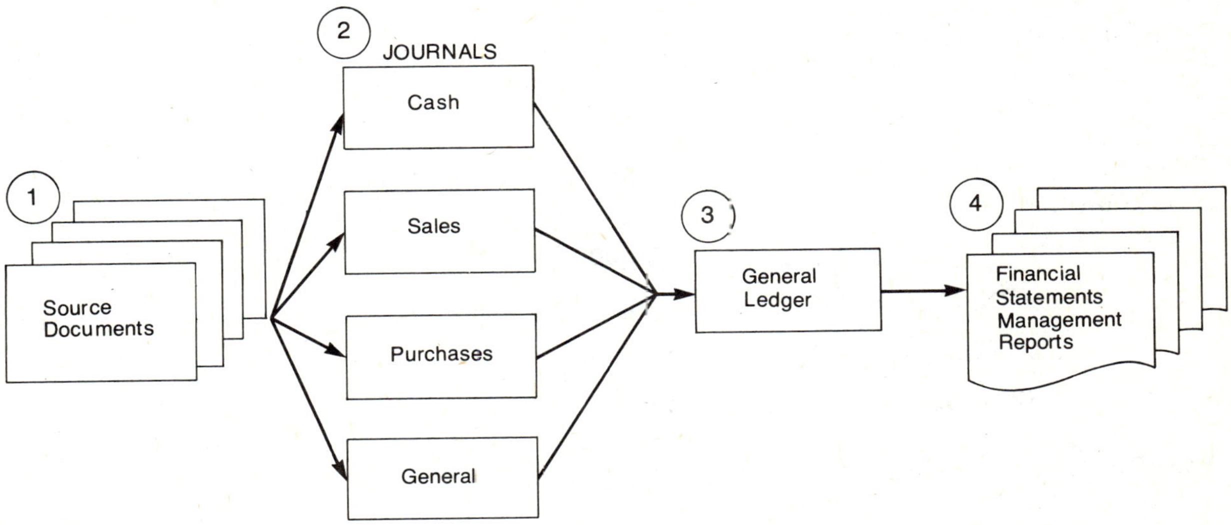

the expressions from the first two chapters and put the entire model together in algebraic notation. We know that:

$$\text{Assets} = \text{Equities}$$
$$A = Eq$$

We also know that:

$$\text{Equities} = \text{Liabilities} + \text{Shareholders' equity}$$
$$Eq = L + SE$$

Further refining this model:

$$\text{Liabilities} = \text{Current liabilities} + \text{Long-term liabilities (longer than one year)}$$
$$L = CL + LL$$

And:

$$\text{Shareholders' equity} = \text{Contributed capital} + \text{Retained earnings}$$
$$SE = CC + RE$$

Putting it all together, we have:

$$\text{Assets} = \text{Current liabilities} + \text{Long-term liabilities} + \text{Contributed capital} + \text{Retained earnings}$$
$$A = CL + LL + CC + RE$$

Rearranging this equation, we can solve for Retained earnings:

$$RE = A - (CL + LL + CC)$$

Try this formula on Exercise 3-1.

EXERCISE 3-1

If we know that:

A (Assets) = $150,000

CL (Current liabilities) = $20,000

LL (Long-term liabilities) = $30,000

CC (Contributed capital) = $25,000

Then RE (Retained earnings) must be $__________.

Now we have the entire balance sheet, which looks like this:

	On the Left Side ASSETS	*On the Right Side* Liabilities and Stockholders' EQUITIES
	Current assets	Current liabilities (CL)
(A)	Property, plant, and equipment	Long-term liabilities (LL)
	Other assets	*Stockholders' Equity (SE):* Contributed capital (CC) Retained earnings (RE)

Yet what, specifically, constitutes Retained earnings? To answer this question, we have to add a little more algebra to our model. In Chapter 2, for balance sheet purposes, we used this definition:

Retained earnings for the end-of-year balance sheet = Retained Earnings at the beginning of the year + Net income earned during the year − Dividends paid out during the year

$$RE_e = RE_b + NI - D$$

So if we know any of the three elements in this equation, we can easily compute the fourth one. Try Exercise 3-2, after reviewing an actual example of a retained earnings statement taken from Transamerica's annual report for 1980 (Figure 3-2 on page 36).

EXERCISE 3-2

Assume that: (1) Retained earnings at the beginning of the year were $65,000; (2) we earned Net income of $10,000 during the current year; and (3) we paid out $5,000 in Dividends during the current year. The Retained earnings balance at the end of the year must then be: $________________.

Most of the relationships among items in financial statements can be expressed algebraically. For example, in chapter 2, we defined Net income as the difference between the Revenues earned during the year and the Expenses related to those Revenues incurred during the year. Again we can express this relationship algebraically as:

$$\text{Net income (NI)} = \text{Revenues (R)} - \text{Expenses (E)}$$

FIGURE 3-2. An example of shareholders' equity taken from Transamerica's annual report (1980)

Note B. Shareholders' Equity

	Common Stock	Additional Paid-in Capital	Retained Earnings
Balance at January 1, 1978	$66,381,000	$345,030,000	$ 643,743,000
Consolidated net income			209,705,000
Dividends declared:			
On preferred stock			(199,000)
On common stock			(59,732,000)
Common stock reacquired	(517,000)	(8,556,000)	
Other changes	276,000	2,318,000	
Balance at December 31, 1978	66,140,000	338,792,000	793,517,000
Consolidated net income			240,202,000
Dividends declared:			
On preferred stock			(155,000)
On common stock			(69,377,000)
Common stock reacquired	(1,238,000)	(20,827,000)	
Other changes	432,000	4,677,000	
Balance at December 31, 1979	65,334,000	322,642,000	964,187,000
Consolidated net income			244,979,000
Dividends declared on common stock			(78,409,000)
Common stock reacquired	(614,000)	(10,125,000)	
Other changes	504,000	5,754,000	
Balance at December 31, 1980	$65,224,000	$318,271,000	$1,130,757,000

At December 31, 1980, 1,200,000 shares of preferred stock ($100 par value) and 5,000,000 shares of preference stock (without par value), both classes issuable in series and cumulative, were authorized, but unissued. All previously outstanding preferred stock has been retired ($3,859,000 in 1979 and $844,000 in 1978) by conversion into common stock and cash redemption.

Note C. Retained Earnings Restrictions

Payment of dividends by Transamerica Corporation and by certain subsidiaries is limited in varying degrees by provisions of loan agreements or by statutory requirements. The combined effect of these matters is not considered to have a practical restrictive effect on consolidated retained earnings.

At December 31, 1980, capital accounts of insurance subsidiaries exceeded capital and surplus reported on a regulatory basis by $516,778,000. Certain accumulations of income included in life insurance statutory surplus ($102,374,000 at December 31, 1980) have not been subjected to income taxes under provisions of the Life Insurance Income Act and might be taxed in whole or in part, if distributed as dividends.

Note D. Stock Option Plans

At December 31, 1980, under the Corporation's stock option plans, 4,983,626 shares of common stock were reserved for sale to key employees of the Corporation and subsidiaries at prices not less than market value on the date options are granted. Options were exercised for 321,406 shares in 1980, 180,125 shares in 1979 and 213,930 shares in 1978 at aggregate option prices of $2,999,000, $1,678,000 and $1,750,000. Of the options for 3,319,674 shares outstanding at December 31, 1980 (aggregate option price $51,033,000), options for 1,509,738 were exercisable.

35

EXERCISE 3-3

If the Net income for the year was $22,500 and the Expenses incurred for the year were $77,500, the Revenues earned during the year must have been $____________.

Now we have expressed the accounting model in several different ways:

1. *by example,* with illustrations of balance sheets, income statements, and statements of retained earnings;
2. *in diagrammatic form,* with Figure 3-1; and
3. *in algebraic notation,* with symbols and arithmetic operators instead of illustrations.

The expression of the accounting model in algebraic notation is a necessary first step to understanding the methodology employed by accountants in entering transactions in the books and records of a business enterprise. So we will make additional use of the accounting model in algebraic form in Chapter 4. Rest assured, however, that you do *not* have to memorize the accounting model in algebraic notation. All you have to do is understand *how* the model was developed. You should be able to start with the basic equation for the balance sheet:

$$\text{Assets} = \text{Liabilities} + \text{Shareholders' Equity}$$

With this formula, and given the appropriate dollar balances, you should be able to develop a balance sheet. Of course, you should also remember the basic equation for the income statement:

$$\text{Net income} = \text{Revenues} - \text{Expenses}$$

This formula enables you to develop a Net income figure, given the appropriate Revenue and Expense amounts.

Similarly, knowing three of the four components of the Retained earnings equation, you should be able to compute the fourth one:

$$\underset{\text{(end of year)}}{\text{Retained earnings}} = \underset{\text{(beginning of year)}}{\text{Retained earnings}} + \underset{\text{(for the year)}}{\text{Net income}} - \underset{\text{(paid or declared for the year)}}{\text{Dividends}}$$

$$RE_e = RE_b + NI - D$$

EXERCISE 3-4

Complete the following expressions:

a. A – L = ________________

b. R – E = ________________

c. CL + LL + SE = ________________

d. A – SE = ________________

e. RE_b + NI – D = ________________

For an example of how the statement of retained earnings appears on an actual annual report, see Figure 3-2. You should now be able to complete the Additional Exercises for Chapter 3.

ADDITIONAL EXERCISES

3-5. Give the equations for each of the following statements in as much detail as possible:

a. Balance sheet:

____

b. Statement of income:

____

c. Statement of retained earnings:

____

3-6. The statement of retained (or reinvested) earnings provides the link between the balance sheet and the income statement. To demonstrate your knowledge of this important statement, complete the following tables relating to the retained earnings account of the three unrelated businesses, a, b, and c.

	(a)	(b)	(c)
Total assets	$100	$____	$200
Total liabilities	____	25	100

Contributed capital	20	25	____
Retained earnings (Beginning of the Year)	20	40	100
Net income (loss) for the year	30	____	(30)
Dividends paid during the year	____	15	10
Retained earnings (End of the Year)	50	40	____

3-7. Indicate the balance sheet classification of each of the following accounts, by placing the appropriate abbreviation in space provided.

CA = Current asset
PPE = Property, plant, and equipment
I = Investments
OA = Other assets
CL = Current liability
LL = Long-term liability
SE = Shareholder's equity

_______ Retained earnings

_______ Goodwill

_______ Patents and processes

_______ Inventories

_______ Land

_______ Current portion of long-term debt

_______ Income taxes payable

_______ Capital in excess of par value

_______ Accounts payable

_______ Cash

_______ Accounts receivable, less allowance for doubtful accounts

_______ Prepaid expenses

_______ Accrued salaries and wages

______ Notes payable to banks (due in 11 months)

______ Construction in progress (to be used as a manufacturing plant)

3-8.

Bizzard One, Inc.
BALANCE SHEET
March 31, 19XX

Assets		*Liabilities and Stockholders' Equities*		
Current Assets:		Current Liabilities:		
Cash and accounts receivable	$ 40,000	Accounts payable		$ 20,000
Inventories	80,000	Income taxes payable		15,000
	120,000	Accrued expenses		5,000
Fixed Assets—Net	100,000			40,000
Other Assets	20,000	Stockholders' Equity		
		Capital stock	100,000	
		Retained earnings	100,000	200,000
	$240,000			$240,000

Compute the following

a. Amount of working capital (CA – CL) $______

b. Quick asset ratio [(CA – Inventory)/CL]______

c. Working capital ratio (CA/CL) ______

d. Debt to equity ratio (CL/SE) ______

3-9. Complete the following equation:

$A + \_\_\_\_ + D = \_\_\_\_ + C_C + R/E_b + \_\_\_\_$

3-10. Quickies:

a. As generally used, the term "stockholders' equity" represents:

i. Retained earnings of a corporation.
ii. changes in Working capital.
iii. Current assets less Current liabilities.
iv. total Assets less total Liabilities.
v. none of the above.

b. Operating expenses are defined as:

i. expenses incurred as a result of borrowing money.
ii. usual expenses incurred in operating the business.
iii. nonoperating losses.
iv. none of the above.

c. $\frac{\text{Cash + Accounts receivables + Temporary investments}}{\text{Total current liabilities}} =$

d. The statement that reflects the financial position of a business at particular point of time is called the

______________________________.

e. The excess of current assets over current liabilities is

called ____________ ____________.

SOLUTIONS

3-1. $75,000

3-2. $70,000

3-3. $100,000

3-4. a. SE (or OE for Owner's equity)
b. NI (Net Income)
c. A (Assets)
d. L (Liabilities)
e. RE_e (Retained earnings at the end of the year)

3-5. a. Balance sheet: CA + PPE + OA = CL + LL + CC + RE
b. Income statement: R – CGS – OE – IT = NI
c. Statement of retained earnings: $RE_e = RE_b + R - E - D$

3-6. a. $30, $0
b. $90, $15
c. $40, $60

3-7.

SE	Retained earnings
OA	Goodwill
OA	Patents and processes
CA	Inventories
PPE	Land
CL	Current portion of long-term debt
CL	Income taxes payable
SE	Capital in excess of par value
CL	Accounts payable
CA	Cash

CA	Accounts receivable, less allowance for doubtful accounts
CA	Prepaid expenses
CL	Accrued salaries and wages
CL	Notes payable to banks (due in 11 months)
PPE	Construction in progress (to be used as a manufacturing plant)
LL	Mortgage payable (due in 5 years)

3-8. a. $80,000
b. 1/1
c. 3/1
d. 0.2/1

3-9. $A + E + D = L + C_C + RE_b + R$

3-10. a. iv
b. ii
c. Quick asset ratio
d. Balance sheet
e. Working capital

4
Debits and Credits

In Chapter 1, we said that assets had to be owned by somebody, either a creditor or a shareholder. So when a business purchases an asset, it must increase either a liability or a shareholders' equity account—as well as the suitable asset account—to indicate the appropriate share of ownership. Let's illustrate this concept by assuming that you wish to start a new plumbing business and that you will need $20,000 capital to get started in business. As the principal shareholder, you plan to invest $7,500, and other shareholders will invest $1,500. The other $11,000 will be borrowed from your friendly banker. The accounting equation would then look like:

Assets = Liabilities + Shareholders' equity
A = L + SE
$20,000 = $11,000 + $9,000

Now let's suppose that we use $5,000 to purchase office equipment. The accounting equation would now look like:

$$\overbrace{\text{Cash} + \text{Office Equipment}}^{\text{Assets}}$$
$$\$15{,}000 + \$5{,}000 \qquad = \$11{,}000 + \$9{,}000$$

Obviously, there is another way to reflect the purchase of an asset; you can change the type of asset by exchanging one asset, Cash, for another asset, Office Equipment.

All accounting transactions could be explained by using the accounting equation, but it would be unduly burdensome and time-consuming. Over the years, accounting has developed a shorthand way of explaining and simultaneously recording business transactions, such as those already described. Once again take the accounting equation:

$$A = L + SE$$

Now observe that "T" with the vertical bar directly below the equals sign (as illustrated). Simply adopt the following twofold convention:

1. Assets will be increased by entering them on the left side of the vertical bar.
2. Liabilities and shareholders' equity accounts will be increased by entering them on the right side of the vertical bar.

Thus we can represent any accounting transaction. For example, the transaction already discussed and represented in Equation 1, would look like:

Cash	
$20,000	

Bank Loan	
	$11,000

Shareholders' Equity	
	$9,000

And our second transaction would change only the assets as follows:

Cash		*Office Equipment*	
$20,000	$5,000	$5,000	

Note that, if we enter the cash payment of $5,000 on the right-hand side of the vertical bar in the Cash account, the effect is the same as if we deducted $5,000, since increases are entered on the left-hand side of the Cash account.

EXERCISE 4-1

Enter transactions a through e in the equation format that follows them. Assume the corporate form of business entity.

- **a. Invest in the stock of the corporation. for $3,500**
- **b. Borrow $15,000 from the bank.**
- **c. Purchase inventory for resale of $10,000.**
- **d. Purchase typewriter for $1,000.**
- **e. Make a $500 payment on the bank loan.**

	Cash		*Inventory*		*Office Equipment*		*Bank Loan*		*Shareholders' Equity*
a.	________	+	________	+	________	=	________	+	________
b.	________	+	________	+	________	=	________	+	________
c.	________	+	________	+	________	=	________	+	________
d.	________	+	________	+	________	=	________	+	________
e.	________	+	________	+	________	=	________	+	________

Note that the total of all the transactions in the account can also be represented in the T-account format. Try it!

Cash		**Inventory**		**Office Equipment**	

Bank Loan		**Shareholders' Equity**	

That's the general approach. Now let's get a bit more rigorous, starting again with the accounting equation:

(1) Assets = Liabilities + Sharesholders' equity

$$A = L + SE$$

(2) Shareholders' equity = Contributed capital + Retained earnings (beginning of year) + Net income − Dividends

$$SE = CC + RE_b + NI - D$$

(3) Net income = Revenues + Expenses

$$NI = R + E$$

Putting all these equations together, we get:

(3A) $$A = L + CC + RE_b + R - E - D$$

Then, by eliminating negatives, we have:

(4) $$A + E + D = L + CC + RE_b + R$$

Now the reason for the decision rule is very clear. Once again:

1. To increase assets, expenses, or dividends, enter the appropriate amount of the *left*-hand side of the account [refer to Equation 4.]
2. To increase liabilities, contributed capital, retained earnings (beginning of the year), or revenues, enter the appropriate amount of the *right*-hand side of the account. (See Figure 4-1.)

Now take one small step—and one giant leap—for your understanding of accounting theory:

DEBIT means LEFT———CREDIT means RIGHT!!
DEBIT means LEFT———CREDIT means RIGHT!!

Any entry made on the left side of a T-account is a debit. For example, a debit to the Cash account is made to the left side; a credit would be made to the right side.

FIGURE 4-1

Now imagine a giant T-account that gives the road map for increasing each of the account categories:

$A + E + D$	$L + CC + RE_b + R$
To increase assets, expenses, or dividends, enter on the left side of the account.	**To increase liabilities, contributed capital, retained earnings at the beginning of the year, or revenues, enter on the right side of the account.**

EXERCISE 4-2

Complete the following table by entering either "Increase" or "Decrease" in the appropriate box:

Classification	*Left Side (Debit)*	*Right Side (Credit)*
Assets		
Liabilities		
Contributed capital		
Revenues		
Expenses		

Now for the tricky part! With an equation, "every action must have an equal and opposite reaction"—to keep the equation in balance. Let's look at some typical entries made by accountants:

a. The purchase of an asset (such as inventory, prepaid insurance, or an automobile) for cash has the following effects:
   1. An increase in one asset (say, Automobile) and a decrease in another asset (Cash).
   2. Since we know that an increase in an asset is a debit and that a decrease in an asset is a credit, the transaction would look like this

Cash		*Automobile*	
	$XXXX	$XXXX	

b. If we purchase that same asset on account (that is, if we don't pay cash), a different result occurs:
   1. We have an increase in the asset (Automobile) and an increase in a liability (Accounts payable).
   2. Since we know that an increase in an asset is a debit and that an increase in a liability is a credit, the transaction would now look like this:

Automobile		*Account Payable*	
$XXXX			$XXXX

c. After a cash sale, the accountant would go through the following reasoning process:

1. An increase in an asset (Cash) and an increase in revenue (Sales).
2. Since we know that an increase in an asset is a debit and that an increase in a revenue account is a credit, the transaction would be reflected as:

Cash	
$XXXX	

Sales	
	$XXXX

d. We make a charge sale—that is, the customer will pay us later—and here is what happens:

1. An increase in one asset (Accounts receivable) and an increas in Revenue (Sales).
2. Since we know that an increase in an asset is a debit and that an increase in a Revenue account is a credit, we would reflect the transaction as:

Accounts Receivable	
$XXXX	

Sales	
	$XXXX

e. We pay the bill that we owe from a previous transaction:

1. We decrease a liability (Accounts payable), and we decrease an asset (Cash).
2. According to the giant T-account, this transaction results in a debit (decrease) to Accounts payable and a credit (decrease) to Cash. In T-account format, it would look like:

Accounts Payable	
$XXXX	

Cash	
	$XXXX

These examples demonstrate that each transaction has an impact on two different accounts. We enter on the left (or debit) side of the account to increase Assets, Expenses, and Dividends. We enter on the right (or credit) side of the account to increase Liabilities, Contributed capital, or Revenue.

Reverse the process. You can then imagine that to *decrease* Assets, Expenses, or Dividends, you must enter on the opposite side from the one that indicates an increase. And conversely, you would enter on the right (credit) side to decrease Assets, Expenses, or Dividends. The same logic is applied to Liabilities, Shareholders' equity, and Revenues. Since you have entered on the right (credit) side to increase these accounts, enter on the left (debit) side to decrease them.

EXERCISE 4-3

Complete the following table by entering either "Debit" or "Credit" in the appropriate box:

Classification	Increase	Decrease
Assets	______	______
Liabilities	______	______
Dividends	______	______
Revenues	______	______
Expenses	______	______
Contributed Capital	______	______

This chapter gives you only a brief look at transaction analysis as practiced by accountants. Reinforce your understanding of these concepts by completing *all* the Additional Exercises that follow. Chapter 5 will give you some additional practice in using T-accounts.

ADDITIONAL EXERCISES

4-4. a. List each of the following categories on the side of the T-account that is appropriate to decrease that account:

Assets
Liabilities
Contributed capital
Dividends
Revenues
Expenses

b. Breaking the giant T-account into mini-T-accounts, we prepare six separate T-accounts. Indicate (with an X or check mark) on which side of each of these accounts an item would be entered to increase the account:

Assets

Liabilities

Contributed Capital

Dividends

Revenues

Expenses

4-5. Using the following format, indicate which categories would be affected by each transaction and whether each account would be debited (Dr) or credited (Cr):*

	Assets	Liabilities	Contributed Capital	Revenues	Expenses
Buy inventory for cash	______	______	______	______	______
Buy stock in your own business	______	______	______	______	______
Receive money from customers	______	______	______	______	______
Buy a truck on credit	______	______	______	______	______
Pay an electricity bill not previously recorded	______	______	______	______	______
Sell merchandise on account	______	______	______	______	______
Pay off a bank loan	______	______	______	______	______
Return merchandise previously sold on account	______	______	______	______	______

4-6. For the indicated changes in the following accounts, circle the appropriate entry to be made by the accountant:

	Circle One Item Only	
a. An increase in cash	Debit	Credit
b. A debit to an Account payable	Increase	Decrease
c. An increase in Accumulated depreciation	Debit	Credit
d. A credit to Capital stock	Increase	Decrease
e. A debit to Notes payable	Increase	Decrease
f. A debit to Sales returns	Increase	Decrease
g. A decrease in the Allowance for doubtful accounts	Debit	Credit
h. A debit to retained earnings	Increase	Decrease

*Note: From the Latin debere (to owe), credere (to be owed).

4-7. Complete the following schedule by entering the word "Increase" or "Decrease."

	Debit	Credit
Revenue	______	______
Expense	______	______
Contributed capital	______	______
Asset	______	______
Liability	______	______
Dividend	______	______

4-8. Indicate, in the blank spaces provided, the appropriate letter signifying the classification of each of the accounts:

a. Current asset
b. Fixed asset (Operational asset) or property, plant and equipment
c. Other asset
d. Contra asset (an asset account used to value another asset)
e. Current liability
f. Noncurrent liability
g. Shareholders' equity

______ Accumulated depreciation (an account used to value property, plant, and equipment)

______ Cash

______ Federal income taxes payable

______ Inventories

______ Capital stock outstanding

______ Retained earnings

______ Mortgage payable

______ Accounts payable

______ Allowance for doubtful accounts (an account used to value accounts receivable)

______ Store equipment

______ Deferred income taxes

______ 90-day note payable to bank

______ Salaries and wages payable

______ Current portion of mortgage payable

______ Goodwill

4-9. Circle the letters of the correct statement(s):

a. Current liabilities = Current assets — Working capital

b. Total assets — Current liabilities = Long-term liabilities

c. Long-term liabilities = Total assets — Current liabilities

d. Owners' equity = Total assets — Long-term liabilities — Current liabilities

4-10. Complete the following sentences by inserting the proper name of the account:

a. If you make a sale of merchandise on account, you *debit* Accounts receivable and you *credit* __________.

b. If you invest money in your own business, you *debit* Cash and you *credit* ________________________.

c. If you pay an account payable, you *debit* Accounts payable and you *credit* ________________________.

d. If you buy a building (to be used in the business) without a down payment and you finance the entire purchase with a mortgage, you *debit* Buildings and you *credit* ____________________________________.

e. If you pay a PG&E bill not previously recorded, you *debit* Utility expenses and you *credit* ____________.

f. If you sell merchandise for cash, you *debit* __________ and you *credit* ____________________.

g. If you pay your employee a weekly salary, you *debit* _______________ and you *credit* ______________.

h. If you repay a bank loan, you *debit* _______________ and you *credit* ____________________.

i. If your customer returns merchandise bought on credit previously, you *debit* ________________ and you *credit* ________________.

j. If you return merchandise that you previously bought for cash, you *debit* ________________ and you *credit* ________________.

k. If your corporation pays a dividend, you *debit* ________________ ________________ and you *credit* ________________.

SOLUTIONS

4-1.

	Cash	Inventory	Office Equipment		Bank Loan	Shareholders' Equity
a.	$3,500			=		$3,500
b.	$15,000			=	$15,000	
c.	($10,000)	$10,000		=		0
d.	($1,000)		$1,000	=		0
e.	($500)			=	($500)	

Cash

(a) $ 3,500	(c) $10,000
(b) 15,000	(d) 1,000
	(e) 500

Inventory

(c) $10,000	

Office Equipment

(d) $1,000	

Bank Loan

(e) $500	(b) $15,000

Shareholders' Equity

	(d) $3,500

4-2.

Left Side (Debit)	*Right Side (Credit)*
Increase	Decrease
Decrease	Increase
Decrease	Increase
Decrease	Increase
Increase	Decrease

4-3.

Increase	*Decrease*
Debit	Credit
Credit	Debit
Debit	Credit
Credit	Debit
Debit	Credit
Credit	Debit

4-4. a.

Liabilities	Assets
Contributed capital	Dividends
Revenues	Expenses

b. Assets—Left side
Liabilities—Right side
Contributed capital—Right side
Dividends—Left side
Revenues—Right side
Expenses—Left side

4-5. Buy inventory for cash – Dr. Assets, Cr. Assets

	Assets	Liabilities	Contributed Capital	Revenues	Expenses
Buy inventory for cash	Dr—Cr				
Buy stock in your own business	Dr		Cr		
Receive money from customers	Dr—Cr				
Buy a truck on credit	Dr	Cr			
Pay an electricity bill not previously recorded	Cr				Dr
Sell merchandise on account	Dr			Cr	
Pay off a bank loan	Cr	Dr			
Return merchandise previously sold on account	Cr			Dr	

4-6. a. Debit
b. Decrease
c. Credit

d. Increase

e. Decrease

f. Increase

g. Debit

h. Decrease

4-7.

	Debit	*Credit*
Revenue	Decrease	Increase
Expense	Increase	Decrease
Contributed capital	Decrease	Increase
Asset	Increase	Decrease
Liability	Decrease	Increase
Dividend	Increase	Decrease

4-8. D Accumulated depreciation
A Cash
E Federal income taxes payable
A Inventories
G Capital stock outstanding
G Retained earnings
F Mortgage payable
E Accounts payable
D Allowance for doubtful accounts
B Store equipment
F Deferred income taxes
E 90-day note payable to bank
E Salaries and wages payable
E Current portion of mortgage payable
C Goodwill

4-9. a and d.

4-10. a. Sales (Revenues)

b. Owners' equity

c. Cash

d. Mortgage payable

e. Cash

f. Cash, Sales (Revenues)

g. Expenses, Cash

h. Bank loan, Cash

i. Sales (Revenues), Accounts Receivable

j. Cash, Purchases (Merchandise)

k. Dividends (Retained earnings), Cash

5

T-Accounts: The Mini-Ledger

In the dark ages, when I was studying accounting, we had to use nicely ruled ledger pages, enter deductions in red ink, and in effect prepare a complete set of books. What a drag! Fortunately for you, this ceremony has been eliminated completely, and the lowly T-account has become a surrogate for the elegantly prepared ledger page. Since the theory is the same in either case, we have lost nothing in the exchange. The use of the T-account has many advantages over the more formal way of presenting accounting information. For example, you don't need to use special paper; you can even do your accounting on the back of an envelope while riding the bus to school or work. A further advantage is that you are able to see all the accounts involved in a transaction on one page, whereas the more formal analysis would require a page for each account. Finally, the more formal method is used today only in very small businesses; with the decreasing cost of micro and minicomputers, only these very small businesses find it economical to maintain the old manual records. Most other businesses keep their ledgers on magnetic tape, disk packs, or floppy disks. Today's electronic systems render obsolete the Charles Dickens version of the bookkeeper, Bob Cratchit, sitting on a high stool at a slanted desk, with a green eye shade and red arm bands, using quill pens to make ciphers with an elegant flourish. So much for the passing of formalism and the coming of the T-account!

So from now on, you will be expected to use T-accounts to solve accounting problems. Here's how: Remember the giant T-account in Chapter 4? All accounts on the left side of the vertical line are increased by entering the appropriate amount of the *left* (or *debit*) side of the account. All accounts on the right side of the vertical line are increased by entering the appropriate amount of the *right* (or *credit*) side of the account.

$$A + E + D = L + CC + RE_b + R$$

To increase assets, and expenses or to record dividends, we enter the amount on this side.	To increase liabilities, shareholders' equity, or revenues, we enter the amount on this side.

EXERCISE 5-1

The accounting model results in a specific set of instructions for increasing and decreasing various categories of accounts. Let's be sure you remember your debits and credits. Demonstrate this by completing the following table, using only the words "Increase" or "Decrease" to complete the matrix:

	Debit	*Credit*
Assets	__________	__________
Liabilities	__________	__________
Contributed capital	__________	__________
Revenues	__________	__________
Expenses	__________	__________
Dividends	__________	__________

Now imagine that this large T-account spawns a bunch of mini-T-accounts, which look like this:

$$A \quad + \quad E \quad + \quad D \quad = \quad L \quad + \quad CC \quad + \quad RE_b \quad + \quad R$$

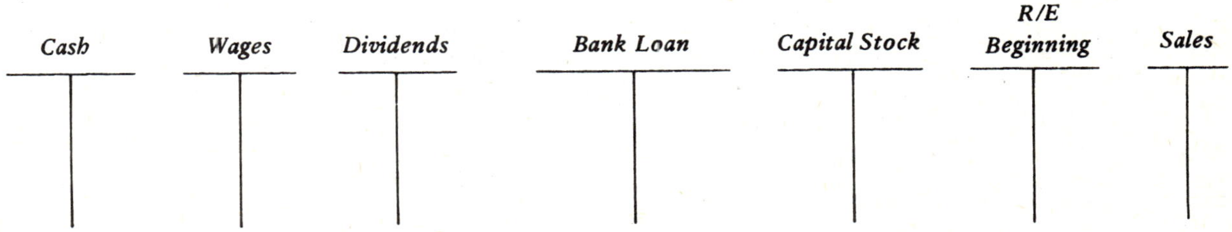

$A + E + D = L + CC + RE_b + R$

A	E	D	=	L	CC	RE_b	R
Accts. Rec.	*Taxes*			*Accts. Pay.*			*Interest Income*
Inventories	*Bad Debts*			*Mortgage Payable*			*Rental Income*

We can't represent all possibilities, but you get the idea.

EXERCISE 5-2

Enter the following transactions in the T-accounts given below. Don't forget to identify the transactions with the appropriate letter.

a. Make a cash sale of $250.
b. Pay an account payable of $100.
c. Buy a new freezer for $750 on account.
d. Borrow $1,000 from the bank.
e. Make a sale on account (credit sale) for $300.

EXERCISE 5-3

Record the following transactions in the T-accounts.

a. The owner invested cash, $7,000.
b. The owner put equipment into the business, $11,000.

c. Bought supplies for cash, $1,200.
d. Bought supplies on account, $2,000.
e. Billed charge customers for services rendered, $2,600.

We can take this drive for simplicity one step further. You don't have to prepare formal journal entries to understand accounting transactions. Remember the flow diagram of the accounting model (Figure 3-1), where transactions were depicted as flowing from source documents into journals and then into ledgers? Well, if you know the transactions, you can skip the journalizing step and proceed directly to the ledger—which is now completely represented by T-accounts. Perhaps an illustration would help. Let's take three related transactions:

a. We invest money in our new popcorn popper ($50).
b. We buy popcorn kernels to pop ($5), and we buy bags, butter, and salt ($3).
c. At the opening football game, we sell out and count the money ($35).

Representing this business in T-account format, we have:

Cash	
(c) 35	(b) 8

Popcorn Popper	
(a) 50	

Owner's Equity	
	(a) 50

Popcorn Sales		Cost of Popcorn Sold (Sales)	
	(c) 35	(b) 8	

In the T-account technique, accounts are increased and decreased directly. We have eliminated the need for a journal because each transaction can be traced (in what is called an *audit trail*) from the ledger back to the transaction (the letter in front of the dollar item refers to the transaction). From the T-accounts we can proceed to the final step—preparing the financial statements. Preparing the income statement is very simple:

Popcorn sales	$35
Cost of sales	8
Net income	$27

Remember the formula for connecting link between the income statement and the balance sheet:

$$SE = CC + RE_b + R - E - D$$

This formula makes preparing the balance sheet just as easy:

Assets			*Liabilities and Owner's Equity*		
Cash	$27	($35 received less $8 paid)	Liabilities	None	
Popcorn popper	50		Owner's equity	$77	(Investment $50 + $27 Net income earned)
Total	$77		Total	$77	

EXERCISE 5-4

Prepare a balance sheet and an income statement from the following T-accounts. Read the accounts from left to right.

Cash		**Accounts Receivable**		**Inventory**	
300		750		1,000	

Fixed Asset (Auto)	
950	

Accounts Payable	
	500

Owner's Equity	
	1,000

Sales	
	3,050

Sales Returns	
50	

Salary Expense	
300	

Rent Expense	
400	

Gas & Electricity	
250	

Advertising Expense	
550	

So that is how the accounting model is translated, through the use of T-accounts, into financial statements. The process remains the same for our mythical popcorn popping enterprise as it is for Safeway Stores, Inc. If you understand this basic model, you eliminate at least 75 percent of your troubles with introductory financial accounting. The rest of the material builds on this basic flow of accounting information.

Speaking of Safeway Stores, Inc., we thought that a review of the Safeway balance sheet would be helpful. So it has been reproduced in Figure 5-2.

ADDITIONAL EXERCISES

5-5. For each of the listed accounts, indicate the following:

* *What is It?* **Asset, liability, and so on?**
* *Which Side?* **Left or right on the T-account?**
* *Debit and Credit?* **Dr or Cr?**

	(1) What is it?	(2) Which side?	(3) Debit or Credit
a. Allowance for doubtful accounts	________	________	________
b. Cash	________	________	________

FIGURE 5-2. A typical balance sheet

Consolidated Balance Sheet

As of January 3, 1981, December 29, 1979 and December 30, 1978
Safeway Stores, Incorporated and Subsidiaries
(thousands)

	Assets	**1980**	**1979**	**1978**
Current assets	Cash	$ 115,758	$ 97,872	$ 136,531
	Receivables	56,633	60,094	52,104
	Merchandise inventories (Note A)	1,012,063	981,305	924,479
	Prepaid expenses	83,777	68,543	70,276
	Total current assets	1,268,231	1,207,814	1,183,390
Other assets	Licenses, notes receivable and investments	31,758	27,391	26,398
	Deferred income tax charges	2,104	1,586	—
	Excess cost of investment in subsidiaries over net assets at date of acquisition, less amortization	3,036	2,180	2,396
		36,898	31,157	28,794
Property (Note G)	Land	139,869	111,238	82,471
	Buildings	183,230	153,202	147,179
	Leasehold improvements	357,732	295,835	223,398
	Fixtures and equipment	1,344,889	1,196,024	1,057,448
	Transport equipment	162,516	153,839	145,777
	Property under capital leases	1,226,900	1,218,270	1,119,957
		3,415,136	3,128,408	2,776,230
	Less accumulated depreciation and amortization	1,381,433	1,266,611	1,152,647
		2,033,703	1,861,797	1,623,583
		$3,338,832	$3,100,768	$2,835,767

See accompanying notes to consolidated financial statements.

FIGURE 5-2. (continued)

	Liabilities and Stockholders' Equity	1980	1979	1978
Current liabilities	Notes payable (Note E)	$ 116,679	$ 136,792	$ 57,342
	Current obligations under capital leases	44,855	44,273	41,084
	Current maturities of notes and debentures	5,880	7,223	6,793
	Accounts payable	726,429	676,263	629,282
	Accrued salaries and wages	129,457	110,928	101,906
	Other accrued expenses	102,074	86,142	76,882
	Income taxes payable	30,108	19,599	56,908
	Total current liabilities	1,155,482	1,081,220	970,197
Long-term debt	Obligations under capital leases (Note F)	844,011	846,179	766,298
	Notes and debentures (Note G)	207,218	109,477	114,436
		1,051,229	955,656	880,734
	Deferred income taxes	—	—	6,202
	Accrued claims and other liabilities	68,023	51,278	42,260
	Commitments and contingencies (Notes B, F, H & I)			
Stockholders' equity (Notes G, J & K)	Common stock—$1.66⅔ par value			
	Authorized 75,000,000 shares			
	Outstanding 26,115,917, 26,115,917 and 26,096,966 shares	43,527	43,527	43,495
	Additional paid-in capital	63,436	63,436	62,690
	Retained earnings	957,135	905,651	830,189
		1,064,098	1,012,614	936,374
		$3,338,832	$3,100,768	$2,835,767

c. Interest income ________ ________ ________

d. Accumulated depreciation ________ ________ ________

e. Bad debts expense ________ ________ ________

f. Store equipment ________ ________ ________

g. Merchandise inventory ________ ________ ________

h. Cost of goods sold ________ ________ ________

i. Income tax payable ________ ________ ________

j. Deferred magazine subscriptions ________ ________ ________

k. Capital stock ________ ________ ________

l. Notes payable ________ ________ ________

m. Prepaid insurance ________ ________ ________

n. Account receivable ________ ________ ________

o. Patents ________ ________ ________

p. Retained earnings ________ ________ ________

q. Land for future plant site ________ ________ ________

r. Loss on sale of fixed assets ________ ________ ________

s. Salaries expense ________ ________ ________

t. Rental income ________ ________ ________

5-6. Describe each of the following T-account entries in words:

a.

Accounts Receivable	
(a) 850	

Sales Revenue	
	(a) 850

____

____

b.

Salary Expense	
(b) 1,000	

Cash	
	(b) 1,000

c.

Purchases	
	(c) 200

Accounts Payable	
(c) 200	

d.

Cash	
(d) 5,000	

Capital Stock	
	(d) 5,000

e.

Retained Earnings	
(e) 6,000	

Cash	
	(e) 6,000

f.

Automobiles	
(f) 7,000	

Cash	
	(f) 1,000

Notes Payable	
	(f) 6,000

g.

Notes Payable	
(g) 10,000	

Cash	
	(g) 10,000

h.

Cash	
(h) 4,500	

Accounts Receivable	
	(h) 4,500

5-7. The accountant for the Half Fast Food Lunch Room became ill from eating a hamburger in the company cafeteria and was taken to the hospital before he had a chance to explain his entries in the following T-accounts:

Cash	
(a) 300	(d) 100
(g) 10	(f) 75
	(h) 35

Accounts Receivable	
(b) 50	(g) 10

Equipment	
(d) 500	

Accumulated Depreciation	
	(e) 25

Accounts Payable	
(h) 35	(c) 220
	(d) 400

Food Sales	
	(a) 300
	(b) 50

Operating Expenses	
(c) 220	
(e) 25	
(f) 75	

Give a concise explanation of each lettered journal entry.

a. ______________________________

b. ______________________________

c. ______________________________

d. ______________________________

e. ______________________________

f. ______________________________

g. ______________________________

h. ______________________________

5-8. The accountant for Bizzad One resigned because she couldn't find her tutor after completing the following T-accounts. The president has asked you to identify the entries made by the accountant and has given you the following possibilities. (Indicate your answer by jotting down the letter of the appropriate entry in the spaces provided below.)

* Investment in the business
* Payment of an account payable

* Cash sale
* Collection of an account receivable
* Sale on account
* Payment of a dividend
* Purchase of office equipment on account
* Sale of office equipment for cash
* Receiving the proceeds from a bank loan
* Repaying a bank loan

Cash	
(4)	(5)
(1)	(6)
(3)	(10)
(7)	
(9)	

Accounts Receivable	
(2)	(3)

Equipment	
(8)	(9)

Accounts Payable	
(10)	(8)

Bank Loan	
(5)	(7)

Capital Stock	
	(4)

Retained Earnings	
(6)	

Sales	
	(1)
	(2)

1. ______________________________

2. ______________________________

3. ______________________________

4. ______________________________

5. ______________________________

6. ______________________________

7. ______________________________

8. ______________________________

9. ______________________________

10. ______________________________

5-9. On a separate piece of paper, write a short essay describing T-accounts to someone unfamiliar with the concept.

5-10. The general ledger T-account for Accounts receivable looks like this:

Accounts Receivable

Debit		Credit
Beginning balance	$42,000	$81,000
	78,000	

What would be the credit sales for the period?

$ __________

SOLUTIONS

5-1.

Debit	*Credit*
Increase	Decrease
Decrease	Increase
Decrease	Increase
Decrease	Increase
Increase	Decrease
Increase	Decrease

5-2.

Cash

Debit	Credit
(a) $250	(b) $100
(d) $1,000	

Accounts Receivable

Debit	Credit
(e) $300	

PP&E

Debit	Credit
(c) $750	

Sales

Debit	Credit
	(a) $250
	(e) $300

Accounts Payable

Debit	Credit
(b) $100	(c) $750

Notes Payable

Debit	Credit
	(d) $1,000

5-3.

Cash	
(a) $7,000	(c) $1,200

Accounts Receivable	
(e) $2,600	

Supplies	
(c) $1,200	
(d) $2,000	

PP&E	
(b) $11,000	

Accounts Payable	
	(d) $2,000

Owner's Equity	
	(a) $7,000
	(b) $11,000

Revenues	
	(e) $2,600

5-4.

A BALANCE SHEET

Asset			*Equities*		
Current Assets:			Current Liability:		
Cash	$ 300		Accounts payable		$ 500
Accounts receivable	750				
Inventory	1,000	$2,050			
Property, Plant, and Equipment:			Owner's Equity:		
Automobile		950	Fred, Owner		2,500
		$3,000			$3,000

AN INCOME STATEMENT

Net Sales:		
Gross sales	$3,050	
Less: returns	50	$3,000
Operating Expenses:		
Salary	300	
Rent	400	
Gas and electricity	250	
Advertising	550	1,500
Net income		$1,500

5-5.

a. Contra asset — Right — Credit
b. Current asset — Left — Debit
c. Revenue — Right — Credit

d.	Contra asset	Right	Credit
e.	Expense	Left	Debit
f.	PP&E	Left	Debit
g.	Current asset	Left	Debit
h.	Expense	Left	Debit
i.	Current liability	Right	Credit
j.	Noncurrent liability	Right	Credit
k.	Contributed capital	Right	Credit
l.	Liability	Right	Credit
m.	Current asset	Left	Debit
n.	Current asset	Left	Debit
o.	Other asset	Left	Debit
p.	Shareholders equity	Right	Credit
q.	Other asset	Left	Debit
r.	Expense	Left	Debit
s.	Expense	Left	Debit
t.	Revenue	Right	Credit

5-6. a. Sale on account (credit sale)
b. Paid salary
c. Returned an item previously bought on credit
d. Invested money in the business
e. Corporation paid a dividend
f. Purchased an automobile with a $1,000 down payment
g. Paid a note payable
h. Customer paid an account

5-7. a. Cash sale
b. Credit sale
c. Recorded liability for expenses incurred
d. Purchased equipment with $100 down
e. Recorded Depreciation on equipment
f. Paid operating expenses
g. Customer paid on account
h. Paid an account payable

5-8. 1. Cash sale
2. Sale on account
3. Collection of an account receivable
4. Investment in the business

5. Payment on bank loan.
6. Payment of a dividend
7. Receiving the proceeds from a bank loan
8. Purchase of office equipment on account
9. Sale of office equipment for cash
10. Payment of an account payable

5-9. A T-account is an informal substitute for a general ledger account. Accounting theory can be demonstrated and transaction problems can be solved by the use of T-accounts, but they would not be used in practice. The T-account method can be used for many other things, such as illustrating the effect of journal entries, serving as the basis for the construction of financial statements, and providing the methodology for making the necessary calculations in connection with the consolidating procedures for financial statements.

5-10. $78,000

6
The Accrual Concept

Although in many ways the hard part of the accounting model is behind us, the accrual concept is still a difficult one for many students. You have already been introduced to the accrual concept without knowing it, because we have talked about such things as accounts receivable and accounts payable.

First let's briefly consider the cash concept. Originally all records were kept on the cash basis. Income was recorded when cash was received, and expenses were recognized at the time the money was paid. Many simple businesses still operate on the "cash basis." As a matter of fact when you prepare your Federal income tax return for Uncle Sam, that return is prepared on a "cash basis." You record as income only the salary that has actually been paid to you, and you can deduct only those contributions, interest payments, and taxes that were actually *paid* during the calendar year.

EXERCISE 6-1

Complete the following table for the cash account:

	Beginning Balance	*Receipts*	*Disbursements*	*Ending Balance*
a.	$4,000	$_____	$ 5,000	$2,000
b.	_____	16,000	18,000	7,000
c.	(1,000)	8,000	3,000	_____
d.	6,000	7,000	4,500	_____
e.	500	1,500	2,000	_____
f.	3,000	9,000	_____	6,500
g.	1,500	2,000	_____	(4,500)

Note: ( ) **indicates overdraft.**

In contrast to the cash method, most businesses today record their income on the accrual basis. In other words, a sale becomes a credit to sales revenues whenever the customer walks home with the merchandise under his or her arm, regardless of whether the payment was made in cash or by credit. Similarly, if businesses recorded expenses only when paid rather than when incurred, the expenses might be understated. Businesses might even increase their income merely by delaying the payment of a bill, and that sort of practice would be unfair. So virtually all businesses are on the accrual basis for both revenues and expenses. This method prevents manipulation of net income and insures that businesses present a uniform and fair picture of their operations to the readers of their financial statements.

We can divide the accrual basis, into three separate parts:

1. accounts receivable and accounts payable,
2. prepayments and deferrals, and
3. depreciation and the cost of goods sold.

We will limit this chapter to the first of these three notions, reserving prepayments and deferrals to Chapter 7 and depreciation and the cost of goods sold to Chapter 8.

Since the foundation of all reporting stems from the cash basis; we can set up a little equation to show how a business can calculate its sales on the accrual basis:

(1) Sales (cash basis) + Sales (not yet collected from customers) − Sales (collected this period but actually made in prior period) = Sales (accrual basis)

Note that sales on the accrual basis are identical to credit sales plus cash sales for the period. So if you know the cash receipts from sales and if you know how much was owed to you at the beginning of the accounting period and at the end of the accounting period, you can easily figure out the amount of sales on the accrual basis. Stating the previous equation in a slightly different way:

(2)

$$\underset{\text{(accrual basis)}}{\text{Sales}} = \text{Cash sales} + \underset{\text{(end-of-period)}}{\text{Accounts Receivable (AR)}} - \underset{\text{(beginning-of-period)}}{\text{Accounts Receivable (AR)}}$$

Note that AR (end-of-period) is simply the Sales (not yet collected from customers) in Equation 1.

EXERCISE 6-2

Supply the missing information:

a. Cash collected on prior credit sales — $ 7,000
Accounts receivable, beginning — 80,000
Accounts receivable, ending — 85,000

Sales (accrual basis) — $______

b. Credit sales — $18,000
Accounts receivable, beginning — 11,000
Accounts receivable, ending — 17,000

Sales (cash basis) — $______

c. Given the T-account illustrated below, the ending Accounts receivable balance is — $______

And the sales (accrual basis for the period are) — $______

Accounts Receivable

Debit		Credit
Balance, 1/1/82	$20,000	$35,000
	70,000	

Similarly we can calculate expenses on an accrual basis if we know the actual cash expenses, along with the amounts owed to creditors at both the beginning and at the end of the accounting period. We can set up an equation (similar to that for sales) as follows:

(3) Expenses (accrual basis) = Cash expenses + Accounts Payable (AP) (end) − Accounts Payable (AP) (beginning)

Note this similarity between Equations 2 and 3.

EXERCISE 6-3

Supply the missing information:

a.	Cash paid for expenses incurred	$18,000
	Accounts payable, beginning	9,000
	Accounts payable, ending	7,000
	Expenses (accrual basis)	$______
b.	Expenses (accrual basis)	$62,000
	Accounts payable, beginning	18,000
	Accounts payable, ending	21,000
	Expenses (cash basis)	$______
c.	Given the following T-account illustration, the ending accounts payable balance is	$______
	And the expenses (accrual basis) for the period are	$______

Accounts Payable

$23,000	Balance, 1/1/82
	$11,000
	$24,000

As you can see, accountants strive to match sales made with the expenses incurred during the same period. In accounting literature, this effort is referred to as the *matching concept.*

This is a good time to sit back and think about the general characteristics of accounts (primarily but not exclusively balance sheet accounts). For one thing, these accounts always have beginning balances (balance sheet accounts). For another, two things can happen to that account: It can increase, or it can decrease. Let's look at the cash account:

Cash in Bank

Balance 9/1/81	$6,000	Disbursements, Sept. '81	$3,000
Receipts, Sept. '81	1,500		

The ending balance in any balance sheet account can always be computed by using the basic formula:

(4) Beginning Balance ($6,000) + Additions ($1,500) − Reductions ($3,000) = $4,500

EXERCISE 6-4

Complete the following expressions:

a. Beginning cash balance + Cash receipts − Cash disbursements =

______________________________.

b. Cash receipts − Cash disbursements = __________________.

c. Net income + Expenses = ______________________.

d. Beginning accounts payable + Merchandise purchased on account − Ending accounts payable = __________________.

e. Beginning accounts receivable − Ending accounts receivable + Credit sales = ____________________________.

With your new-found knowledge of how to convert from a cash to an accrual basis of accounting (or vice versa), you can tackle the Additional Exercises.

ADDITIONAL EXERCISES

6-5. Net income (cash basis) for the Rationed Gas Station, Inc. is $6,500. You determine that the unpaid Accounts receivable at the end of the accounting period is $2,200. There

were no Accounts receivable at the beginning of the period. You also learn that unpaid bills amounted to $1,700 at the beginning of the accounting period and $2,700 by the end of the period. No bills were paid during the period. What was the net income (accrual basis)?

$__________

6-6. Supply the missing data for each of the following independent situations:

a.	Accounts payable, 12/1/81	$ 1,600
	Accounts payable, 12/31/81	1,700
	Merchandise purchased on credit, 12/31/81	10,500
	Cash paid on account, December	$______
b.	Revenues	$40,000
	Cost of goods sold	20,000
	Other expenses except taxes	6,000
	Income tax expense	1,400
	Income tax rate	______%
c.	Supplies on hand, 12/1/81	$ 500
	Supplies on hand, 12/31/81	520
	Supplies purchased	300
	Supplies used	$______
d.	Prepaid insurance, 12/1/81	$ 200
	Prepaid insurance, 12/31/81	350
	Insurance expense, December	1,000
	Insurance purchased, December	$______
e.	Net income before taxes, 1981	$ 8,000
	Income tax expense, 1981	1,000
	Dividends paid, 1981	2,000
	Retained earnings, 12/31/81	11,000
	Retained earnings, 1/1/81	$______

The next three questions can be answered by referring to the following company's annual report (income statement) for the year 19XX.

Income Statement Year 19XX

Sales		$500,000
Less: Cost of goods sold	$310,000	
Depreciation	10,000	
Other expenses	100,000	420,000
Net income		$ 80,000

The company's balance sheets at the beginning and end of the year were as follows:

	January 1		December 31	
Cash		$ 40,000		$ 50,000
Accounts receivable		80,000		100,000
Merchandise inventory		60,000		70,000
Store equipment:				
Original cost	$200,000		$260,000	
Less: Accumulated depreciation	70,000	130,000	90,000	170,000
Total assets		$310,000		$390,000
Accounts payable		$ 50,000		$ 30,000
Capital stock		110,000		140,000
Retained earnings		150,000		220,000
Total liabilities and owners' equity		$310,000		$390,000

6-7. How much cash was collected from customers in 19XX?

$____________

6-8. How much was paid out in dividends during 19XX?

$____________

6-9. How much cash was disbursed in payment of accounts able during 19XX? (Assume that the Cost of goods sold and other expenses in total represent expenses on the accrual basis). $____________

6-10. From the following information prepare a statement of cash receipts and disbursements:

a. Cash balance beginning of year, $17,000
b. Cash balance end of year, $19,000
c. Salary expense for the year, $30,000
d. Advertising expense for the year, $14,000
e. Unpaid advertising bills increased by $6,000 during the year
f. There were no unpaid salaries at the beginning of the year
g. The unpaid salaries at the end of the year were $4,000
h. Cash collections from customers were $32,000
i. There were no other cash receipts or disbursements during the year.

STATEMENT OF CASH RECEIPTS AND DISBURSEMENTS

Cash sales		$________
Less: Operating Expenses paid in cash:		
Salary expense	$________	
Advertising expense	________	
Net income (cash basis)		$________
Add:		
Cash balance (beginning of year)		________
Cash balance (end of year)		========

SOLUTIONS

6-1. a. $3,000
b. $9,000
c. $4,000
d. $8,500
e. –0–
f. $5,500
g. $8,000

6-2. a. $12,000
b. $12,000
c. $55,000; $70,000

6-3. a. $16,000
b. $59,000
c. $12,000; $24,000

6-4. a. Ending cash balance
b. Income on cash basis (excess of receipts over disbursements)
c. Revenues
d. Cash payments made to suppliers
e. Sales on the cash basis

6-5. $6,500 + $2,200 + $1,700 – $2,700 = $7,700

6-6. a. $10,400
b. 10%
c. $280
d. $1,150
e. $6,000

6-7. $480,000

6-8. $10,000

6-9. $430,000

6-10.

Cash sales		$32,000
Salary	$26,000	
Advertising	8,000	
	30,000	30,000
Net income (cash basis)		$ 2,000
Cash balance (beginning of year)		$17,000
Cash balance (end of year)		$19,000

7
Prepayments and Deferrals

For some unknown reason, accounting texts spend an inordinate amount of time on this subject, and it sound so complicated. Maybe these concepts have a certain elegance that is intellectually satisfying. But you will probably be better off with the attitude that these items constitute a relatively insignificant part of the total balance sheet picture.

The usual listing of prepayment and deferrals includes two types of revenues and two types of expenses:

1. prepaid expense,
2. accrued expense,
3. deferred revenue, and
4. accrued revenue.

PREPAID EXPENSE

Prepaid expense is perhaps the best known of the four categories, and the typical example is prepaid insurance. If you have ever purchased insurance, you quickly discover that insurance brokers want their money before the policy is issued. So insurance is typically prepaid. Since an insurance policy provides protection for the future, it is an asset. If you buy the policy for one year, it is worth one-half of what you paid for it at the end of six months. What happened to the other half—it is expense!

Example: You buy a one-year auto insurance policy for $200 on January 1. It is now September 30. How much of the $200 is expense, and how much is prepaid insurance (an asset)? The expense is $150, and the policy is worth $50 (prepaid expense). The appropriate balances in the affected accounts after the adjustment are as follows:

Prepaid Insurance	
$50	

Insurance Expense	
$150	

EXERCISE 7-1

On July 1, 19X1, the Maxe Corporation paid in advance a three-year fire insurance premium of $3,000. At that time, the full amount was recorded as Insurance expense. On December 31, 19X1, the end of Maxe's accounting year, the required adjusting entry should be:

Prepaid Insurance	

Insurance Expense	
$3,000	

ACCRUED EXPENSE

The other category that you are likely to encounter is accrued expense. Accrued expenses are very similar to accounts payable, you have received an actual bill; in the case of accrued expense, although it is a liability, you do not legally have to pay it now.

Example: Real estate taxes will always be with us. Suppose that your real estate tax is based on a year beginning April 1 and ending March 31 and that it will be payable on that March 31. We are now at December 31, three months earlier.

Even though we don't have a tax bill in hand, clearly three-quarters of the real estate tax expense is allocable to the period ending on December 31. So we estimate what the real estate tax is likely to be—say, $480. On December 31, after letting the estimated tax have its effect, the accounts would look like this:

Accrued Real Estate Taxes Payable (a liability)

	$360

Real Estate Tax Expense (an expense)

$360	

Another common example of an accrued expense is Accrued wages payable. Only rarely does the end of an accounting period coincide with the weekly payroll period. So, to properly reflect expenses (accountants call it "matching expenses and revenues"), we must include in this year's expense any amounts that will be paid next year. If the year ends on a Tuesday and payday is Friday, we must accrue two-fifths (2/5) of the weekly payroll that will be paid on Friday. With a (weekly payroll of $5,000), the accounts look like this:

Accrued Wages Payable (a liability)

	$2,000

Wage & Salary Expense (an expense)

$2,000	

EXERCISE 7-2

From each of the following accounts, determine:

a. What were the amounts of the wages actually paid to employees during the year? $____________________

b. How much new insurance was actually purchased during the year? $____________________

Accrued Wages Payable

\$44,000	\$ 7,000 Balance 1/1/XX
	42,000

Prepaid Insurance

Balance 1/1/XX \$ 7,000	\$60,000
63,000	

DEFERRED AND ACCRUED REVENUE

The other two categories—deferred and accrued revenue—are less important. Mentally cross out the word "deferred" in deferred revenue and substitute the word "unearned." Relatively few companies have to deal with unearned revenue, but for them it is important. Some examples are:

* *Airline tickets:* For the airline, at the time a ticket is sold, assume a liability to provide a ride.
* *Magazine subscriptions:* Subscriptions must be paid in advance. So when you mail the company a check, the publisher assumes a liability to provide you with twelve or so future issues of the magazine.
* *Lay-away sale:* The customer paid a part of the purchase price, but the store cannot record it as earned revenue until the sale is consummated.

As you can see, the concept of unearned revenue is not central to an understanding of accounting, although it does occur occasionally in special circumstances.

The same thing goes for accrued revenue—revenue earned but not yet due. Due to the nature of the agreement with the customer, the business has not yet sent a bill to the customer. (Hence accrued revenue is sometimes called unbilled revenue). Typical cases include interest earned on an investment or time expended by a Certified Public Accountant on client matters. But, again, examples of accrued revenue are few and far between.

For starters, let's concentrate on the concepts of:

1. prepaid expenses, and
2. accrued expenses.

EXERCISE 7-3

Complete the following table:

Description of Account	*Asset or Liability?*
Prepaid expense	______
Accrued expense	______
Unbilled revenue	______
Unearned income	______

EXERCISE 7-4

Match the following definitions (on the left) to the appropriate titles (on the right). Indicate your answers by placing the letters of account titles in the answer blanks on the left:

	Brief Definition	*Account Title*
______	A revenue collected, but not earned	a. Accrued expense
______	An expense incurred, but not yet due to be paid	b. Prepaid expense
______	An expense paid, but not incurred	c. Unbilled revenue
______	A revenue earned, but not collected	d. Unearned revenue

ADDITIONAL EXERCISES

7-5. These accounts, among others, appear in the chart of accounts for BART:

Accounts Number	*Name of Account*	*Accounts Number*	*Name of Account*
10	Cash	150	Unearned revenue
20	Accounts receivable	200	Ticket revenue
30	Supplies inventory	300	Salary expense
40	Prepaid insurance	320	Insurance expense
50	Store equipment	350	Interest expense
55	Accumulated depreciation	400	Income tax expense
60	Other assets	410	Depreciation expense
100	Accounts payable	450	Electricity expense
110	Interest payable	460	Supplies expense
120	Accrued salaries	470	Payroll tax expense

For the following transactions (or adjustments), indicate, in the spaces provided below the Account Number (Acc. #), the amount of the adjustment as of year-end on 12/31/XX:

	Debits		Credits	
	Acc. #	Amount	Acc. #	Amount
a. An insurance policy, originally entered in Acc. #40 for $750 covering one year beginning 7/1/XX.				
b. Tickets purchased during December of 19XX were $2,500,000. This amount was entered in Acc. #10 and Acc. #200. Tickets actually used during December totaled $2,400,000.				

7-6. The term "revenue recognition" conventionally refers to (circle the correct answer):

a. The process of identifying transactions to be recorded as revenue in an accounting period.

b. The process of measuring and relating revenue and expenses of an enterprise for an accounting period.

c. The earning process that gives rise to revenue realization.

d. The process of identifying transactions that result in an inflow of assets from customers.

7-7. By using the following T-accounts, indicate the balances in the accounts following the indicated adjustments in parts a and b.

a. The term of the insurance policy is three years. If the total premium is $1,200, then one year after purchase the *account balances* would be:

Prepaid Insurance		Insurance Expense	
$1,200			

b. Interest earned on an investment amounts to 6 percent per annum of the principal, although the interest will not be received for two months. The principal of the note is $7,000, and the date of the note, 10/31/XX. The date for which accounting is to be done is 12/31/XX.

Accrued Interest Receivable	

Interest Revenue	

7-8. By using the following T-accounts, indicate the balance in the accounts after the indicated adjustments in parts a and b.

a. The Pelican magazine has decided to accept subscriptions for one year. In the first subscription drive they collected $3,600. Since there are four issues a year, after the first magazine has been issued, the balances in the respective accounts would be as follows:

Earned Revenue	

Unearned (Deferred) Magazine Subscriptions	
	$3,600

b. Royalties have been earned in the amount of $600. They will not be billed until next month. The balances in the accounts prior to billing are as follows:

Unbilled Royalty Income	

Royalty Income	

7-9. On a separate sheet of paper, write an explanation of unearned (deferred) income to someone unfamiliar with accounting.

7-10. On a separate sheet of paper, write an explanation of accrued revenue as you understand it.

SOLUTIONS

7-1.

Prepaid Insurance	
$2,500	

Insurance Expense	
$3,000	$2,500

Note: To properly reflect the asset and expense accounts, you have to increase the asset by $2,500 (5/6 of $3,000) and decrease the expense account to 1/6 of $3,000 (or $500).

7-2. a. $44,000

b. $63,000

7-3.

Prepaid expense	Asset
Accrued expense	Liability
Accrued income	Asset
Unearned income	Liability

7-4. d A revenue collected, but not earned

a An expense incurred, but not yet due to be paid

b An expense paid, but not incurred

c A revenue earned, but not collected

7-5. a. Dr #320, $375; Cr #40, $375

b. Dr #200, $100,000; Cr #150, $100,000

7-6. c. The earning process which gives rise to revenue recognition.

7-7. a. Prepaid insurance, $800; Insurance expense, $400

b. Accrued interest receivable, $70; Interest revenue, $70

7-8. a. Earned revenue, Cr balance, $900; Unearned magazine subscriptions, Cr balance, $2,700

b. Unbilled royalty income, Dr balance, $600; Royalty income, Cr balance, $600.

7-9. Unearned income represents amounts that have been collected by a business entity but for which the business owes a liability of some kind, such as the rendering of a service or the shipment of merchandise.

7-10. Accrued revenue is revenue earned but not yet billed as, for example, work done by an attorney for a client which has not been submitted to the client in the form of a bill.

8

Depreciation and The Cost of Goods Sold

DEPRECIATION

Of the two major concepts in this chapter, let's begin with depreciation. Depreciation is the accountant's way of allocating the cost of an asset over its useful life and of charging it as an expense in the corresponding income statement.

> *Example:* If we buy a truck for the business for $7,000 and if the truck has a useful life of five years, we allocate $1,400 ($7,000 ÷ 5 years) of the cost to each of the succeeding five years. Each year, of course, the depreciation expense of $1,400 finds its way into Retained earnings via the net income route (remember NI = R – E). At the end of the first year, the accounts would look like:

Truck		*Accumulated Depreciation—Truck*		*Depreciation Expense*	
$7,000			(1) $1,400	(1) $1,400	

By the start of the fifth year, they would look like:

Truck		*Accumulated Depreciation—Truck*		*Depreciation Expense*	
$7,000			$5,600 balance prior years	(1) $1,400	
			(1) $1,400		

Each year an entry would be made to debit the depreciation expense and credit the accumulated depreciation in the amount of $1,400. At the end of five years, the balance in the truck account would be $7,000, and the balance in the Accumulated depreciation account for the truck would be a credit balance of $7,000.

EXERCISE 8-1

a. **If we have a truck that was used when we purchased it at $3,500, and if it is expected to last only two years, indicate the balances in the respective T-accounts at the end of the first year of use.**

b. Complete the following depreciation schedule for a new truck with a five-year life and a scrap value = $0:

End of Year	Original Cost	Depreciation Expense	Accumulated Depreciation
0	$15,000	$0	$0
1			
2			
3			
4			
5			

Actually, of course, depreciation has quite a few more wrinkles than we've shown you. But the essential theoretical basis for depreciation is the same. [Chapter 10 is devoted to a detailed discussion of Property, plant, and equipment and related depreciation problems.] For the moment, just consider depreciation as the accountant's way of allocating costs to successive accounting periods. Remember that you (meaning the company) pay the $7,000 at the time the asset is purchased and that the subsequent depreciaion entries do not require the expenditure of funds. In other words, depreciation is a noncash expense.

EXERCISE 8-2

You start a new business and buy an apartment building for $100,000 with a 25-year life. You have no other assets in the business. The rental income (net of operating expenses except depreciation) is $5,000 per year. What would the balance sheet look like at the end of the twenty-fifth year?

New Business
BALANCE SHEET
19XX

Assets			*Equities*	
Cash		$______		
			Owner's equity	$______
Apartment Building:				
Original Cost:	$______			
Less: Accumulated depreciation	______	______		
Total assets		$______	**Total equities**	$______

The federal income tax laws were changed in 1981, allowing automobiles and trucks to be depreciated in three years and buildings to be depreciated in fifteen years, among other changes in the depreciation rates. This change in the federal income tax regulations may have an influence on depreciation rates in financial statements, although the useful economic life of an asset should be the criterion for the accountant in allocating a portion of the cost of an asset to the income statement.

COST OF GOODS SOLD

The other basic concept in this chapter involves the relationship between inventory and the cost of goods sold. (You might have noticed that occasionally we use "cost of sales," which means the same.)

An ongoing business usually has a *beginning inventory* (I_b). During the year the business buys more merchandise for resale, and these amounts are called *purchases* (P). It is pretty easy to see that the beginning inventory plus the purchases for the year add up to the total amount of *goods available for sale* (G). Algebraically:

$$I_b + P = G$$

But an onging business also makes sales during the year, and these sales have to be reflected in this equation. If you know your end-of-year inventory (I_e) and deduct that figure from the goods available for sale, you reflect the year's sales and at the same time arrive at your *cost of goods sold* (CGS). Algebrically, that line of thought looks like this:

$$G - I_e = I_b + P - I_e = CGS$$

Example: Your beginning inventory (I_b) is \$750. By the end of the year, during which you made purchases (P) of \$2,250, your ending inventory (I_e) is \$1,000. What is the cost of goods sold (CGS)? Solution:

$$\begin{aligned} CGS &= I_b + P - I_e \\ &= \$750 + \$2{,}250 - \$1{,}000 \\ &= \$2{,}000 \end{aligned}$$

Conversely, if you know the cost of goods sold, you can deduct that amount from goods available (G) to arrive at the ending inventory (I_e):

$$I_e = I_b + P - CGS$$

EXERCISE 8-3

Complete the following table for cost of goods sold:

	(a)	(b)	(c)	(d)
Beginning inventory	7	______	15	22
Purchases	20	17	30	28
Goods available	______	23	______	______
Ending inventory	12	______	______	25
Cost of goods sold	______	20	25	______

Periodic Inventory Method

The *periodic inventory method,* commonly used by smaller businesses, is an easy method to understand. In elementary financial accounting it is the only method that I require my students to learn. The periodic method means simply that we take the ending inventory (I_e) at specific points of time, usually at the end of the business' fiscal year. Since we did the same thing last year, we also have the beginning inventory (I_b). Then we can just add up the purchases during the year, and—presto—we have an equation with one unknown, the cost of goods sold. Just as simple as falling off a log.

Example: Assume the same information as in the preceding example:

Inventory		*Purchases*		*Cost of Goods Sold*	
$ 750	(a) $750	$2,250	(a) $2,250	(a) $3,000	(b) $1,000
(b) $1,000					

Now we transfer beginning Inventory and Purchases to Cost of goods sold (a) and set up the ending inventory (b).

Now that you have all the requisite knowledge to complete the exercises, go to it. But be aware that some repetition (or review, if you prefer) is incorporated intentionally into the exercises.

One last note: Chapter 8 is the last chapter before taking the First Progress Test. Normally, the first eight chapters of an introductory accounting course would cover the first third of the required material. But we have spent a little more-than-the-normal amount of time on these fundamental topics to give you a firmer grasp of the material at the outset. A sound knowledge of the topics covered in these last eight chapters will make studying the balance of the course all the easier. So remember that, when you have completed the exercises for Chapter 8, take the First Progress Test that begins on page 109.

ADDITIONAL EXERCISES

8-4. For each of the following transactions, indicate which account should be debited and which account should be credited:

a. Accrual of real estate taxes for the current fiscal year:

Debit ____________________ Credit ____________________

b. Recording depreciation on office furniture for the year:

Debit ____________________ Credit ____________________

c. Inventory is counted at the end of the year. Since this is a new business, there was no inventory at the beginning of the year.

Debit ____________________ Credit ____________________

8-5. You have been requested to make a calculation of the gasoline used during the past year ending December 31, 1981. The following data is considered reliable.

Cost per Gallon	*$1.25 Regular*	*$1.35 Unleaded*	*$1.40 Unleaded Premium*
Physical Inventories (gals):			
July 1, 1980	5,200	2,000	1,000
January 1, 1981	2,400	3,000	1,500
December 31, 1981	1,400	4,000	1,500
Purchases (gals):			
1/1 - 6/30/81	10,000	6,000	5,000
7/1 - 12/31/81	12,000	7,000	8,000
a. 1981 usage (gals)	______	______	______
b. 1981 usage ($)	$______	$______	$______

Review Problem

8-6. Enter the following transactions regarding the Cincus Ferry Company into the appropriate T-accounts provided Prepare the balance sheet as of 11/30/XX and an income statement for the month of November 19XX. The trial balance of the Cincus Ferry Company on October 31, 19XX is as follows:

	Dr	*Cr*
Cash	$ 85,000	
Supplies/inventory	9,000	
Prepaid insurance	6,000	
Cincus ferry boat	900,000	
Accumulated depreciation		$ 300,000
Accounts payable		50,000
Interest payable		6,000
12% mortgage notes (payable) in annual installments of $50,000)		300,000
Capital stock ($30 par value/share)		300,000
Retained earnings		44,000
	$1,000,000	$1,000,000

The following transactions occurred during the month of November:

1. Fares collected and deposited in the bank, $15,000
2. Payroll for the month:

Ferry captain	$1,200
Ferry crew	800
Secretary	500
	2,500
Less: Income tax withheld	500
Balance paid by check	$2,000

3. Amount paid on accounts payable, $20,000
4. Interest accrued on mortgage for October, $3,000
5. Monthly depreciation on ferry boat, $2,500
6. Diesel fuel for October paid by check, $3,000
7. $500 of prepaid insurance was expensed during October

a. Prepare T-accounts to record 10/31/XX balances and November 19XX transactions for Cincus Ferry Company:

b. On a separate sheet of lined paper, prepare a statement of income for November 19XX and a balance sheet as of 11/30/XX.

8-1. a.

Truck		Accumulated Depreciation Truck		Depreciation Expense	
$3,500			$1,750	$1,750	

b.

End of Year	Original Cost	Depreciation Expense	Accumulated Depreciation
0	$15,000	-0-	-0-
1	15,000	$3,000	$ 3,000
2	15,000	3,000	6,000
3	15,000	3,000	9,000
4	15,000	3,000	12,000
5	15,000	3,000	15,000

8-2.

BALANCE SHEET

Assets			*Equities*	
Cash		$125,000	Owner's equity	$125,000
Apartment Building:				
Original cost	$100,000			
Less: Accumulated depreciation	100,000			
Total assets		$125,000	Total equities	$125,000

8-3. Reading from top to bottom:

a. 27,15

b. 6, 3

c. 45, 20

d. 50, 25

8-4. a. Dr Real estate tax expense; Cr Accrued real estate tax payable

b. Dr Depreciation expense; Cr Accumulated depreciation

c. Dr Inventory (asset); Cr Cost of goods sold

8-5.

	Regular	*Unleaded*	*Premium Unleaded*
a.	23,000 gals	12,000 gals	13,000 gals
b.	$28,750	$16,200	$18,200

8-6. a.

Cash	
$85,000	(2) $ 2,000
(1) $15,000	(3) $20,000
	(6) $ 3,000

Withholding Tax Payable	
	(2) $500

Salaries	
(2) $2,500	

Supplies Inventory	
$9,000	

Accrued Interest Payable	
	$6,000
	(4) $3,000

Fuel Expense	
(6) $3,000	

Prepaid Insurance	
$6,000	(7) $500

Mortgage Payable	
	$300,000

Depreciation Expense	
(5) $2,500	

Ferry Boat	
$900,000	

Capital Stock	
	$300,000

Insurance Expense	
(7) $500	

Accumulated Depreciation—Ferry Boat	
	$300,000
	(5) $ 2,500

Retained Earnings	
	$44,000

Interest Expense	
(4) $3,000	

Accounts Payable	
(3) $20,000	$50,000

Fare Revenue	
	(1) $15,000

b.

Cincus Ferry Company
BALANCE SHEET
November 30, 19XX

Assets			*Equities*		
Current Assets:			Current Liabilities:		
Cash	$ 75,000		Accounts payable	$ 30,000	
Inventory	9,000		Tax payable	500	
Prepaid insurance	5,500	$ 89,500	Interest payable	9,000	$ 39,500
Ferry Boat	$900,000		Mortgage Payable Shareholder's Equity:		
Accumulated			Capital stock	300,000	
depreciation	302,500	597,500	Retained earnings	47,500	347,500
		$687,000			$687,000

Cincus Ferry Company
INCOME STATEMENT
November, 19XX

Fare Revenues		$15,000
Operating Expenses:		
Salaries	$2,500	
Fuel	3,000	
Insurance	500	
Depreciation	2,500	
Interest	3,000	11,500
Net income		$ 3,500

First Progress Test

This test, as well as the two other Progress Tests, should be taken without references to the book. The First Progress Test is designed to be completed in one and one-half hours. More important than finishing on time, however, is doing a good job. So if it takes you longer than the allotted time, remember that time is not the foremost goal.

This test is divided into four parts:

* Quickies (multiple choice questions)—26 points,
* The Balance Sheet—24 points,
* The Income Statement—20 points, and
* Accounting Mechanics—30 points.

The answers are given at the end of the test. As a minimum, you should score at least 75 points (which is exactly 75 percent) on the test. If you do better, congratulations! You may proceed to Chapter 9. If you score lower, determine where your weaknesses are, and review the appropriate sections before going on.

QUICKIES (2 points each)

1. T-accounts are substitutes used in the classroom for:

   a. journal entries.
   b. source documents.
   c. general ledger accounts.
   d. closing journal entries.
   e. none of the above.

2. "Debit" means:

   a. left-hand side of an account.
   b. increase in an account.
   c. decrease in an account.
   d. right-hand side of an account.
   e. an increase from a credit.

3. Which of the following is the correct statement of the accounting equation?

   a. $A = EX + R + L + S/E$
   b. $A + EX = D + L + R + R/E_b$
   c. $A + EX - L = D + R - R/E_b + C/C$
   d. $A + EX + D = L + C/C + R + R/E_b$
   e. None of the above

4. All of the following business transactions have the effect of increasing assets and of increasing liabilities *except*:

   a. buying merchandise on credit.
   b. receiving advance payment for rent.
   c. issuing bonds.
   d. receiving payment for services rendered last year.
   e. obtaining a bank loan.

5. All of the following business transactions have the effect of increasing expenses *except*:

   a. recorded expense for rent for the month.
   b. recorded depreciation for the year.
   c. paid employee salaries.
   d. purchased items for merchandise inventory.
   e. paid the auditors' bill, which was not previously recorded on the books.

6. Assets are customarily presented on the balance sheet:

   a. on the basis of cost, because cost is usually factual and can be objectively verified.
   b. on the basis of cost, because in the event of liquidation, the assets would probably not sell for more than cost.

c. on the basis of cost as adjusted by a price index reflecting changes in the purchasing power of the dollar.
d. on the basis of current fair market value established by independent appraisals.
e. on the basis of the lower of cost or market because in case of liquidation, this amount is the most likely amount realizable from the sale.

7. A balance sheet:

a. reports a company's financial position at a specific time.
b. may be represented by the model: Assets = Liabilities − Owner's equity.
c. both a and b.
d. covers a period of time, usually one year.
e. neither a or b.

8. Shareholders' equity for a corporation consists of:

a. contributed capital.
b. contributed capital in excess of par value.
c. retained earnings.
d. only the sum of a and b.
e. the sum of a, b, and c.

9. Several balance sheet asset classifications follow. The first one out of sequence (going from a through d) is:

a. current assets.
b. long-term investments and funds.
c. other assets.
d. property, plant, and equipment.
e. none of the above classifications are out of sequence.

10. Net income divided by the shares of common stock outstanding is the computation for:

a. earnings per share.
b. return on investment.
c. current ratio.
d. debt to equity ratio.
e. none of the above.

11. The effect of recording a two-for-one stock split* would be to:

a. decrease the current ratio, decrease working capital, and decrease book value per share.

*A stock split is merely an exchange of shares. In this case, shareholders receive from the issuing company one share for every one they hold. A stock split does not involve any change in the dollar totals of shareholder's equity.

b. leave inventory turnover unaffected, decrease working capital, and decrease book value per share.
c. leave working capital unaffected, decrease earnings per share, and decrease book value per share.
d. leave working capital unaffected, decrease earnings per share, and decrease the debt to equity ratio.
e. none of the above.

12. Generally, revenues should be recognized at a point when:

a. management decides it is appropriate to do so.
b. the product is available for sale to the ultimate consumer.
c. an exchange has taken place and the earnings process is virtually complete.
d. an order for a definite amount of merchandise has been received for shipment FOB destination.
e. there is minimum likelihood of a bad debt occurring.

13. Classification as an extraordinary item on the income statement would be most appropriate for the:

a. abnormal increase in an operating expense.
b. substantial write-off of obsolete inventories.
c. sale of investments acquired for resale.
d. substantial loss resulting from flood damage.
e. none of the above.

THE BALANCE SHEET

14. (8) points

Bizzard One, Inc.
BALANCE SHEET

Assets		*Liabilities and Stockholders' Equity*		
Current Assets:		Current Liabilities:		
Cash and accounts receivable	$ 40,000	Accounts payable		$ 5,000
Inventories	80,000	Income taxes payable		10,000
	120,000	Accrued expenses		5,000
				20,000
Fixed Assets-Net:	100,000	Long-Term Debt		20,000
Other Assets:	20,000	Stockholders' Equity		20,000
		Capital stock	100,000	
		Retained earnings	100,000	200,000
	$240,000			$240,000

Compute the following:

a. Amount of working capital: $____________________

b. If net income is $50,000, what is the ROI? ____________________ %

c. Working capital ratio: ______________________________

d. Long-term debt to equity ratio: ______________________________

15. (6 points) The statement of retained (or reinvested) earnings provides the link between the balance sheet and the income statement, complete the following tables relating to the retained earnings account of the three unrelated businesses, a, b, and c.

	(a)	(b)	(c)
Total assets	$100	$_____	$200
Total liabilities	_____	25	100
Contributed capital	20	25	_____
Retained earnings (beginning of the year)	20	40	100
Net income (loss) for the year	30	_____	(30)
Dividends paid during the year	_____	15	10
Retained earnings (end of the year)	50	40	_____

16. (6 points) Rearrange the following asset accounts in correct balance sheet order:

Cash ______________________________

Property, plant, and equipment ______________________________

Long-term investments ______________________________

Accounts receivable ______________________________

Other assets ______________________________

Merchandise inventories ______________________________

Prepaid expense ______________________________

17. (4 points) Complete the following balance sheet:

Saturday Night Fever, Inc.
BALANCE SHEET
September 30, 19XX

Assets		*Liabilities and Stockholders' Equity*	
Current Assets:		Current Liabilities:	
Cash	$4,100	Notes payable to banks	$4,000
Amounts due from customers	900	Wages payable	3,000
Items purchased for resale	1,500	Taxes payable	2,500
Prepaid insurance	300		
Total current assets	$_____	Total current liabilities	$_____
Property, plant, and equipment:		Stockholders' Equity	$_____
Machinery	$8,000		
Automobile	1,500		
	_____		
Total assets	$_____	Total equities	$_____

THE INCOME STATEMENT

18. (5 points) Answer the following short questions relating to the income statement (assume sales are always $250,000) and consider each question independently:

a. If sales are $250,000 and the gross margin percentage is 40 percent, the cost of goods sold is $____________.

b. If the operating income is $50,000, the percentage of operating income to sales is ________ percentage.

c. If the gross margin percentage is equal to the cost of goods sold percentage, the gross margin is $____________.

d. If the income tax *rate* (for all operating income) is 50 percent and the net income is $25,000, then operating income is $____________.

e. If operating expenses total $75,000, and if the gross margin percentage is 40 percent, operating income is $____________.

19. (11 points) Complete the following algebraic expressions:

a. Assets = Liabilities + ______________________________

b. Retained earnings (end of year) = Net income − Dividends + ______________

c. Stockholders' equity = Contributed capital + ______________________

d. Sales − Cost of goods sold = ______________________________

e. Operating income − Income taxes = __________________________

f. Gross margin − Operating expenses = __________________________

g. Revenues − All expenses = ______________________________

h. Assets − Liabilities = Retained earnings + ______________________

i. Revenues − Cost of goods sold − Operating expenses = ______________

j. Gross margin − Operating expenses − Income taxes = ______________

k. $\dfrac{\text{Net income}}{\text{Stock outstanding}}$ = ______________________________

20. (4 points) Complete the following income statement:

	Dollar Amount	*Percentage of Net Sales*
Net sales	$__________	100%
Cost of sales	__________	60
Gross margin	__________	40
Operating expenses	__________	15
Operating income	__________	25
Income taxes	__________	15
Net income	$200,000	10

ACCOUNTING MECHANICS

21. (10 points) Your roommate, who is taking Bus. Ad. 1, has just completed the following T-accounts for the Cincus Ferry Company. But since he rushed off to watch "Wall Street

Week" on TV, he left the explanations for the entries for you to complete. Please explain your roommate's entries in the spaces provided.

Cash	
(a) $15,000	(b) $ 2,000
(e) $25,000	(c) $20,000
	(g) $ 1,000
	(i) $ 1,500
	(j) $ 100

Income Tax Withheld	
	(b) $500

Rental of Ferry	
(d) $10,000	

Prepaid Insurance	
(g) $1,000	(h) $500

Capital Stock	
	(e) $25,000

Payroll Expense	
(b) $2,500	

Ferry Terminal Equipment	
(f) $30,000	

Retained Earnings	
(i) $1,500	

Diesel Fuel	
(j) $900	

Accounts Payable	
(c) $20,000	(d) $10,000
	(f) $30,000
	(j) $ 800

Ferry Revenue	
	(a) $15,000

Insurance Expense	
(h) $500	

a. ______________________________

b. ______________________________

c. ______________________________

d. ______________________________

e. ______________________________

f. ______________________________

g. ______________________________

h. ______________________________

i. ______________________________

j. ______________________________

22. (9 points) Indicate the normal balance (Dr or Cr) for each of the following accounts. Also indicate whether each should appear on the income statement or on the balance sheet. To mark your answers enter checkmarks in the appropriate columns.

Accounts	*Normal Balance* *Debit*	*Credit*	*Balance Sheet*	*Income Statement*
a. Accumulated depreciation	______	______	______	______
b. Purchase discount allowed	______	______	______	______
c. Dividends paid	______	______	______	______
d. Sales returns	______	______	______	______
e. Allowance for doubtful accounts	______	______	______	______
f. Amortization of patents	______	______	______	______
g. Depeciation expense	______	______	______	______
h. Land	______	______	______	______
i. Amount paid in excess of par value of common stock	______	______	______	______

23. (11 points) Complete the following table by entering either "Increase" or "Decrease" in the appropriate box:

Classification	*Left Side (Debit)*	*Right Side (Credit)*
a. Assets	__________	__________
b. Liabilities	__________	__________
c. Contributed capital	__________	__________
d. Revenues	__________	__________
e. Expenses	__________	__________

Complete the following table by entering either "Debit" or "Credit" in the appropriate box:

Classification	*Increase*	*Decrease*
f. Assets	__________	__________
g. Liabilities	__________	__________
h. Dividends	__________	__________
i. Revenues	__________	__________
j. Expenses	__________	__________
k. Contributed Capital	__________	__________

SOLUTIONS

1. c
2. a
3. d
4. d
5. d
6. a
7. a
8. e
9. c
10. a
11. c
12. c
13. d
14. a. $100,000
    b. 25 percent
    c. 6 to 1
    d. 1 to 10, or 0.10, or 10 percent
15. Reading from top to bottom:
    a. $30, 0
    b. $90, 15
    c. $40, 60
16. Cash
    Accounts receivable
    Inventories
    Prepaid expense
    Long-term investments
    Property, plant, and equipment
    Other assets

17. Reading from top to bottom:
Assets: \$6,800, \$9,500, \$16,300.
Equities: \$9,500, \$6,800, \$16,300.

18. a. \$150,000
 b. 20 percent
 c. \$125,000
 d. \$50,000
 e. \$25,000

19. a. Shareholders' equity
 b. Retained earnings (beginning of year)
 c. Retained earnings (end of year)
 d. Gross margin
 e. Net income
 f. Operating income
 g. Income, "bottom line," Net income
 h. Contributed capital
 i. Operating income
 j. Net income
 k. Earnings per share (EPS)

20. \$2,000,000; \$1,200,000; \$800,000; \$300,000; \$500,000; \$300,000

21. a. Revenue received
 b. Paid payroll of \$2,500 with a withholding tax of \$500
 c. Paid accounts payable
 d. Accrued ferry rental
 e. Sold capital stock
 f. Bought equipment on account
 g. Bought insurance for cash
 h. Recorded expiration of insurance
 i. Paid dividend
 j. Paid for diesel fuel; Cash \$100, Accounts payable, \$800

22.

	Debit	*Credit*	*Balance Sheet*	*Income Statement*
a.		X	X	
b.		X		X
c.	X		X	
d.	X			X
e.		X	X	
f.	X			X
g.	X			X
h.	X		X	
i.		X	X	

23.

a.	Increase	Decrease
b.	Decrease	Increase
c.	Decrease	Increase
d.	Decrease	Increase
e.	Increase	Decrease
f.	Debit	Credit
g.	Credit	Debit
h.	Debit	Credit
i.	Credit	Debit
j.	Debit	Credit
k.	Credit	Debit

9
Sales Revenue

NET SALES

The single most important barometer of business success is revenue. "Revenue" is a general term that includes income from services as well as from the sale of merchandise. "Sales," on the other hand, is used to designate revenues arising just from the sale of tangible items. Without an increase in sales, income cannot increase unless the managers are somehow able to cut expenses. "Expenses," in turn, are generally expressed as a percentage of net sales; for the example, the expense of advertising might be running at a rate of 4 percent of net sales. In fact, a percentage column alongside the money column in income statements is fairly common (Figure 9-1).

FIGURE 9-1

Quiet Disco, Inc.
INCOME STATEMENT
Month Ended October 31, 19XX

			Percentage to Net Sales
Net Sales:			
Gross Sales	$3,100		
Less: Returns and allowances	100	$3,000	100%
Cost of Goods Sold:		1,800	60
Gross margin		1,200	40
Operating Expenses:			
Salaries and wages	$ 600		
Rent	300		
Office supplies	150		
Insurance	75		
Miscellaneous	75	1,200	40
		-0-	0

EXERCISE 9-1

Complete the following table:

	$	%
Net sales	$10,000	
Cost of goods sold		75
Gross margin		
Operating expenses		10
Net income (before income taxes)		
Federal taxes on income (50% rate)		
Net income		

In Figure 9-1, for example, Quiet Disco is operating at a "breakeven" point, that is, its sales are precisely equal to its expenses. But let's assume that the managers are somehow, during the month of November, able to increase their Net sales by $1,000. What happens to Net income? Assuming that the Operating expenses for November remain at $1,200, the Cost of goods sold increases by $600 (60 percent of the increase in sales of $1,000), and the Gross margin increases by $400 (40 percent of the increase in sales of $1,000). Since the Operating expenses remain constant at $1,200, Net income increases from zero to $400 and, in the percentage column, rises to 10 percent of Net sales.

But what if the November sales dropped to $2,000? Just apply the same logic in reverse. The Cost of goods sold is $600 less, and the Gross margin drops to $800. Since we again assume that the Operating expenses remain constant at $1,200, the net result of the operation for November is a Net loss of $400.

EXERCISE 9-2

If the Operating expenses are $5,000, and if the Gross margin percentage is 25 percent, at what sales volume would we have to operate to break even? $____________

All businesses can be analyzed in a similar fashion providing only that we are able, by historical analysis, to separate those expenses that vary directly with sales (such as Cost of goods sold) from those that are independent of the level of Net sales (such as Operating expenses) in our illustration.

ACCOUNTING FOR BAD DEBTS

Bad debts and the allowance for doubtful accounts present a problem in calculating sales revenue. Virtually all the business done in the United States relies on some form of credit. In other words, not every dollar reported as net sales necessarily finds its way into the bank account, because some accounts are more collectible than others. Most businesses that have an historical perspective on their customers can predict with reasonable accuracy the percentage of net sales that is likely to be uncollectible. A simple historical ratio gives the accountant a working percentage:

$$\frac{\text{Bad debts during the year}}{\text{Net sales during the year}} = \text{Percentage of uncollectibles}$$

EXERCISE 9-3

The advantage of relating a company's bad debt experience to its net sales for the period is that this approach:

a. gives a reasonably correct statement of receivables in the balance sheet.

b. relates bad debts experience to the period of sale.
c. is the only generally accepted method for valuing accounts receivable.
d. makes estimates of uncollectible accounts unnecessary.

Calculating this ratio for several years will reveal trends that might call for changes in the percentage used, but for our purposes let's assume that the average percentage remains constant over time and approximates 1 percent. Using our old friend, the T-account, we can illustrate the entries that are normally made in such a situation.

> *Example:* All of Quiet Disco's sales were on credit; so during the month of October 19XX the provision for doubtful accounts would have been $30 (1 percent of Net sales of $3,000). If November credit sales were $4,000, and if December's were $4,500, we would then have the following entries:

Accounts Receivable

(1) $3,000	
(3) $4,000	
(5) $4,500	

Allowance for Doubtful Accounts

	(2) $30
	(4) $40
	(6) $45

Net Sales

	(1) $3,000
	(3) $4,000
	(5) $4,500

Bad Debts

(2) $30	
(4) $40	
(6) $45	

A brief description of each of the entries follows:

1. Net credit sales are recorded.
2. 1 percent of credit sales of $3,000 is recorded as a provision for bad debts.
3. Net credit sales are recorded for November.
4. November provision for bad debts is entered.

5/6. Similar entries for the month of December.

7. This entry records the write-off of a $10 account that is uncollectible. (See following page.)

Now what happens if sometime during the year, say in December, a $10 account receivable becomes uncollectible? In that case, the accounts would appear as follows:

Accounts Receivable		*Allowance for Doubtful Accounts*	
$11,500	(7) $10	(7) $10	$115

EXERCISE 9-4

Given the following journal entries:

Bad debts expense	**$1,200**	
Allowance for doubtful accounts		**$1,200**
Allowance for doubtful accounts	**100**	
Accounts receivable		**100**
Cash	**100**	
Recovery of bad debts		**100**

What might you conclude? (Indicate the correct statement or statements.)

a. Net income is decreased by $1,000.
b. The net amount of accounts receivable is decreased by $1,200.
c. The allowance for doubtful accounts is increased by $1,100.
d. Gross accounts receivable is reduced by $100.

Note that entry 7—the write-off of the uncollectible $10 account—does *not* affect income since it is merely a credit to Accounts receivable and a debit to Allowance for doubtful accounts. It has no effect on the balance sheet either. An illustration of the balance sheet presentation will make this point clear. But let's first present the accounts as they would appear before entry 7.

Accounts Receivable:		
Accounts receivable—trade	$11,500	
Less: Allowance for doubtful accounts	115	$11,385

After entry 7, the same accounts would appear as follows:

Accounts Receivable:		
Accounts receivable—trade	$11,490	
Less: Allowance for doubtful accounts	105	$11,385

So entry 7 changes neither the total assets, nor the current ratio, nor the net amount of accounts receivable as stated on the balance sheet.

What if a bad debt is eventually collected? For example, what if the company receives a payment of the $10 that was written off by the entry 7? In that case, the simplest treatment is just to debit Cash and credit Miscellaneous income for the amount of $10.

EXERCISE 9-5

For the month of November, your credit sales are $7,000. Your bad debt experience indicates a bad debt rate of 0.5 percent of credit sales. Your collections on accounts receivable for the month are $2,500, and the accounts receivable determined to be worthless during the month total $15. Enter this information in the T-accounts:

PERIODIC INVENTORIES AND THE COST OF GOODS SOLD

What are periodic inventories? In simple terms, they are nothing more than inventories taken periodically. Here's how they work: During the month (or year), the accountant merely records the additions to inventory in an account called "purchases" (P). At the end of the accounting period, a physical inventory (I_e) is taken. The dollar amount representing the physical inventory is then deducted from the total of the beginning inventory (I_b) and the purchases to arrive at the cost of goods sold (CGS). In other words:

$$CGS = I_b + P - I_e$$

Conversely:

$$I_e = I_b + P - CGS$$

Since either of these equations is linear, if you know three of the components, you can determine the fourth. Although we will meet the inventory problem again in Chapter 10, remember that the periodic inventory method provides the necessary information to determine: 1. the ending Inventory, which appears on the balance sheet, and 2. the Cost of goods sold, which appears as a deduction from Net sales on the income statement.

Sales are not the only variable. Unlike the Cost of good sold, which remains fixed regardless of the sales level, Operating expenses can vary with the level of sales. Although we assumed earlier that all expenses remained constant, such is not always the case. Nevertheless, you can analyze any business as long as you are able, by historical analysis, to separate expenses that vary directly with sales (such as Cost of goods sold) from those that are independent of the level of Net Sales (such as Operating expenses).

As an example of how important it is for sales revenue to grow, compare the sales growth of Tandem Computers, Inc. and Subsidiaries for the five years ended September 30, 1980, as given in their annual report (Figure 9-2). Note also the impact on EPS over the same period.

Example: Let's continue the illustration started in Chapter 8 (page 102):

Inventory		*Purchases*		*Cost of Goods Sold*	
$ 750	(a) $750	$2,250	(a) $2,250	(a) $3,000	(b) $1,000
(b) $1,000					

Entry a is the transfer to Cost of goods sold; entry b is the set-up of ending inventory. This is a basic illustration of the four component elements of all accounts:

1. Beginning Inventory balance	$750
2. Increases in the account (Purchases)	$2,250
3. Decreases in the account (Cost of goods sold)	$2,000
4. Ending Inventory balance	$1,000

ADDITIONAL EXERCISES

9-6. Complete the following table (continued on page 131):

	(a)	*(b)*	*(c)*
Beginning Inventory	**$100**	**$ 80**	**$ 50**
Purchases, gross	**40**	**120**	**250**

TANDEM COMPUTERS INCORPORATED AND SUBSIDIARIES

CONSOLIDATED STATEMENT OF OPERATIONS

For the Five Years Ended September 30, 1980

(Dollars in Thousands Except Per Share Amounts)

	Year Ended September 30				
	1980	1979	1978	1977	1976
REVENUES	$108,989	$55,974	$24,305	$7,692	$ 581
COSTS AND EXPENSES:					
Cost of revenues	40,831	20,786	9,096	3,514	482
Product development	8,786	4,654	2,169	1,094	979
Marketing, general and administrative	40,049	20,828	8,803	2,719	1,327
Interest, net	(1,759)	(398)	(253)	36	(38)
	87,907	45,870	19,815	7,363	2,750
INCOME (LOSS) BEFORE INCOME TAXES AND EXTRAORDINARY CREDIT	21,082	10,104	4,490	329	(2,169)
Provision for Income Taxes	10,395	5,184	2,337	171	—
INCOME (LOSS) BEFORE EXTRAORDINARY CREDIT	10,687	4,920	2,153	158	(2,169)
Extraordinary Credit—Tax benefit of net operating loss carryforwards	—	—	1,218	167	—
NET INCOME (LOSS)	$ 10,687	$ 4,920	$ 3,371	$ 325	$(2,169)
INCOME (LOSS) PER COMMON SHARE:*					
Income (loss) before extraordinary credit	$ 1.06	$ .59	$ .30	$ .03	$ (2.17)
Extraordinary credit	—	—	.17	.03	—
Net income (loss)	$ 1.06	$ .59	$ .47	$ .06	$ (2.17)
Weighted average shares outstanding*	10,080,372	8,356,756	7,179,948	5,359,846	1,060,540

*Adjusted for a two-for-one stock split in June, 1980.

FIGURE 9-2. A historical pattern of growth in revenue

Reprinted by permission of Tandem Computers, Inc.

Purchases returns	**5**	**10**	**0**
Freight-in	**5**	______	**10**
Total goods available	**140**	**200**	______
Ending inventory	______	**90**	______
Cost of sales	**$100**	**$ ______**	**$300**

9-7. A local furniture store carries an average inventory of $50,000, which it turns over (or sells out) three times a year at a gross profit of 40 percent and a net profit of 10 percent of sales.* If a 10-percent reduction in selling prices will result in four turnovers per year with a 10-percent increase in operating expenses, will the company make more or less net profit? How much?

a. More or Less (circle one).

b. How much? $____________

9-8. If business conditions are stable, a decline in the number of sales outstanding from one year to the next (based on a company's accounts receivable at year-end) might indicate which of the following?

a. A stiffening of the company's credit policies.
b. That the second year's sales were made at lower prices than the first year's sales.
c. That a longer discount period and a more distant due date were extended to customers in the second year.
d. A significant decrease in the volume of sales of the second year.

9-9. a. Complete the following table using the same bad debt experience rate for each year. Begin your solution by solving for 19X3 first:

	19X1	*19X2*	*19X3*
Net credit sales	250,000	______	400,000
Bad debt expense	______	1,500	______
Balance in Allowance for doubtful accounts at end of year	1,600	2,600	2,850
Bad debt write-offs	150	______	1,750

b. What is the balance in the Allowance for doubtful accounts as of 1/1/X1?

9-10. In connection with a fire loss suffered by your client on March 31, 19X1, you have been asked to compute the amount of the inventory lost during the fire for insurance purposes. The following relevant data has been obtained.

*Inventory turnover is defined as:

$$\frac{\text{Cost of goods sold}}{\text{Average inventory}} = \text{Inventory turnover}$$

Disregard income tax effects. All the data is for the fiscal year ended December 31, 19X0 unless specified otherwise:

Sales	$1,000,000
Cost of goods sold	$ 700,000
Operating expense	$ 125,000
Income taxes	50%
Inventory, 12/31/X0	$ 150,000
Purchases 1/1-3/31/X1	$ 175,000
Sales 1/1-3/31/X1	$ 300,000
Physical inventory, 3/31X1 (after fire)	$ 37,500

a. What is your best estimate of the inventory immediately before the fire at 3/31/X1? $__________

b. What is your opinion on the amount of the fire loss that should be claimed at 3/31/X1? $__________

SOLUTIONS

9-1.

	$	%
Net sales	$10,000	100%
Cost of goods sold	7,500	75
Gross margin	2,500	25
Operating expenses	1,000	10
Net Income (before taxes)	1,500	15
Federal taxes on income	750	7.5
Net income	$ 750	7.5

9-2. $20,000

9-3. b

9-4. b, c, and d are all correct.

9-5.

Cash	
(3) $2,500	

Accounts Receivable	
(1) $7,000	(3) $2,500 (4) $ 15

Allowance for Doubtful Accounts	
(4) $15	(2) $35

Sales	
	(1) $7,000

Bad Debt Expense	
(2) $35	

9-6. Reading from top to bottom:

a. 40

b. 10, 110

c. 310, 10

9-7. a. Less

b. $7,500

9-8. a

9-9. a.

	19X1	19X2	19X3
Net credit sales		$300,000	$2,000
Bad debt expense	$1,250	500	
Bad debt expense			
Bad debt write-offs			

b. $500

9-10. a. $115,000

b. $77,500

10
Inventory Costing

To understand inventories as they appear on the balance sheets of larger corporations, you must be familiar with several problems in valuation. These problems break down into two general classes: inventory flow assumptions and inventory valuation conventions.

INVENTORY FLOW ASSUMPTIONS

If we have a group of items in inventory and we sell one, which one did we sell? The answer to that problem is not as obvious as it seems. Accountants have reacted to the problem by making assumptions about the particular item that is sold. You can make four main assumptions, each of which has a different impact on net income and balance sheet presentation. So we will discuss each separately.

Assumption 1: Specific Identification

Suppose the items of inventory are different or identifiable enough (such as by serial number) that we know which one we sold. In that case, if the cost has been identified with that particular item, you simply charge the costs of goods sold with a specific amount and relieve the inventory account by an identical amount. This method is possible only in very specialized circumstances, and so it is used only infrequently. For example, a used car dealer might employ this method since each car is individual. The specific identification method is particularly appropriate to this kind of situation.

Assumption 2: Average Cost

Let's say that we don't know which item we sold. In that case, the cost of the entire group of similar items, divided by the total number of items in that group, gives the average cost of that item. So all the accountant needs to know is the average unit cost and the number of items sold. This method, for example, might be appropriate for a grain elevator operation, where all the grain is mingled and ascertaining the exact flow of the kernels in or out is impossible. In periods of rising prices, this method tends to understate the value of the Inventory on the balance sheet and to overstate the amount contained in Cost of goods sold.

Assumption 3: FIFO (First-In First-Out)

This inventory flow assumption is probably closer to reality than any of the others. A good manager would always rotate stock, that is, sell the oldest items first. In an inflationary period, this method would allocate the most recent (higher) costs to the balance sheet Inventory, so the total amount of this inventory is closer to current value. On the other hand, with the oldest costs allocated to it, the Cost of goods sold tends to be understated, and consequently net income tends to be overstated.

Assumption 4: LIFO (Last-In First-Out)

This method is attractive in periods of rising prices. The reason is that the most recent costs are allocated to the Cost of goods sold account, and so these current costs are matched with current selling prices, thus creating a reasonably realistic picture of gross margin and net income. As a drawback, the balance sheet suffers since the oldest costs are allocated to the balance sheet valuation, resulting in an understatement of current assets.

EXERCISE 10-1

If inventory levels are stable or increasing, which of the following is not an argument in favor of the LIFO method as compared to FIFO?

a. **Income taxes tend to be reduced in periods of rising prices.**
b. **Cost of goods sold tends to be stated at approximately current cost in the income statement?**
c. **Cost assignments typically parallel the physical flow of the goods.**
d. **Income tends to be smoothed as prices change over time.**

Students become very confused with the impact of these various inventory flow assumptions and their effect on taxes, net income, and other items. Our best advice is to encourage you to build a very simple model, like the one in Figure 10-1, and use it to figure out the various ramifications. Note that in all cases the Goods available for sale are the same (3 units at a total price of $6). The difference in the three cases stems from the fact that, as the value for the one item remaining in inventory declines, the amount allocated to expense (Cost of goods sold) increases. Remember, by definition, Goods available for sale is identically equal to the ending inventory plus the Cost of goods sold.

FIGURE 10-1 An inventory flow chart

	FIFO	*Average Cost*	*LIFO*
In Jaunary purchase 1 item ($1)	**$1**	**$1**	**$1**
In June purchase 1 item ($2)	**2**	**2**	**2**
In December purchase 1 item ($3)	**3**	**3**	**3**
Goods available (3 units)	**6**	**6**	**6**
Ending inventory (1 unit)	**3**	**2**	**1**
Cost of goods sold	**3**	**4**	**5**

In this model we have a rising price level—one item costs three times as much in December as it did in January. Under the FIFO assumption the most recent ($3) item is left and the $1 and $2 items are sold. Thus this method understantes Cost of goods sold, but leaves the inventory valuation approximately correct. Under the LIFO assumption, the two most recent items ($3 and $2) are sold, leaving the $1 item in inventory. Thus it understates the inventory but approximately matches the current cost of $3 with current selling prices (actually ($2 + $3) ÷ 2= $2.50 per item). So if we use FIFO in an inflationary period, Cost of goods sold is lowest of all three methods. And, if Cost of goods sold is lowest, then Net income would correspondingly be the highest. A higher Cost of goods sold under LIFO would result in the lowest net income and a consequent income tax saving, since income taxes are calculated on net income.

EXERCISE 10-2

Given a beginning inventory at 1/1/81 of 4 units @ $20, and purchases during 19XX of the following units:

1/28/XX	6 units @ $21
3/1/XX	4 units @ $22
6/15/XX	8 units @ $23
8/21/XX	5 units @ $24
10/5/XX	2 units @ $25

And sales of the following units:

February, 19XX	7 units
May, 19XX	3 units
July, 19XX	2 units
November, 19XX	5 units
December, 19XX	1 unit

Answer the following questions:

a. **What is the inventory (in units) as of 12/31/XX?** ________

b. **What is the inventory (in dollars) using FIFO?** $________

c. **What is the inventory (in dollars) using LIFO?** $________

d. **What is the inventory (using average cost)?** $________

EXERCISE 10-3

The Harry Carry Ferry Mfg. Co.'s inventory cost on the balance sheet was lower using first-in first-out than last-in first-out. Assuming no beginning inventory, what direction did the cost of purchases move during the period?

a. **Up**
b. **Down**
c. **Steady**
d. **Cannot be determined**

INVENTORY VALUATION CONVENTIONS

Having determined which cost flow assumption is used by the company that you are trying to evaluate, you must then understand the lower of cost or market convention to complete the valuation picture. Ordinarily inventory is valued at cost, but, if for some reason current market is less than cost, we would be carrying an asset in the balance sheet that is overvalued and that could not be sold for a normal markup. Accountants feel that, in this situation, the inventory should be valued at market. The definition of market used is rather complicated:

> Market is defined as replacement cost, but not more than current selling price, less the cost to complete and sell the item, nor less than net realizable value reduced by a normal profit margin.

This definition is a difficult one to understand, so let's break it into three parts:

1. replacement cost,
2. net realizable value (ceiling), and
3. normal profit margin (floor).

Replacement Cost

Replacement cost is the price than the item can be purchased for on the open market today. Suppose that, as owner of a camera shop, you purchased a camera six months ago but that between them and now there was a price increase of 10 percent. If your cost was \$250, the replacement cost would be \$275 (\$250 + 0.10 of \$250).

Net Realizable Value (NRV)

Assuming a retail sale price of \$400, what amount can you realize on the sale? Let's say that the sales clerk is entitled to 5-percent commission on the sale and that packing the camera for shipment is \$5. Then the ceiling or net realizable value (NRV) can be calculated as follows:

$$\$400 - \$20 - \$5 = \$375$$

Normal Profit Margin

Finally, the *floor* consists of the NRV reduced by a normal profit margin. Let's assume that by looking at last year's income statement for the camera shop we observe that the Net income, as a percentage of Net sales, was 20 percent. Computing that 20 percent of $400 is $80, the floor can be calculated rather easily:

$$\$375 - \$80 = \$295$$

Figure 10-2 illustrates this definition graphically. It assumes that:

* the selling price of an item is $1,
* the cost to complete and sell the item is 10¢, and
* the normal profit margin is 10¢ per item.

So the net realizable value (NRV)—or ceiling—is 90¢. The floor is NRV (90¢) less a normal profit margin (10¢)—or 80¢. Figure 10-2 presents five different cases in which to apply the decision rules: [ ] indicates the selected value. Each case involves a different decision rule:

		Case 1	Case 2	Case 3	Case 4	Case 5	
Ceiling (NRV)	90¢		[90]				Ceiling 90¢
Floor	80¢			[80]			Floor 80¢
Cost		[70¢]	95¢	95¢	95¢	[78¢]	
Replacement cost		80¢	92¢	75¢	[85¢]	75¢	

FIGURE 10-2 Lower of cost or market

* *Case 1:* **If cost is lower than replacement cost, take cost.**
* *Case 2:* **Otherwise, check to see if replacement cost is more than 90¢. If so, take 90¢.**
* *Case 3:* **Otherwise, check to see if replacement cost is less than 80¢. If so, take 80¢.**
* *Case 4:* **Otherwise take replacement cost.**
* *Case 5:* **After selecting a market price as determined in steps 2, 3, or 4, make a final check to be sure that market is not higher than cost. For example see case 5 in the figure. Re-**

placement cost, although less than cost, is less than the floor. So replacement cost, as redefined, is 80¢. It is nothing more or less than the market price, which is now higher than cost. So 78¢ cost is selected.

EXERCISE 10-4

To understand the concept of cost or market, whichever is lower, we must have rigorous definition of market value. Let's say that the selling price of an item is $10, that the normal gross profit margin of 10 percent is earned, and that the cost to prepare and sell the item is $1. Complete the following table, assuming that the lower of cost or market doctrine is applied:

	(a)	*(b)*	*(c)*	*(d)*	*(e)*
Cost price	**$9.00**	**$7.00**	**$6.00**	**$10.00**	**$8.00**
Replacement cost	**8.00**	**8.00**	**4.00**	**8.50**	**7.00**
Market value	**$_____**	**$_____**	**$_____**	**$_____**	**$_____**
Inventory value	**$_____**	**$_____**	**$_____**	**$_____**	**$_____**

Why is all this important? For one very simple reason—it demonstrates the conservatism of accountants and of accounting theory. Without the floor of 80¢, the cost or market rule would allow the accountant to write down an item excessively this period for an abnormal loss, which results in an abnormal profit next period. Similarly, if the accountant were permitted to value an item higher than 90¢, a loss would be capitalized, since the most that can be realized from the sale is $1 − 10¢ or 90¢.

Inventories are extremely important to the calculation of Net income. On the balance sheet they have more impact on current ratios and on working capital than any other single item in the current asset section. A traditional presentation of inventories is given in the Tandem Computers annual report (Figure 10-3).

A different kind of inventory evaluation is exemplified by the footnote in Figure 10-4 excerpted from the 1979 Ford Motor Company's annual report.

ADDITIONAL EXERCISES

The student Corp. began business on 1/1/XX. Information about its year-end inventories under different valuation methods is given. Using this information, you are to

TANDEM COMPUTERS INCORPORATED AND SUBSIDIARIES

NOTES TO CONSOLIDATED FINANCIAL STATEMENTS

1. SUMMARY OF SIGNIFICANT ACCOUNTING POLICIES

CONSOLIDATION

The consolidated financial statements include the accounts of Tandem Computers Incorporated and its wholly owned subsidiaries after elimination of intercompany accounts and transactions. Foreign exchange gains and losses are not significant and are reflected in the results of operations.

REVENUE RECOGNITION

The Company generally recognizes equipment sales revenues at the time of shipment.

INVENTORIES

Inventories are stated at the lower of cost (first-in first-out) or market and include material, labor, and manufacturing overhead. The components of inventory used to determine cost of revenues were:

(In Thousands)	September 30		
	1980	1979	1978
Purchased parts and subassemblies	$11,832	$ 6,207	$4,196
Work-in-process and finished systems	9,069	5,097	2,123
	$20,901	$11,304	$6,319

INCOME TAXES

The Company provides for income taxes on total DISC income and accounts for investment tax credits as a reduction of the provision for taxes on income in the year in which the related credits are realized.

PROPERTY AND EQUIPMENT

Systems spares are depreciated using the double declining balance method. All other property and equipment are depreciated using the straight-line method. The estimated useful lives are:

	Years
Production and test equipment	5-10
Computer equipment	5-7
Office furniture and equipment	5-10
Systems spares	5
Leasehold improvements	Lease Term

Expenditures for maintenance and repairs are charged to operations as incurred. Expenditures for major betterments and renewals are capitalized and depreciated over the estimated remaining useful life of the asset. The net gain or loss on assets retired or otherwise disposed of is credited or charged to operations and the asset cost and related depreciation are removed from the accounts.

FIGURE 10-3. A description of FIFO inventory valuation, Tandem Annual Report for 1980. Reprinted by permission of Tandem Computers, Inc.

Inventory Valuation

Inventories are stated at the lower of cost or market. The cost of most U.S. inventories is determined by the Last-In, First-Out (LIFO) method. The cost of the remaining inventories is determined substantially on a First-In, First-Out (FIFO) basis.

If the FIFO method of inventory accounting had been used exclusively by the Company, inventories would have been $824 million and $564 million higher than reported at December 31, 1979 and December 31, 1978 respectively.

FIGURE 10-4. Ford Motor Company and LIFO inventory valuation

choose the phrase that most accurately completes each of the statements numbered 10-5 through 10-8:

Date	*LIFO Cost*	*FIFO Cost*	*Average Cost*
12/31/X1	$5,100	$5,000	$5,050
12/31/X2	$4,550	$4,500	$4,525
12/31/X3	$5,150	$5,500	$5,250

10-5. The inventory method that would show the highest net income for 19X2 is:

a. LIFO cost.

b. FIFO cost.

c. average cost.

10-6. The inventory method that would show the lowest net income for 19X2 is:

a. LIFO cost.

b. FIFO cost.

c. average cost.

10-7. The inventory method that would show the highest income for all three years combined would be:

a. LIFO cost.

b. FIFO cost.

c. average cost.

10-8. The information given seems to indicate that the movement of prices for the items in the inventory was:

a. up in 19X2 and down in 19X3.

b. up in both 19X2 and 19X3.

c. down in 19X2 and up in 19X3.

d. down in both 19X2 and 19X3.

10-9. A company using a periodic inventory system neglected to record a purchase of merchandise on account at year-end. This merchandise was omitted from the year-end physical count. How will these errors affect assets, liabilities, and stockholders' equity at year end and net earnings for the year?

	Assets	*Liabilities*	*Stockholders' Equity*	*Net Earnings*
a.	No effect	Understate	Overstate	Overstate
b.	No effect	Overstate	Understate	Understate
c.	Understate	Understate	No effect	No effect
d.	Understate	No effect	Understate	Understate

10-10. Market value is defined as replacement cost, but not more than selling price less cost to complete and sell, nor less than selling price less cost to complete and sell and a normal profit margin. Based on this definition, complete the following table:

	(a)	*(b)*	*(c)*	*(d)*
Historical cost	$25.00	$25.00	$25.00	$25.00
Replacement cost	20.00	30.00	15.00	15.00
Cost to complete and sell	10%	10%	20%	20%
Normal profit margin	10%	10%	20%	10%
Current selling price	$25.00	$40.00	$20.00	$15.00
The ceiling price is	$____	$____	$____	$____
The floor price is	$____	$____	$____	$____
The inventory value should be	$____	$____	$____	$____

SOLUTIONS

10-1. c

10-2. a. 11 units

b. 4 × $23; 5 × $24; 2 × $25 = $262

c. 4 × $20; 6 × $21; 1 × $22 = $228

d. (4 × 20) + (6 × 21) + (4 × 22) + (8 × 23) + (5 × 24) + (2 × 25) = 648/29 = 22.34

10-3. b

10-4.

	(a)	*(b)*	*(c)*	*(d)*	*(e)*
Market value	$8.00	$8.00	$8.00	$8.50	$8.00
Inventory value	$8.00	$7.00	$6.00	$8.50	$8.00

10-5. b. FIFO cost

10-6. a. LIFO cost

10-7. b. FIFO cost

10-8. c. Down in 19X2 and up in 19X3.

10-9. c.

10-10.

	(a)	*(b)*	*(c)*	*(d)*
Ceiling	$22.50	$36.00	$16.00	$12.00
Floor	$20.00	$32.00	$12.00	$10.50
Inventory	$20.00	$25.00	$15.00	$12.00

11
Cash and Near-Cash Assets

Cash itself is perhaps the easiest of all accounts on the balance sheet to understand. As you all know, it comes in two forms: the cash that you have in your pocket or purse *(cash on hand)* or cash that you have deposited in your friendly banking establishment.

BANK RECONCILIATION

The cash in the bank causes most of the problems in this chapter. The bank is required by law to furnish you with a bank statement at specified intervals, which is usually one month. If you assume that the ending balance on the bank statement, is what you actually have in the account, you are ignoring two things:

1. any deposits that you have made but that are not yet credited* to your account by the bank (we call these items *deposits in transit*); and

*The use of "credit" in this context is confusing to students. From the bank's point of view, the money you deposit is a liability. The bankers owe it to you. So when you deposit additional funds in your account, they credit an account on their books

2. any checks that you might have written and that have not found their way back to your bank as yet (we call these *outstanding checks*).

Now both the deposits in transit and the outstanding checks are entered in your own checkbook (hopefully). So to reconcile your checkbook balance—that is, make it agree—with the balance that appears on the bank statement, you have to go through the computation shown in Figure 11-1.

Balance per bank statement	$400
Add: Deposit not yet credited by bank	50
	$450
Deduct: Checks written but not yet returned to the bank	150
	$300

FIGURE 11-1. A simple bank reconciliation

All problems associated with cash should be as simple as they appear in this Figure. Unfortunately, reconciliation is always complicated by a number of problems: mistakes in the checkbook, arithmetic and otherwise; bank debits not recorded, such as an NSF check* (which that "fink," your roommate, gave you last week); bank charges you had forgotten about; and so on. But be persistent and hold fast to the basic underlying theory, and you will prevail over the numbers. Some people suggest the technique demonstrated in Figure 11-2.

FIGURE 11-2. Dual form of bank reconciliation

Balance per bank	$400	Balance per checkbook	$505
Add: Deposits in transit	50	Deduct: Error in subtraction	35
	450		470
Deduct: Outstanding checks	150	Roommate's bum check	50
Adjusted balance per bank	$300		420
		Bank charges not deducted	20
			$400
		Whoops, another adding mistake	$100
			$300

called Depositor's Liability. Similarly, when the bank issues a debit memo, they deduct something from what they owe you. An example of a debit memo (DM) would be the monthly bank charges.

*These initials are commonly used by the banking community to describe a check returned to the depository because the person originally writing the check did not have sufficient funds in the account.

Unfortunately most textbooks get things much more complicated than they need to be by including petty cash, undeposited cash, and other fiendish and improbable items in the ledger balance of cash in the bank. Any accountants worth their salt would have separate accounts for undeposited cash, change funds, petty cash, or whatever. Our suggestion is that you ignore these spurious factors in your cash work. The exercises in this manual are free of that kind of extraneous stuff.

EXERCISE 11-1

Your roommate, having trouble balancing a personal bank account, has requested your assistance. Using the following information, reconcile the checkbook balance at October 31, 19XX:

Balance per October 31, 19XX bank statement			**$60**
Weekly allowance check mailed directly to the bank by parents on October 31, 19XX:			**70**
Checks not presented to bank for payment according to your rommate:			
Kutrate Kleaners	**#42**	**$20**	
Friendly Finance Co.	**43**	**90**	
Smooth Movers, Inc.	**45**	**9**	
Balance per checkbook			**$60 (overdraft)**

In addition you discover the following:

***You are holding an uncashed check given to you by your roommate, which was not entered in the checkbook ($10).**

***An arithmetic error in the checkbook, which, when corrected, will reduce the $60 overdraft to $59 overdraft.**

***The deposits are never entered by your roommate until the notice is received from the bank that the allowance check has arrived.**

a. The total of the outstanding checks is $________________.

b. The correct checkbook balance is $ __________________.

We have described two different ways to reconcile a bank statement with the cash balance as it appears on the books. There is still another way. In this approach, you make up what is called a *proof of cash statement.* The essentials of this method include:

1. a reconciliation of the bank balance at the beginning of the month (which you already have from last month), and

2. separate columns for reconciling deposits—as well as disbursements (checks, written)—per the bank and per year books during the month, and
3. a column for the bank reconciliation at the end of the month, which is identical to the first method that we described.

The best way to understand a *proof of cash statement* is to work one. Please do just that in Exercise 11-2.

EXERCISE 11-2

Complete the following proof of cash statement:

	(a) *10/1/XX*	*(b)* *Deposits*	*(c)* *Withdrawals*	*(d)* *10/31/XX*
Balance per bank	**$5,000**	**$______**	**($7,500)**	**$1,000**
Deposits in transit	**500**	**$______**		**$3,500**
Outstanding checks	**($3,500)**		**$____**	**$______**
Balance per book	**$____**	**$______**	**($5,500)**	**$______**

SHORT-TERM INVESTMENTS

The section on short-term investments can be mercifully short. You should remember just two things:

1. The definition of short-term (temporary) investments: The investment must be regularly traded on a recognized exchange so that the market price is readily determinable (from reading the *Wall Street Journal,* for example) and consequently can be sold at the drop of a hat. The intention of the company must also be to hold it for a short-term, usually one year or less. No floors and no ceilings to worry about! (See Figure 11-3.)
2. Short-term investments are valued on a lower of cost or market basis. Add up all the costs of all such securities, and add up all the market values. Then pick the lower one for balance sheet purposes. Do *not* make the choice on an item-for-item basis. If a write-down to market is required, the entry would take the following form:

Loss on short-term investments	$XXXX	
Allowance to reduce investments to LCM*		$XXXX

Now we can challenge those exercises on cash!

*LCM means lower of cost or market.

Marketable securities are carried at the lower of aggregate cost or market. To adjust their carrying value to approximate market, equity securities included in the portfolio have been reduced by unrealized losses (net of insignificant unrealized gains). During 1980, the allowance for decline in market value of equity securities was reduced by $679,000, primarily due to the realization of losses of $640,000. Charges against income for unrealized losses in 1979 and 1978 were $522,000 and $361,000, respectively. Net realized losses on sales of marketable securities in such years, based on average cost, were $48,000 and $172,000, respectively.

FIGURE 11-3. Illustration of how marketable securities are treated in published financial statements

Excerpted from Prentice-Hall, Inc. 1980 Annual Report.

ADDITIONAL EXERCISES

Use the following data for Bora Bora for Exercises 11-3 through 11-5:

BANK RECONILIATION
September 30, 19XX

Bank balance		$5,397.50
Less: Outstanding checks		
69	$100.00	
72	416.10	
78	56.20	
81	14.70	587.00
Ledger balance		$4,810.50

The bank statement on October 31, 19XX from the First National Bank for Bora Bora reveals:

Date		*Debits*		*Deposits*	*Balance*
October 1					$5,397.50
4	$416.10	$65.40		$115.10	
11	$ 76.70	$56.20	$69.25	$315.60	
16	$ 10.15	$25.40			
18	$115.60			$195.90	
22	$101.20				
24	$ 74.25	$64.80		$211.60	
30	$ 3.85	(service charge			$5,156.80

The deposits in the Bora Bora cash receipts book for October were:

Oct. 4	$115.10	Oct. 18	$195.90	Oct. 31	$215.60
11	$315.60	24	$211.60		

The cash disbursements book of Bora Bora contained the following checks:

82	**$65.40**	**85**	**$69.25**	**88**	**$ 42.90**	**91**	**$74.25**
83	**$99.80**	**86**	**$10.15**	**89**	**$115.60**	**92**	**$64.80**
84	**$76.70**	**87**	**$25.40**	**90**	**$101.20**		

Bora Bora balance of cash on October 31 was $5,118.85.

11-3. What were the outstanding checks at 10/31/XX?

Number	*Amount*
________	________
________	________
________	________
________	________
________	________

11-4. What were the deposits in transit at 10/31/XX?

Date	*Amount*
________	________
________	________

11-5. What is the corrected ledger balance at 10/31/XX?

$____________

11-6.

	Balance 11/30/XX	*Deposits*	*Withdrawal*	*Balance 12/31/XX*
Per bank	**$1,170**	**$5,620**	**($4,935)**	**$1,855**
Deposits	**265**	**(265)**		**125**
Outstanding checks	**(315)**	**125**	**315**	**(190)**
			(190)	
Other reconciling items				
NSF check		**30**		**30**
December bank charges			**15**	**15**
Per books	**$1,120**	**$5,510**	**($4,795)**	**$1,835**

The correct ledger balance per books on 12/31/XX should be:

a. **$1,835**

b. **$1,790**

c. $1,880

d. $1,820

e. None of the above.

11-7. The Kiwi Computer Company had some extra cash on June 30, 19X1 and purchased the following securities, all of which are regularly traded on a recognized stock exchange:

Name of Security	*Number of Shares*	*Per Share Cost Price 7/1/X1*	*Per Share Market Value 12/31/X1*
Moonlite Mining Co.	100	20	17
Heckled Mining Co.	100	40	34
Goldbug Mining Co.	100	10	9
Kewpie Computer Co.	300	5	15
Pineapple Computer Co.	100	30	40
National Oil Co.	500	20	10

a. What is the total cost price of the securities purchased?

$____________

b. What is the value for balance sheet purposes at 12/31/X1?

$____________

The following data have been taken from the financial statements of Maxe, Inc., a calendar-year retailer:

	12/31/X0	*12/31/X1*
Trade accounts receivable—net	$21,000	$19,500
Merchandise inventory	$37,500	$35,000
Accounts payable—merchandise	$23,700	$24,500

Total sales for 19X1 were $300,000 and for 19X0 were $275,000.
Cash sales were 20% of total sales for each year.
Cost of goods sold was $210,000 for 19X1.
General and administrative expenses, including $8,750 depreciation, totaled $25,000 each year. The amount of such expenses involving cash payments was paid 80% in the year incurred and 20% in the following year. There were no bad debts in either year. Unpaid general and administrative expenses are not included in the preceding accounts payable data.

11-8. How much cash did Maxe collect during 19X1 resulting from sales in 19X0 and 19X1? $____________

11-9. What were the purchases (net) for the year ended December 31, 19X1? $____________

11-10. How much cash was disbursed for general and administrative expenses during this year? $___________

SOLUTIONS

11-1. a. $129.00
b. $1.00

11-2. Reading down the columns:
a. $2,000
b. $3,500, $3,000, and $6,500
c. $3,500 and ($1,500)
d. $3,500, ($1,500), $3,000

11-3. #69, $100; #81, $14.70; #83, $99.80; #88, $42.90

11-4. 10/31/80, $215.60

11-5. $5,115

11-6. b

11-7. a. $21,500
b. $19,500

11-8. $301,500

11-9. $207,500

11-10. $16,250

12

Property, Plant, and Equipment

Property, plant, and *equipment* is the label for the long-lived physical assets of a business entity, which are known by other descriptions such as Fixed assets, Plant assets, and Operational assets. Whatever their name, just remember that this generic category of assets includes long-lived tangible assets such as buildings, machinery, equipment, land, natural resources, automobiles, and trucks—among others (Figure 12-1).

Accounting for property, plant, and equipment entails two issues:

* One is the identification and measurement of the asset's *cost* at the acquisition date.
* The other is the allocation of this cost over future accounting periods during which the asset will be owned and used. We call this allocation *depreciation,* and it is an important example of the matching of costs and revenues.

6. PROPERTY AND EQUIPMENT

	1980	1979
Land and improvements	$ 4,362,000	$ 4,123,000
Buildings and building equipment	33,431,000	27,753,000
Furniture and equipment	19,376,000	16,885,000
	57,169,000	48,761,000
Less accumulated depreciation	18,464,000	15,705,000
	38,705,000	33,056,000
Prepublications costs, less accumulated depreciation of $33,277,000 and $28,567,000, respectively	27,729,000	23,608,000
Acquired copyrights and publication and distribution rights, less accumulated depreciation of $3,087,000 and $690,000, respectively	10,964,000	13,391,000
Property and equipment—net	$77,398,000	$70,055,000

FIGURE 12-1. Example of property, plant, and equipment on an annual report

Excerpted from Prentice-Hall, Inc. Annual Report for 1980.

THE COST OF PROPERTY, PLANT, AND EQUIPMENT

Historical cost is not a difficult concept to grasp. The cost of a plant asset includes all the items necessary to put the asset into operation, such as its invoice price, sales tax, freight, installation cost, and any preliminary set-up costs. These costs would be reduced by any discounts earned by paying for the asset in a timely fashion (purchase discounts). If the asset is constructed by the company, it is appropriate to include in the cost of the asset, the material, labor, and overhead incurred in the construction process. Some companies have the policy of "expensing" items worth less than a certain dollar amount—such as waste baskets—simply because they are not "material" (that is, of significant value) and because the cost of keeping track of them is more trouble than they are worth. In ordinary circumstances, such items as waste baskets are long-lived assets, but, at a cost of $10 or so to capitalize and to depreciate them over time, the accounting benefits are simply not worth the effort. This is an example of the *materiality concept.* Furthermore, since an established company buys items like waste baskets fairly uniformly over time, the distortion of the financial statements, if any, is inconsequential. In a well-run company, the accounting department maintains an individual record on each item of equipment, places identification tags on each item, and conducts periodic sampling tests of the physical existence of the assets by members of the internal audit staff.

EXERCISE 12-1

Decide whether each of the following items should be classified as Property, plant, and equipment or expensed during the current accounting period. Assume that the materiality criterion is $250 per item:

	Total Cost	*Capital Item or Expense?*
a. 10 venetian blinds @ $150	$1,500	________
b. Air conditioning installation for new data processing facility	$7,000	________
c. Cleaning rugs in reception area and conference room	$1,600	________
d. Down payment on new photocopier	$ 225	________
e. Replacement of heavy-duty truck tires (4 @ $275)	$ 900	________
f. Purchase of new welding machine	$5,900	________
g. Freight on new welding machine	$ 600	________
h. Sales tax on new welding machine	$ 354	________

DEPRECIATION EXPENSE AND ACCUMULATED DEPRECIATION

Most assets classified as property, plant, and equipment are subject to physical deterioration and technological obsolescence. (The one notable exception is land, other than land containing mineral resources.) To account for this factor, the accountant is faced with a twofold problem: One has to do with valuing the item for the balance sheet, and the other involves allocating the asset's cost over its useful economic life. For balance sheet purposes, a contra asset account, called *Accumulated depreciation* (Credit balance), serves as a valuation account; it is deducted from the original cost of the operational asset. To allocate the cost of the asset over the years of use, an expense account is provided for deducting from the income statement that portion of the cost of the asset that is deemed to have expired during the accounting period. A typical entry used to record the dual aspects of this problem follows:

Depreciation expense	$XXXX	
Accumulated Depreciation		$XXXX

Noted that the cash outflow is made when the asset is acquired. Since subsequent charges to Depreciation expense involve no additional outflow of cash, depreciation (or amortization, as it is called in the case of intangible assets) is known as a *noncash expense.* Either, of course, is a legitimate deduction in computing Net income and in calculating income taxes.

EXERCISE 12-2

As generally used in accounting, what is depreciation?

a. It is primarily a process of asset valuation for balance sheet purposes.
b. It applies only to long-lived intangible assets.
c. It is used to indicate a decline in market value of a long-lived asset.
d. It is an accounting process that allocates long-lived asset cost to accounting periods.
e. All of the above.

Straight-Line Depreciation

Depreciation is classified either as accelerated depreciation or as straight-line depreciation. The easier way is the straight line method, which can be calculated from the formula:

$$\text{Annual depreciation expense} = \frac{\text{Original cost} - \text{Salvage value}}{\text{Years of useful life}}$$

Accelerated Depreciation

In the case of accelerated depreciation, the expense is greater during the early years of the economic life of the asset than in the later years. From a realistic standpoint, certain items may, in fact, depreciate faster during the early years of their economic life, such as Cadillacs. But the bulk of depreciable items do not follow this pattern. Why, then, has there been so much emphasis on accelerated depreciation methods in the accounting literature? The answer is that, since the tax effects of the higher expense are so favorable, business managers favor accelerated depreciation in their attempts to save on income taxes. Accelerated depreciation can be calculated in two basic ways: the double-declining balance (DDB) method, the sum-of-the-years-digits (softy) method. Since they both come to roughly the same time profile of expense for a given asset, let's begin with the SOFTY method.

* *Step 1:* Add up all the digits in the useful economic life of the asset—say 8 years:

$$1 + 2 + 3 + 4 + 5 + 6 + 7 + 8 = 36$$

* *Step 2:* Calculate the depreciable portions of the asset:

Depreciable Portion = Original cost − Salvage value

* *Step 3:* Calculate the first year's depreciation by multiplying:

First year's depreciation = 8/36 × Depreciation portion

* *Step 4:* Calculate subsequent years (years 2 through 8) as follows:

Year 2 = 7/36 × Depreciable portion
Year 3 = 6/36 × Depreciable portion
.
.
.
Year 8 = 1/36 × Depreciable portion

Example: Let's assume that we buy a sewing machine to be used in our sail-making business for $4,000. After an estimated useful life of 8 years, the machine can be resold for $400. Applying the formula given on the preceding page:

* *Step 1:* 1 + 2 + 3 + 4 + 5 + 6 + 7 + 8 = 36
* *Step 2:* $4,000 − $400 = $3,600
* *Step 3:* 8/36 × $3,600 = $800 (First year's depreciation)
* *Step 4:*

7/36 × $3,600 = $ 700
6/36 × $3,600 = $ 600
5/36 × $3,600 = $ 500
4/36 × $3,600 = $ 400
3/36 × $3,600 = $ 300
2/36 × $3,600 = $ 200
1/36 × $3,600 = $ 100
Total depreciation = $3,600

EXERCISE 12-3

Compute the annual depreciation for a truck. Use the sum-of-the-years'-digits (SOFTY) method. Assume an original cost of $20,000,

a salvage value of $500, and a 5-year economic life. Repairs for the first year were $100; for the second and third years, $300 each year; and $500 for each of the two remaining years.

	Depreciation Expense	*Net Asset Value at End of the Year*
Year 1	______	______
2	______	______
3	______	______
4	______	______
5	______	______

The other method for accelerated depreciation is the *double-declining balance* (DDB) method. Let's illustrate this method by using the same information contained in Exercise 12-3.

Year	*Calculation*	*Depreciation Expense*	=	*Net Asset Value at End of the Year*
1	2 X 20% X $20,000	$8,000		$12,000
2	2 X 20% X $12,000	$4,800		$ 7,200
3	2 X 20% X $ 7,200	$2,880		$ 4,320
4	2 X 20% X $ 4,320	$1,728		$ 2,592
5	($2,592 – $500)	$2,092		$ 500

The DDB method, as the name implies, doubles the straight-line rate and applies that rate to the net asset value at the end of the preceding year. The last year is adjusted to reduce the net asset value to the salvage value at the end of the year.

ACCOUNTING FOR SALES AND TRADE-INS

When accounting for the sale or disposal of PP&E assets, all such transactions fall into two categories:

1. *Assets that are traded in for assets of like kind:* In this case take the net asset value (original cost less the accumulated depreciation) and add on the cash paid for the new like asset. This total then becomes the basis for the new asset. So no gain or loss is recognized on the exchange.

Example:

Cash

	(1) $9,500

Printing Press

Bal. $10,000	(1) $10,000
(1) $12,000	

Accumulated Depreciation

(1) $7,500	Bal. $7,500

Explanation of these T-accounts is as follows: Bal. indicates the balance in the accounts before the trade-in of the old press. (1) This is a compound journal entry reflecting the purchase of the new press for a cash outlay of $9,500 and the trade-in of the old printing press. Note that no gain or loss is recognized on the trade.*

2. *Assets that are either traded for unlike assets or simpy sold.* This case is best explained by the following example:

   Example: An asset with an original cost of $4,000 and an accumulated depreciation balance of $3,300 was sold for $1,000:

Sewing Machine

Bal. $4,000	(1) $4,000

Accumulated Depreciation

(1) $3,300	Bal. $3,300

Cash

(1) $1,000	

Gain on Sale of Sewing Machine

	(1) $300

The explanation of these T-accounts is as follows:

*This method is called the tax method because it has been acceptable for income-tax purposes, but the Economic Recovery Act of 1981 may change its tax status.

* "Bal. $4,000" indicates the original cost of $4,000 in the Sewing machine account
* "Bal. $3,300" in Accumulated depreciation indicates the depreciation accumulated to the date of sale
* "(1)"—this is a compound journal entry that consists of four parts:
  a. to record the retirement of the asset at $4,000,
  b. to record the elimination of the Accumulated depreciation portion of asset,
  c. the entry in cash that records the $1,000 received from the sale, and
  d. the gain on the sale of $300, which is computed as follows:

Sales price		$1,000
Original cost of asset	4,000	
Accumulated depreciation	3,300	700
Gain on Sale		$ 300

EXERCISE 12-4

The following journal entries in Property, plant, and equipment could be due to:

Cash

(1) 1,700	(2) 6,000

Delivery Trucks

Bal. 14,760	(1) 3,670
(2) 6,000	

Accumulated Depreciation Delivery Trucks

(1) 1,670	Bal. 6,820

Gain/Loss on Fixed Assets

(1) 300	

a. A delivery truck traded in on another delivery truck and a purchase of second new truck.
b. Sale of delivery truck without a trade in and the purchase of a second new truck.
c. The sale of a delivery truck without a trade in and the trade in of a second delivery truck on a new truck.
d. No firm conclusion can be drawn from these entries.

ADDITIONAL EXERCISES

12-5. The net book value of an automobile was $960 when it was sold for a loss of $600. What was the selling price of the car? $____________

12-6. Blacker Company exchanged a business automobile for a new automobile. The old automobile had an original cost of $3,500, an undepreciated cost of $1,600, and a market value of $2,000 when exchanged. In addition, Blacker paid $2,200 cash for the new automobile. The list price of the new automobile was $4,300. At what amount should the new automobile be recorded for financial accounting purposes?

a. $3,500   c. $4,200

b. $3,800   d. $4,300

12-7. In January of 1974 the Idea Company purchased a patent for a new consumer product for $170,000. At the time of purchase, the patent was valid for 17 years. Due to the competitive nature of the product, the patent was estimated to have a useful life of 10 years. During 1978, the product was removed from the market under governmental order because of a potential health hazard present in the product. What amount should Idea charge to amortization expense during 1978, assuming that amortization is recorded at the end of each year?*

a. $10,000   d. $102,000

b. $17,000   e. $130,000

c. $34,000

12-8. An addition made to a machine increased its fair market value and its production capacity by 25 percent without extending the machine's useful life. The cost of the improvement should be:

a. expensed.

b. debited to Accumulated depreciation.

c. capitalized in the Machine account.

d. allocated between Accumulated depreciation and the machine account.

*Amortization is similar to depreciation. The formula is: $\frac{\text{Cost of patent}}{\text{Useful life in years}}$ = Annual amortization expense.

12-9. A 26-foot sailboat of the Thunderbird class was built with the intention of renting the boat to weekend sailors on San Francisco Bay at Berkeley Boatbuilders, Inc. It was started in 1976 and completed on January 2, 1978. It has an estimated economic life of ten years. It was decided in 1978 to use the double-declining balance method of accelerated depreciation. The estimated salvage value of the vessel in 1988 is $1,000. The following listing gives the relevant amounts spent during the construction period and during the operating years, 1978 through 1981.

1976:	
Cost of lumber	$1,700
Rental of loft space	$ 150
Insurance on loft	$ 75
Paint, glue, and fiberglass	$ 325
Labor—carpenters	$1,150
1977:	
Cost of lumber	$1,100
Fittings	$ 500
Sails	$1,200
Labor	$2,200
1978:	
Rental income	$2,000
Cost of berth	$ 720
Insurance	$ 200
Taxes (personal property)	$ 100
1979:	
Rental income	$2,900
Cost of berth	$ 720
Taxes and insurance	$ 350
1980:	
Rental income	$3,500
Repair of hull damaged by lessee	$ 750
Cost of berth	$ 800
Taxes and insurance	$ 400
1981:	
Rental income	$4,500
New set of sails	$1,100
Cost of berth	$ 800
Taxes and insurance	$ 500

Answer the following questions relating to the Thunderbird:

a. What was the depreciation expense for 1977?

____

b. What is the total asset cost at the beginning of 1978?

____

c. What was the depreciation expense for 1978?

____

d. What was the income (net) from the rental of the sailboat for 1979? ______________________________

e. What was the net book value of the boat at the end of 1980? ______________________________

f. What was the income (net) from the rental of the sailboat in 1981? ____________________

g. What was the net book value of the boat at the end of 1981? ____________________

12-10. On July 1, 19XX Miller Mining, a calendar-year corporation, purchased the rights to a copper mine. Of the total purchase price, $2,800,000 was appropriately allocable to the copper. Estimated reserves were 800,000 tons of copper. Miller expects to extract and sell 10,000 tons of copper per month. Production began immediately. The selling price is $25 per ton. To aid production, Miller also purchased some new equipment on July 1, 19XX. The equipment cost $76,000 and had an estimated useful life of 8 years. But after all the copper is removed from this mine, the equipment will be of no use to Miller and will be sold for an estimated $4,000.

a. If sales and production conform to expectations, what is Miller's depletion expense on this mine for financial accounting purposes for the calendar year 19XX?*

a. $105,000
b. $210,000
c. $225,000
d. $420,000
e. Some other amount

b. If sales and production conform to expectations, what is Miller's depreciation expense on the new equipment for financial accounting purposes for the calendar year 19XX. Use straight-line depreciation.

a. $4,500
b. $5,400
c. $9,000
d. $10,800
e. Some other amount

SOLUTIONS

12-1. a. Expensed
b. Capitalized
c. Expensed
d. Capitalized

*Depletion is similar to depreciation. The formula is: $\frac{\text{Cost of land}}{\text{Estimated reserves (in tons)}}$ = Depletion expense per ton.

e. Expensed
f. Capitalized
g. Capitalized
h. Capitalized

12-2. d

12-3.

Year	*Depreciation Expense*	*Net Asset Value*
1	$6,500	$13,500
2	$5,200	$ 8,300
3	$3,900	$ 4,400
4	$2,600	$ 1,800
5	$1,300	$ 500

12-4. b

12-5. $360

12-6. b

12-7. d

12-8. c

12-9. a. 0
b. $8,400
c. (20% of $8,400) = $1,680
d. $2,900 – $1,070 – $1,344 = $486
e. $8,400 – $1,680 – $1,344 – $1,075 = $4,301
f. $4,500 – $2,400 – $860 = $1,240
g. $4,301 – $860 = $3,441

12-10. a. b–$210,000
b. b–$5,400 ($\frac{\$76{,}000 - \$4{,}000}{80 \text{ months}}$ = $900/month; 6 months = $5,400)

13

Liabilities: Current and Noncurrent

Liabilities can be defined simply as *claims by creditors on the assets of a business entity.* They can be divided into two general classifications: current and noncurrent. The definition of a current liability follows closely the definition of a current asset: *A current liability is a liability that will require the expenditure of cash during the normal operating cycle of a business entity, usually one year.*

EXERCISE 13-1

One of the following statements describing a current liability is not correct. Circle the incorrect statement.

a. Normally paid within a 12-month period.

b. Represents, conceptually, the present value of the future outlays of assets required to pay the liability in full.

c. Has a definite and known payment date.

d. Is directly related to a specific current asset.

A *noncurrent liability* differs from a current liability only in timing. Since noncurrent liability includes all liabilities except current liabilities, it includes all those obligations that will require the expenditure of cash sometime beyond one year from the date of the balance sheet.

Both classifications of liabilities are very important to the user of financial statements. Let's consider Current Liabilities first.

CURRENT LIABILITIES

Some of the major reasons why the classification of current liabilities is important are:

* for the calculation of working capital,
* for the calculation of short-term liquidity ratios,
* as a measure of the short-term solvency of a business, and
* for the determination of the debt equity ratio.

Working capital is defined as follows:

Working capital = Current assets − Current liabilities

Current assets are assets that are or will be converted into cash during the normal operating cycle of a business entity (usually one year), while current liabilities are those that require the expenditure of cash within the same period. So working capital, if you look again at that formula, is clearly a measure of the safety margin of the business. Without adequate working capital, a business entity would be unable to survive the claims of creditors. Working capital is also important because changes in working capital are the subject of one of the financial statements that must be included in reports to the Securities and Exchange Commission, as well as in the annual reports of publicly held corporations. This statement is called the *statement of changes in financial position.* (Chapter 17). In the absence of any absolute measure of adequate working capital, you must consider the amount of working capital available in terms of the relative magnitudes of current assets and current liabilities. This ratio is called the *working capital ratio* or *current ratio* (Current ratio = Curret assets ÷ Current liabilities, see Chapter 18).

Another short-term liquidity ratio is called the *quick asset ratio.* Because this ratio will also be discussed in detail in Chapter 18, suffice it to say for now that current liabilities are an important ingredient of each of these common liquidity measures.

EXERCISE 13-2

Select the correct statement(s):

a. Current ratio = Working capital ratio
b. Current liabilities + Working capital = Current assets

c. Current ratio = Current assets ÷ Current liabilities

d. Quick asset ratio = (Cash + Temporary investments) ÷ Current liabilities.

EXERCISE 13-3

Indicate by a check (√) which of the following accounts are normally classified as current liabilities:

a. ______ Bank overdraft

b. ______ Accumulated depreciation

c. ______ Allowance for doubtful accounts

d. ______ Federal income taxes payable

e. ______ Bonds payable, maturing within a year

f. ______ Accrued salaries and wages

g. ______ Accounts receivable credit balances

h. ______ Deferred income taxes

Finally, current liabilities comprise an important criterion for potential creditors in forming an opinion of the ability of the business enity to repay its debts. In this respect, current liabilities are called "a measure of th short-term solvency of a business."

All these considerations are very important in financial statement analysis, and they depend on a proper understanding and computation of current liabilities. The most important classifications of current liabilities are:

* Current maturities of long-term debt,
* Short-term bank loans,
* Accounts payable,
* Income taxes payable, and
* Accrued expenses.

Most of these classifications are self-explanatory, but some might require a bit of explanation. Current Maturities of long-term debt is the portion of long-term debt (usually bonds or mortgages) that is due in one year or less. Short-term bank loans are customarily used to finance inventories or accounts receivable for a 3- to 6-month period. Accounts payable are the amounts owed to trade creditors. Income taxes are self-explanatory, and accured expenses have already been explained in connection with accrual accounting in Chapter 6.

EXERCISE 13-4

Select the one account of the following four that does not belong with the other three.

a. Accounts payable.
b. Accrued federal income taxes.
c. Deferred magazine subscriptions.
d. Current maturities of long-term debt.

OTHER LIABILITIES

Other special classes of liabilities include:

* *deferred revenues*—more appropriately called "unearned revenues," as in "unearned" magazine subscriptions,
* *returnable container accounts*—Coke bottles, for example, for which a deposit is owed if the bottle is returned, and
* *deferred income taxes or deferred taxes on income*—since income taxes are computed on net income as defined by GAAP, the actual federal tax payments may be for a different amount. This timing difference gives rise to another type of liability, which is shown separately in the financial statement between long-term debt and shareholders' equity.

EXERCISE 13-5

According to financial accounting principles, net income (before income taxes) is computed to be $50,000. The actual federal income taxes paid for the same period are $15,000. Assume that the income tax rate is 40 percent. In the following T-accounts, make the appropriate entries to reflect the deferred income tax liability.

Hint: **Enter the Income tax expense (based on accounting income) in an expense account; enter the actual tax liability in an Income tax payable account (a liability); and enter the difference in these two amounts in the Deferred taxes on income account (a liability).**

LONG-TERM DEBT

By contrast with current liabilities, long-term debt represents debt that is to be discharged or paid off in than one year from the date of the balance sheet. As mentioned, the current portion of long-term debt is deducted from the total long-term debt and shown in the Current liability section of the balance sheet. The reader of financial statements should be aware that long-term debt is normally collateralized, that is, its payment is secured by some or all of the assets of the business, usually Property, plant, and equipment. Typically, when we purchase a home that is subject to a mortgage, we do not obtain title to the property until the entire mortgage is paid off. Businesses often have the same sort of long-term debt. The property so encumbered should be clearly identified either in the balance sheet or in the appended notes.

EXERCISE 13-6

Given the following payment schedule of a mortgage, answer the questions posed:

	Principal Amount	*Annual Payment*	*Principal Portion*	*Interest Portion*
Original loan, 1/1/X1	**$10,000**			
Payment, 1/1/X2	**$ 7,093**	**$4,307**	**$2,907**	**$1,400**
Payment, 1/1/X3	**$ 3,779**	**$4,307**	**$3,314**	**$ 993**
Payment, 1/1/X4	**-0-**	**$4,307**	**$3,779**	**$ 528**

a. What amount should be shown as a current liability on December 31, 19X1? $____________

b. What amount should be shown as accrued interest payable on December 31, 19X1? $____________

c. What is the Long-Term Debt at December 31, 19X1? $____________

If a business plans to finance its operations by issuing debt instruments (as opposed to issuing capital stock), it issues *bonds*, usually in denominations of $1,000. These bonds carry a stated *(nominal)* interest rate payable usually in semiannual installments. In addition, these obligations have a fixed maturity date at which time the company must pay the principal amount to the holder of the bond. The market rate of interest may fluctuate as much as 2 percent per week between the time that the bonds are printed and issued. No investor would be willing to buy a bond with a nominal interest rate of 12.7 percent when the market rate of interest is fluctuating around 15 percent. So such a bond sells at a *discount*.

Example: A bond issued by Pacific Telephone is selling at "88." An investor pays $880 for a bond with a face amount of $1,000. What is the *effective* rate of interest? In the numerator we put the interest the investor will receive ($1,000 × .127 = $127) and in the denominator the price the investor must pay ($880).

$$\frac{\$127}{\$880} = 14.43\% \text{ effective interest rate}$$

Now the Pacific Telephone investment account must mirror this transaction. To do so, it must record not only the actual interest payment, but also the discrepancy (discount) between the purchase price and the face amount of the bond. It must also attempt to express in the income statement something approximating the effective interest rate. The only method for accomplishing all this that we will consider is called *straight-line amortization.* This approach results in a fixed amortization of the bond discount over the life of the bond (until the maturity date, which in this case is 2019).

The Pacific Telephone example can be illustrated by using T-accounts:

Cash	
(1) $880	(2) $127

Bond Discount	
(1) $120	(3) $3.15

Bond Payable	
	(1) $1,000

Interest Expense	
(2) $127 (3) $ 3.15	

* Entry 1 is the sale of the bond by the corporation.
* Entry 2 is the payment of the annual interest at 12.7 percent.
* Entry 3 is the straight-line amortization of the bond discount.

As the bond gets closer and closer to the year 2019, investors will be willing to pay amounts closer to the redemption value of the bond. For example, one day before the due date an investor would be willing to pay very close to $1,000. Further, the balance sheet at the end of year 1 reports the bond value at $883.15, and the income statement shows the interest expense at $130.15 ($127 cash payment + 3.15 amortization of bond discount):

$$\frac{\$130.15}{\$883.15} = 14.73\% \text{ effective interest}$$

So effective interest is the amount ($130.15) that Pacific Telephone must pay to have the use of $883.15 for one year. Some of the exercises will address this problem of bond discount and expense.

Bond premium is just the reverse of bond discount. If the market interest rate drops below the nominal interest rate for the bond, then the investor would be willing to pay a premium for the bond. The effective interest rate would then fall below the nominal rate of interest.

Figure 13.1 the consolidated balance sheet of Tandem Computers for 1979 and 1980. Note particularly the classification of liabilities in connection with the description in this chapter.

ADDITIONAL EXERCISES

13-7. a. An *overstatement* of net income may result from the failure to record

a. dividends declared on common stock.

b. an accrued expense.

c. amortization of premium on bonds payable.

d. a contingent liability.

b. Assume that the current market rate of interest is 18¼ percent. You are interested in purchasing a subordinated debenture bond of American Telephone and Telegraph Company which matures in 1990 and carries a coupon rate of 12%. The face value of the bond is $5,000. Would you expect to pay:

a. more than $5,000.

b. less than $5,000.

c. exactly $5,000.

13-8. a. Of the following items, the *one* that should be classified as a current liability is:

a. a law suit against the company that will come to trial in 1984. Our attorney says the suit has little merit.

TANDEM COMPUTERS INCORPORATED AND SUBSIDIARIES

CONSOLIDATED BALANCE SHEETS

As of September 30, 1980 and 1979

	(In Thousands)	
ASSETS	**1980**	**1979**
CURRENT ASSETS:		
Cash (Note 4)	$ 9,265	$ 2,198
Cash investments	6,980	4,560
Accounts receivable, net of $1,016,000 allowance for doubtful accounts in 1980, none in 1979	42,552	19,881
Inventories (Note 1)	20,901	11,304
Prepaid expenses	1,965	1,385
Total current assets	81,663	39,328
PROPERTY AND EQUIPMENT, at cost (Notes 1 and 3):		
Production and test equipment	4,135	1,982
Computer equipment	4,702	2,417
Office furniture and equipment	1,083	382
Systems spares	4,391	2,141
Leasehold improvements	4,054	1,597
	18,365	8,519
Less—Accumulated depreciation and amortization	4,327	1,900
	14,038	6,619
	$95,701	$45,947

	(In Thousands)	
LIABILITIES AND STOCKHOLDERS' INVESTMENT	**1980**	**1979**
CURRENT LIABILITIES:		
Current maturities of capitalized lease obligations	$ 476	$ 375
Accounts payable	11,063	5,675
Accrued expenses	3,216	1,269
Accrued income taxes	5,676	4,913
Total current liabilities	20,431	12,232
CAPITALIZED LEASE OBLIGATIONS, net of current maturities (Note 3)	1,651	1,144
DEFERRED INCOME TAXES	3,325	1,041
COMMITMENTS (Note 6)		
STOCKHOLDERS' INVESTMENT (Note 5):		
Preferred stock—$.10 par value, authorized 2,400,000 shares; none outstanding	—	—
Common stock—$.025 par value, authorized 20,000,000 shares; outstanding 8,339,498 shares in 1979 and 10,024,918 shares in 1980	251	209
Additional paid-in capital	53,555	25,520
Retained earnings	16,488	5,801
Total stockholders' investment	70,294	31,530
	$95,701	$45,947

The accompanying notes are an integral part of these balance sheets.

FIGURE 13-1. Classification of liabilities

Reprinted by permission of Tandem Computers, Inc.

b. a cash dividend declared before the balance sheet date when the date of record is subsequent to the balance sheet date.

c. deferred income taxes.

d. all of the above.

b. The stated interest rate on the face of a debt instrument affects the issue price of that instrument. If the instrument is issued at a premium (assuming no other marketplace variable), the stated interest rate is:

a. at the prevailing market rate.

b. above the prevailing market rate.

c. below the prevailing market rate.

d. not determinable from the information given.

13-9. Merchandise is normally shipped to the Maxe Company, FOB shipping point. The December 31, 19X1 physical inventory of Maxe Company appropriately included $3,800 of merchandise that was not recorded as purchases until January, 19X2. What effect will this error have on December 31, 19X1 assets, liabilities, retained earnings, and earnings for the year then ended? (Circle one answer on each of the four lines below.)

a. On assets: overstate, understate, no effect

b. On liabilities: overstate, understate, no effect

c. On retained earnings: overstate, understate, no effect

d. On net earnings: overstate, understate, no effect

13-10. On July 1, 1969, a corporation issued at face value $100,000 in serial bonds with 5-percent interest payable on January 1 and July 1 of each year and principal repayments in increments of $10,000 on July 1 of each year from 1973 through 1982.

a. Transactions related to this issue decreased working capital during 1977 by:

a. $13,500

b. $13,250

c. $12,500

d. $12,750

e. $13,000

b. Decreased income during 1977 by: $______________

SOLUTIONS

13-1. d

13-2. a, b, and c are correct. d omits Accounts receivable in the numerator.

13-3. a, d, e, f, and g.

13-4. Deferred magazine subscriptions (not a current liability).

13-5.

Federal Income Tax Payable	
	$15,000

Deferred Income Taxes	
	$5,000

Income Tax Expense	
$20,000	

13-6. a. $2,907
b. $1,400
c. $7,093

13-7. a. b—an accrued expense
b. b—less than $5,000

13-8. a. b
b. b

13-9. a. No effect on assets
b. Understate liabilities
c. Overstate retained earnings
d. Overstate net earnings

13-10. a. d—$12,750

b. Decreased income during 1977 by $2,750

Calculations:

Date	*Balance*	
7/1/69	$100,000	
12/31/69	$100,000	
12/31/72	$100,000	
7/1/73	$ 90,000	
7/1/74	$ 80,000	
7/1/75	$ 70,000	
7/1/76	$ 60,000	
12/31/76	$ 60,000 × 2.5% =	$ 1,500
7/1/77	$ 50,000 × 2.5% =	$ 1,250
12/31/77	$ 50,000	
		$ 2,750
	+ Principal repayment	$10,000
		$12,750

14

Owners' Equity

With its broadest possible definition, the term "Owners' equity" means:

Owners' equity = Assets − Liabilities

Since this definition says nothing about the business entity's form of organization, it could refer to a sole proprietorship, a partnership, or a corporation.

FORMS OF ORGANIZATION

Many small businesses take the form of sole proprietorships, that is, they have single owners. My wife's pottery studio, for example, operates as a sole proprietorship. In her case the Owners' equity section of the general ledger contains one account entitled:

Y. Boutell, capital

This account would be credited for the initial investment in the business, as well as yearly for the profits of the studio. It is also debited for the drawings (disinvestment) by which the owner takes money out of the business.

If, however, the pottery business expanded, she might wish to take in a partner, in which case the following considerations become relevant:

* the amount of investment the new partner will make,
* the profit and loss sharing ratio, and
* the share of the assets upon dissolution of the business.

Most such matters would be settled by a partnership contract, and the operation of the business also becomes subject to the Uniform Partnership Act. Little accounting theory is involved in partnerships. Instead of one capital account, as in the case of sole proprietorship, there would be as many capital accounts as there are partners. Owners' equity would be the sum of all of the balances in the partners' capital accounts. Typical firms that operate as partnerships are professional organizations, such as medical groups, public accounting firms, and law firms.

But to the accountant the most important form of business organization is the corporation. The *corporation* is an artificial person created by state law; it can do business, make contracts, borrow and lend money, and sell shares of ownership. The stock certificate is the evidence of ownership in the corporation. We call the Owner's equity section of the balance sheet Stockholders' equity. If a group of investors wish to form a corporation, the scenario goes something like this:

* From the state of incorporation they obtain a charter, which authorizes the issuance of a certain number of shares of stock. This stock is called *authorized stock.*
* They sell the shares of stock to the investors for cash or for the fair market value of property or of other assets contributed to the corporation. This is called *issued stock.*
* They commence business operations by having the shareholders elect a board of directors, who in turn whould elect the officers of the corporation.

Of course, things are never as simple as they first appear, particularly with respect to corporations. For example, most states require corporations to set a par value on their shares of stock. Let's assume that we set a par value of $1 per share. Let's further assume that the stock will be sold for $5 per share. The entries in the T-account would look like this for each share sold:

Cash	
$5	

Capital Contributed in Excess of Par Value	
	$4

Capital Stock Issued (par value)	
	$1

EXERCISE 14-1

The New Data Corp. began business on January 1, 19X2 and sold 5,000 shares of capital stock at $10 per share for cash to investors. The par value of the stock was $5 per share. One month later New Data sold an additional 2,000 shares at $11 per share. Record these in the following T-accounts:

In some cases, for good business reasons, corporations re-acquire stock that was previously issued. This reacquired stock is known as *treasury stock*. Since it is recorded at cost, the entry is simply:

Cash	
	$ XXXX

Treasury Stock (at cost)	
$ XXXX	

Two additional facts should be noted in connection with *treasury stock:*

1. The balance in the treasury stock account is deducted from the total of Shareholders' equity on the balance sheet.
2. Since treasury stock is held by the corporation, it is not outstanding. So, when and if dividends are declared, they are declared and paid only on outstanding shares.

We can also define treasury stock as:

Treasury stock = Issued stock − Outstanding stock

EXERCISE 14-2

Treasury stock involves shares that are:

a. **issued but not currently outstanding.**
b. **subscribed but not yet issued.**
c. **authorized but not yet issued.**
d. **outstanding but cannot accrue dividends.**

LEVERAGE

If you plan to start a business, you can finance your operations in two ways. The first is to borrow money, through either bank financing or bond issuances. The second way is to ask other investors to put their funds at risk along with your own and thereby become part owners of this business. This second method is called *equity financing.* Actually most businesses finance their operations by a combination of the two methods, because each has its advantages and disadvantages.

On the one hand, debt financing through the bond market provides funds for the business with a fixed and known interest obligation. The interest expense is deductible for federal and state income tax purposes, so the actual cost is closer to one-half of the contractual interest rate. Yet debt financing has the disadvantage of requiring specified interest payments to be made on a semiannual basis, at the risk of foreclosure by the bondholders. Further no payments can be made to the equity holders until the bondholders have been paid. At the same time the bondholders have no say in the operations of the business. Neither do they not participate in the growth in earnings of the business. They are entitled to their interest payments and to the principal payments, when due—and that's all!

On the other hand, in equity financing, the stockholders bear all the risk, and share all the profits. The corporation may not deduct any distributions to the shareholders in the form of dividends, so equity financing is much more of a drain on the business' cash resources than debt financing. Further, if the business goes into bankruptcy, the bondholders must be paid off before any payments can be made to the shareholders. In fact, in cases of bankruptcy, the shareholders might even receive nothing, despite the fact that they initially invested as much or more than the bondholders.

So the question really boils down to whether the business is going to make money and be successful. Let's say that, as a shareholder, you invest only 25 percent of the capital required to operate the business, relying on the bondholders to supply the other 75 percent. In this situation, you may be able to double or triple your money in a relatively short time—or, if there is a slowdown or a recession in the economy, lose everything. With a healthy earnings growth, results might look like this:

Bondholders $750,000 invested (10% interest rate)
Stockholders $250,000 invested

	19X0	*19X1*	*19X2*
Earnings	$100,000	$125,000	$150,000
To bondholders	75,000	75,000	75,000
Amount available for shareholders	$ 25,000	$ 50,000	$ 75,000

This situation is an example of "leverage." Initially, in 19X0, with $100,000 in earnings, both bondholders and shareholders are earning 10 percent on their investment. In 19X1, stockholders are earning 20 percent, and in 19X2 they are earning a whopping 30 percent—an increase of 200 percent over what they were earning just two years ago, while the actual total earnings only increased by 50 percent! This is known as *leveraging your investment* or *trading on the equity.*

EXERCISE 14-3

a. Company X (which is in the 50 percent tax bracket) is currently studying the economic effects of a proposed bond issue (8-percent, 10-year bonds), as contrasted with a possible issue of preferred stock. Assuming the bond is sold at par, the net interest rate that Company X would pay is:

a. 8.0 percent.
b. 5.0 percent.
c. 4.0 percent.
d. 0.08 percent.
e. None of the above.

b. If a company decides to sell preferred stock (instead of bonds) to finance the building of a new plant, one of the following statements would *not* hold. Which one?

a. The debt to equity ratio will decrease.
b. Working capital will increase at least temporarily.
c. Net income will be reduced in subsequent years.
d. The new issue of preferred stock will provide additional leverage for common stockholders.

PREFERRED STOCK

Preferred Stock retains some of the characteristics of bonds while adding some of the attributes of common stock equity.* For example, the dividend is expressed in a percentage, and the stock is redeemable at par. On the other hand, since preferred stock receives a dividend, it is subordinate to the claims of the bondholders. In addition, corporations may not deduct dividends for income tax purposes. And, in case of liquidation, preferred shareholders are in a much riskier position than the bondholders.

To make preferred stock more attractive to investors, the issuing corporation can stipulate in the contract that the stock will be *cumulative.* In other words, if the preferred dividend is missed for any year, before any dividends can be paid to common stockholders, all the preferred dividends in arrears must be paid.

Some corporations have attempted to overcome some of the objections to preferred stock by making it convertible, under specified terms, into common stock. Convertible preferred stockholders could then retain the preferred stock if things did not look particularly good, since they would be better off than common shareholders with respect to dividends and in case of liquidation. On the other hand, if it looked like the company had really "taken off," they could jump on the "bandwagon" by exercising their conversion privileges and converting their holdings to common stock.

EXERCISE 14-4

1. A company wishes to raise funds by issuing either bonds or *cumulative* preferred stock, but they are forecasting a loss for next year. How will the annual interest or dividend affect total liabilities? (Assume no dividends have been declared.)

a. Interest is a current liability each year (until paid).
b. Cumulative preferred dividends are a current liability each year (until paid).
c. *Both* interest and cumultive preferred dividends are current liabilities each year (until paid).
d. Interest and cumulative preferred dividends in arrears are current liabilities each year (until paid).
e. None of the above.

2. A company wishes to raise funds by issuing either bonds or preferred noncumulative stock. How will the annual interest or dividend affect annual net earnings available to common stockholders each year?

a. Annual net earnings available to common stockholders are reduced by annual interest but *not* by preferred dividends.

*Common stock is the portion of the capital stock of a corporation that comprises the residual equity.

b. Annual net earnings available to common stockholders are reduced by preferred dividends but not by annual interest.

c. Annual net earnings available to common stockholders are reduced by annual interest and preferred dividends.

d. Annual net earnings available to common stockholders are *not* reduced by annual interest or preferred dividends.

SOME CHARACTERISTICS OF ACCOUNTING FOR STOCKHOLDERS' EQUITY

The reader should bear in mind three important dates with respect to dividend payments. Here they are, in chronological order and usually separately by at least two or three weeks:

* *Declaration date*—the day the board of directors meet and declare a dividend. On this date, a Current liability is created on the balance sheet.
* *The record date*—the date on which the investor must own the stock to receive the dividend (no accounting entry is required by the corporation).
* *The payment date*—the date the corporation is required to mail the payments to the stockholders of record (debit Dividends payable, credit Cash).

The only group that has the power to declare dividends is the board of directors. No court or group of stockholders can force the board to declare a dividend, but once it is declared the corporation then has a legal obligation to pay it.

Finally, a corporation may want to pay a dividend despite a severe cash shortage. In that case, it can pay a stock dividend (such as a 5-percent stock dividend.) If you, the investor, hold 100 shares of the stock on the record date, you would be entitled to receive an additional 5 shares of stock (5 percent of 100 shares). The accounting on the part of the corporation for this transaction is simple:

* Retained earnings is debited for the fair market value of the stock dividend.
* The Common stock account is credited for the par value of the stock issued.
* Capital contributed in excess of par Value is credited for the difference.

Example: A firm declares a stock dividend of 5 percent. Before the stock dividend, 10,000 shares of stock are issued and outstanding, with par value $1 per share and a market value of $10 per share.

Capital Stock		*Excess of Amounts Contributed over Par Value*		*Retained Earnings*	
	Bal. $10,000		Bal. $1,000	(1) $5,000	Bal. $25,000
	(1) $ 500		(1) $4,500		

Only a single entry is needed to increase Capital stock by 500 shares (or 5 percent of 10,000 shares). The debit to Retained earnings is $5,000 (500 shares at $10 per share). The balance ($5,000 – $500) is credited to Excess of amounts contributed over par value.

A *stock split* should be distinguished from a stock dividend. In a stock split, a corporation issues several shares of stock for each share outstanding—such as a three-for-one stock split. If you, the investor, hold 100 shares you would receive an additional 200 shares. Thus you wind up with three shares for every one you owned originally. For a stock split, you need not make any accounting entry. You simply increase the number of authorized, issued, and outstanding shares by the appropriate multiple.

EXERCISE 14-5

a. The effect of recording a two-for-one stock split would be to:

a. decrease the current ratio, decrease working capital, and decrease book value per share.
b. leave inventory turnover unaffected, decrease working capital, and decrease book value per share.
c. leave working capital unaffected, decrease earnings per share, and decrease book value per share.
d. leave working capital unaffected, decrease earnings per share, and decrease the debt to equity ratio.
e. none of the above.

b. The directors of Corel Corporation, whose $40 par value common stock is currently selling at $50 per share, have decided to issue a stock dividend. The corporation has an authorization for 200,000 shares of common, has issued 110,000 shares,

of which 10,000 shares are now held as treasury stock, and desires to capitalize $400,000 of the Retained earnings balance. To do so, the directors should declare a stock dividend of:

a. 10 percent.
b. 8 percent.
c. 5 percent.
d. 2 percent.
e. None of the above.

c. A stock is said to go "ex-dividend" on the day

a. the dividend is declared.
b. of record.
c. the corporation mails the dividend check.
d. the stockholder receives the dividend check.
e. none of the above.

Figure 14-1 shows an example of a statement of stockholders' investment taken from Tandem Computer's annual report. Not that the statement is comprehensive in that it covers the three years from September 30, 1977 through September 30, 1980. Also note that it describes the changes not only in the Contributed capital but also in Retained earnings for this period. This statement gives a complete picture of Stockholders' equity for Tandem Computers.

Reminder: When you have completed the exercises for Chapter 14, take the Second Progress Test, which is found immediately after the Additional Exercises.

ADDITIONAL EXERCISES

On November 30, 19X1, when the Maxe Company's stock was selling at $40 per share, its Stockholders' equity accounts were as follows:

Stockholders' Equity:	
Capital stock—common, authorized 1,000,000 shares issued and outstanding 100,000 shares with a par value of $20 per share	**$2,000,000**
Premium on capital stock	**600,000**
Retained earnings	**3,000,000**
Total	**$5,600,000**

TANDEM COMPUTERS INCORPORATED AND SUBSIDIARIES

CONSOLIDATED STATEMENT OF STOCKHOLDERS' INVESTMENT

For the Years Ended September 30, 1979 and 1980

(In Thousands)

	Preferred Stock		Common Stock		Additional Paid-in	Retained	Total Stockholders'
	Shares	Amount	Shares*	Amount	Capital	Earnings	Investment
Balance, September 30, 1978	—	$ —	7,352	$ 184	$14,473	$ 881	$15,538
Sale of common stock, net of related expenses	—	—	840	21	10,054	—	10,075
Sale of stock under stock option and stock purchase plans, net	—	—	148	4	758	—	762
Income tax benefit resulting from exercises of non-qualified stock options and early disposition of shares acquired under qualified stock option and stock purchase plans	—	—	—	—	235	—	235
Net income	—	—	—	—	—	4,920	4,920
Balance, September 30, 1979	—	—	8,340	209	25,520	5,801	31,530
Sale of common stock, net of related expenses	—	—	1,430	36	24,243	—	24,279
Sale of stock under stock option and stock purchase plans, net	—	—	255	6	2,986	—	2,992
Income tax benefit resulting from exercises of non-qualified stock options and early disposition of shares acquired under qualified stock option and stock purchase plans	—	—	—	—	806	—	806
Net income	—	—	—	—	—	10,687	10,687
Balance, September 30, 1980	—	$ —	10,025	$ 251	$53,555	$16,488	$70,294

*Adjusted for two-for-one stock split in June, 1980.

The accompanying notes are an integral part of this statement.

FIGURE 14-1. An example of stockholders' investment

Reprinted by permission of Tandem Computers, Inc.

14-6. The book value of a share of Maxe Company's stock is:*

- **a. $2 per share.**
- **b. $20 per share.**
- **c. $26 per share.**
- **d. $56 per share.**
- **e. None of the above.**

*See Glossary/Index for definitions.

14-7. The board of directors of Maxe Company voted to issue two shares of stock for each share presently outstanding and to reduce the par value to $10 per share.

a. no entry for the stock dividend is required.
b. capital stock would increase to $2,400,000.
c. capital stock would increase to $4,000,000.
d. shareholder's equity would increase by $1,000,000.
e. none of the above.

14-8. Assuming the issuing company has only one class of stock, a transfer from Retained earnings to Capital stock equal to the market value of the shares issued is ordinarily a characteristic of:

a. either a stock dividend or a stock split.
b. neither a stock dividend nor a stock split.
c. a stock split but not a stock dividend.
d. a stock dividend but not a stock split.
e. a cash dividend.

14-9. The stockholders' equity of Slumber Company at July 31, 19XX, is as follows:

Common stock, par value $10, authorized 400,000 shares; issued and outstanding 150,000 shares	$1,500,000
Capital in excess of par value	70,000
Retained earnings	195,000
Total	$1,765,000

On August 1, 19XX, the board of directors of Slumber declared a 4-percent stock dividend on common stock, to be distributed on September 15. The market price of Slumber's common stock was $20 on September 15, 19XX. What is the amount of the charge to Retained earnings as a result of the declaration and distribution of this stock dividend?

a. $120,000.
b. $60,000.
c. $105,000.
d. $0.
e. None of the above.

14-10. From the annual report for Tandem Computers in Figure 14-1:

a. What was the book value per share on September 30, 1980? $__________

b. How many shares of common stock were outstanding on September 30, 1979? __________

c. What was the average price that Tandem Computers received for the sale of its common stock? (*Hint*: Be sure to add par amounts as well as addition paid-in capital amounts.) $__________

d. What was the total amount of Shareholders' equity as of September 30, 1980? $__________

e. Was there any treasury stock held by the company on September 30, 1980? $__________

SOLUTIONS

14-1.

Cash	
(1) $50,000	
(2) $22,000	

Capital Contributed in Excess of Par Value	
	(1) $25,000
	(2) $12,000

Capital Stock Issued (Par Value)	
	(1) $25,000
	(2) $10,000

14-2. a

14-3. a. a—4 percent

b. c—preferred stock dividends have no effect of net income.

14-4. a. a—Dividends are not a liability until declared by the board of directors even if preferred stock dividends are cumulative.

b. a—Similar reasoning to part a.

14-5. a. c—Only effect is on EPS and book value per share.

b. b—Since 400,000/50 = 8,000 shares or 8 percent of shares presently outstanding.

c. b—The record date.

14-6. d—$56 per share.

14-7. e—This is a stock split.

14-8. d—A stock dividend only.

14-9. a—$120,000 (150,000 shares × 4 % = 6,000 shares × $20 per share).

14-10. a. $70,294 ÷ 10,025 = $7.01 per share

b. 8,340,000 shares

c. $251,000 + $53,555,000 / 10,025,000 = $5.37 per share

d. $70,294,000

e. No

Second Progress Test

The Second Progress Test covers Chapters 9 through 14. So the emphasis in this test is concentrated primarily on the major balance sheet items such as Accounts receivable, Inventories, Property, plant, and equipment, and Liabilities.

Like the First Progress Test, you should do your best to complete the test within one and one-half hours. But, again, correct answers, rather than speed, should be your overriding goal. This test is also divided into several different segments which, together with the assigned points, are as follows:

* (Quickies—multiple choice questions—30 points),
* Inventories—(30 points),
* Property, Plant, and Equipment—(20 points), and
* Liabilities and Stockholders' Equities—(20 points).

As in the First Progress Test you should score at least 75 (75 percent) to say that you are making satisfactory progress. Good luck on the test.

QUICKIES (2 points each)

1. The write-off of a bad debt affects:

   a. the current ratio.
   b. the amount of working capital
   c. the quick asset ratio.
   d. EPS.
   e. none of the above.

2. A bad debt recovery affects all of the following ratios except:

   a. long-term debt to equity ratio.
   b. the current ratio.
   c. EPS.
   d. book value per share.
   e. accounts receivable turnover ratio.

3. Given the following list of short-term investments, the appropriate balance sheet valuation is:

	Cost	*Market Value*
Common stock A	$1,000	$1,200
Common stock B	$5,000	$5,700
Bond C	$2,000	$1,700
Preferred stock D	$3,000	$2,300

   a. $11,000.
   b. $10,000.
   c. $10,900.
   d. $11,900.
   e. some other amount.

4. If a company holds *only one* short-term investment in a class A bond that was purchased at a face value of $10,000 and that has a current market value of $9,000, then the proper financial statement presentation of this item would not:

   a. affect the current ratio.
   b. affect the quick asset ratio.
   c. affect ROI.
   d. affect EPS.
   e. all of the above statements are false.

5. Information from Maxe Company's financial statements is as follows:

	19X1	*19X0*
Current assets at December 31	$2,000,000	$2,100,000
Current liabilities at December 31	1,000,000	900,000
Stockholders' equity at December 31	2,500,000	2,700,000
Net sales for year	8,300,000	8,800,000
Cost of goods sold for year	6,200,000	6,400,000
Operating income for year	500,000	550,000

What is the current ratio at December 31, 19X1?

a. 1.20 to 1
b. 2.25 to 1
c. 2.33 to 1
d. 7.33 to 1
e. 2.00 to 1

6. If inventories are stable but prices are rising, which of the following statements is true?

a. Using FIFO would result in the lowest current ratio.
b. Using LIFO (as opposed to FIFO) would result in an increase in federal income taxes, other things being equal.
c. Using average cost to value inventories would result in the highest balance sheet valuation for inventory.
d. Using FIFO would result in the highest ratio of net income to sales.
e. Using LIFO would result in the highest net income.

7. Using LCM valuation for inventory and given the following data, which of the following amounts should appear on the balance sheet?

Sales price (each)	$5.00
Replacement cost (each)	$2.50
Cost price (each)	$3.00
Cost to complete and sell	$1.00
Normal profit margin	$2.00

a. $3.00
b. $2.50
c. $1.50
d. $2.00
e. $4.00

8. Using an accelerated depreciation method would accomplish all of the following except:

a. provide adequately for the obsolesence factor.
b. lower income taxes in the early years.

c. provide the highest long-term debt to equity ratio in the first year.
d. shorten the economic life of the asset.
e. provide a lower ROI in the first year.

9. The Dredge-Em-Up Gold Mining Co., Inc. acquired a piece of property with an old river bed, which is thought to contain small amounts of gold. But it was purchased with the understanding that the land must be restored to a condition suitable for recreational use after it extracts the low-grade gold ore. Geological surveys estimate that recoverable reserves will be 3,000,000 tons (from which approximately 3,000 ounces of gold will be extracted after further processing), and that the land will have a value of $600,000 after restoration. Relevant cost information follows:

Land (including river bed)	$6,000,000
Restoration cost	$ 900,000
Geological surveys	$ 300,000

If Dredge-Em-Up Gold Mining Co., Inc. maintains no inventories of extracted material, what should be the charge to depletion expense per ton of material extracted?

a. $1.80.
b. $1.90.
c. $2.00.
d. $2.10.
e. $2.20.

10.

Cash, 9/30/XX	$__________
Cash, 10/31/XX	365
Withdrawals, October, 19XX	1,900
Deposits, Ocotber, 19XX	1,350

11.

Accounts receivable, 9/30/XX	$__________
Accounts receivable, 10/31/XX	1,000
Sales revenues, October, 19XX	135,000
Collections on account, October, 19XX	97,000
Cash sales, October, 19XX	45,000

12.

Accumulated depreciation, 9/30/XX	$ 61,000
Accumulated depreciation, 10/31/XX	90,000
Depreciation expenses, October, 19XX	$__________
Original cost of fully depreciated machine destroyed 10/15/XX	6,000

13.

Inventory, 9/30/XX	$ 12,500
Inventory, 10/31/XX	10,000
Cost of goods sold	250,000
Net purchases, October, 19XX	$__________

14.

Interest income, October, 19XX	$__________
Accrued interest Income, 9/30/XX	700
Accrued interest income, 10/31/XX	900
Interest collected, October, 19XX	2,300

15.

Allowance for doubtful accounts, 2/28/XX	$ 950
Allowance for doubtful accounts, 1/31/XX	860
Provision for doubtful accounts, February, 19XX	480
Bad Debts writeoffs, February, 19XX	__________

INVENTORIES (10 points each)

The following information is available from your firm's accounting records pertaining to the purchases of General television sets (the 19-inch color table model):

Purchasing Data:

November 30, 19X1 (100 sets @ $170)
February 20, 19X2 (25 sets @ $180)
June 15, 19X2 (50 sets @ $200)
October 30, 19X2 (100 sets @ $205)

Sales Data (by quarters):

Quarter ended January 31, 19X2, 125 sets
April 30, 19X2, 40 sets
July 31, 19X2, 30 sets
October 31, 19X2, 50 sets

Inventory of 19-inch color TV sets on October 31, 19X1, 30 sets @ $160.

As the firm's accountant, you have been asked to answer the following questions:

16. Using a LIFO costing method, what would the value of the inventory of TV sets be on October 31, 19X2? $__________

17. How much would the inventory increase/decrease if the company adopted a FIFO inventory valuation? __________ (increase/decrease) $__________.

18. Consider question 18 independently of the foregoing questions. Assuming a FIFO basis of inventory costing, you have been informed that there has been a sharp drop in the price of TV sets because of an influx of imported sets, reducing the current replacement cost to $175. Assuming that the current selling price of the set is $250 and that the costs to complete and sell one set is 10 percent of the selling price. The profit margin based on selling price is also 10 percent of the selling price. How would this affect your answer to question 17? Specify the direction of the change (up or down), as well as the amount of the change in your answer.

________________ $________________

up/down

PROPERTY, PLANT, AND EQUIPMENT (20 points)

19. (15 points) You have just acquired a drilling rig, which is going to be used to rent out to various wildcat drilling companies. The rig cost $200,000 with an estimated salvage value of $40,000 and an estimated life of 4 years. In attempting to decide which method of depreciation to use, you want to calculate the impact of accelerated depreciation on the statement of income, as opposed to that of straight-line depreciation, as well as any potential tax savings that might arise from using accelerated depreciation. Your accountant has provided you with the following schedule to assist in making your decision. Please complete the schedule:

	Depreciation Expense			*Tax Savings*
Year	*Straight-Line*	*SOFTY*	*Difference*	*50% Rate*
1981	______	______	______	______
1982	______	______	______	______
1983	______	______	______	______
1984	______	______	______	______
Totals	______	______	______	______

20. (5 points) You have just traded in an old delivery van, whose original cost was $4,800 and whose accumulated depreciation at the date of trade-in was $4,300. You traded for a new electric delivery vehicle with a net cash price of $8,900. At what price should this vehicle be put on the book of your corporation? ____________

LIABILITIES AND STOCKHOLDERS' EQUITIES (20 points)

21. For each of the following events (at the instant the event occurs), you are to decide whether or not a liability is created. If so, indicate the title of the liability account and the amount in the space provided; if not, write "None" in the space provided. (2 Points each)

_________________________ a. A check for $900 is received from a new tenant for 6 months' rent in advance on a room.

_________________________ b. A contract is signed to buy 50 tons of coal a week for 20 weeks at a cost of $50/ton, payment to be made in 30 days.

_________________________ c. During January, the employer paid $6,000 in wages subject to Social Security. By February 27 the employer must pay 6 percent of those wages to the federal government as Social Security taxes.

_________________________ d. 7-percent, 20-year bonds with a face value of $1,000,000 are issued at par. The interest is payable at 6-month intervals.

_________________________ e. The payment of cash by a passenger ($450) to the Low and Slow Airline, Inc. for an airline ticket. The flight is scheduled for 6 weeks from today.

22. From following the excerpt from the balance sheet of PSA, Inc. (December 31, 1979), answer these questions:

Stockholders' Equity (in thousands):	*December 31*	
	1979	*1978*
Preferred stock, par value $1 per share; 500 shares authorized, none issued		
Common stock, par value $1 per share; 9,500 shares authorized, 3,426 shares issued and outstanding (3,346 in 1978)	$ 3,426	$ 3,346
Additional paid-in capital	36,840	36,392
Retained earnings	59,957	36,860
Total stockholders' equity	100,223	76,598

a. (1 point) The number of shares of stock outstanding at December 31, 1979: ____________

b. (2 points) The total contributed capital as of December 31, 1979: $____________

c. (1 point) The number of unissued shares of common stock as of December 31, 1979: ____________

d. (3 points) The book value per share as of December 31, 1979: $____________

e. (3 points) The book value per share as of December 31, 1979: $____________

SOLUTIONS

1. e
2. e
3. c
4. e
5. e
6. d
7. b
8. d
9. e
10. $915
11. $8,000
12. $35,000
13. $247,500
14. $2,500
15. $390
16. 30 sets at $160, 30 sets at $170 = $9,900
17. 60 at $205 = $12,300 – 9,900 = $2,400
18. Replacement cost is less than the selling price less the cost to complete and sell ($250 – 25 – 25 = 200). So the valuation would be $200 per set, which is $5 less than the answer to 17. Down: $5 × 60 sets = $300.
19.

	Straight-Line	*SOFTY*		*Difference*		*Tax Savings*
1981	$ 40,000	$ 64,000	+	$24,000	+	$12,000
1982	40,000	48,000	+	8,000	+	4,000
1983	40,000	32,000	–	8,000	–	4,000
1984	40,000	16,000	–	24,000	–	12,000
Total	$160,000	$160,000		-0-		-0-

20. $4,800 – $4,300 + $8,900 = $9,400

21. a. Unearned rent income, $900
    b. None
    c. Accrued taxes payable, $360
    d. Bonds payable, $1,000,000
    e. Unearned ticket revenue, $450

22. a. 3,426,000 shares
    b. $40,266,000
    c. 9,500,000 − 3,426,000 = 6,074,000 shares
    d. $76,598 ÷ 3,346 = $22.89 per share of common stock
    e. $100,223 ÷ 3,426 = $29.25 per share of common stock

15
Long-Term Investments

For the most part, the phrase "long-term investments" means "equity securities." A business may invest in the equity securities (that is, in the ownership) of another for a number of reasons, but the main ones, rather succinctly, are:

* to obtain control of the acquired corporation,
* to eliminate competition,
* to grow,
* to guarantee sources of supply, or
* to use excess cash.

The different levels of investment in equity securities can be divided basically, into two distinct categories:

* acquiring enough shares of stock to assure control of the acquired corporation, and
* investments of lesser amounts.

Control of the acquired corporation is assured when the acquiring corporation owns more than 50 percent of the outstanding voting stock of the company. In this case the acquiring corporation must consolidate its financial statements with those of the acquired corporation, presenting both corporations as one economic entity. The consolidation procedure is complicated enough to be given special attention in Chapter 16.

So we'll leave consolidation alone in this section, confining our discussion to situations in which the acquiring corporation owns 50% or less of the outstanding voting stock of the acquired corporation.

Investments of 50 percent or less can be further subdivided into two situations:

* the acquiring corporation owns less than 20 percent of the acquired corporation's stock, and
* the acquiring corporation owns at least 20 percent but 50 percent or less.

First, when the acquiring corporation owns less than 20 percent of the acquired corporation's stock, it cannot exercise significant influence, and the accounting for the investment is relatively straightforward. The balance sheet presentation is based on historical cost at time of acquistion. As you might expect from the conservative approach of the accounting profession, accountants use the lower of cost or market rule to value the investment in later balance sheet presentations. On the income statement, the acquiring corporation reports dividends as received. Dividends declared by the acquired corporation become a liability of that corporation at the time they are declared, and, correspondingly, they become a receivable to the acquiring corporation. Consequently, as soon as the paying corporation declares a dividend, the acquiring corporation realizes income on the income statement.

The accounting for this class of investments can be summarized in the following T-accounts, below where: (1) is the investment, and (2) is the payment of the investor's share of the first year's dividend:

Cash		*Investment in A*		*Income from A*	
(2) \$700	(1) \$6,000	(1) \$6,000			(2) \$700

When the investment is at least 20 percent but not more than 50 percent, significant influence *is* exercised over the acquired corporation, according to generally accepted accounting principles. This case is sometimes referred to as *effective control*—that is, although control is less than absolute, it allows the exercise of significant influence. So such influence must be recognized in the accounting treatment of this class of investments. So the balance sheet must show two things:

* the original cost of the investment in the acquired corporation, *plus*
* the proportionate share of the next income, that the acquired corporation earns since the date of acquisition, reduced by the proportionate share of dividends that the acquired corporation pays or declares.

This method of accounting for income and dividends is called the *equity method.*

EXERCISE 15-1

a. Which of the following describes the amount at which a parent company should carry its long-term investment in companies of 40 percent on its separate financial statements in periods subsequent to acquisition?

a. Original cost of the investment to the parent company.
b. Original cost of the investment adjusted for the parent's share of the subsidiary's earnings, losses, and dividends.
c. Current market value of the investment adjusted for dividends received.
d. Current market value of the investment.
e. None of the above.

b. If a long-term investment (a bond) is acquired at a discount, the amount of the long-term investment on the balance sheet would:

a. remain constant from year to year.
b. decrease each year.
c. increase each year.
d. change from year to year depending on the market rate of interest.
e. none of the above.

Example: We acquire 40 percent of KKWT (Knock, Knock, Who's There?), a Country Western radio station for $50,000. During the first year of operation, KKWT earned net income of $10,000 and paid total dividends of $5,000. These transactions would be reported as follows:

Cash		*Investment in KKWT*		*Income from KKWT*	
(3) $2,000	(1) $50,000	(1) $50,000	(3) $2,000		(2) $4,000
		(2) $ 4,000			

Entry 1 reflects the investment in KKWT for cash. Entry 2 records the proportionate share of income (40 percent of $10,000) earned by KKWT. Finally, entry 3 summarizes the dividends paid KKWT ($5,000 × 40 percent).

EXERCISE 15-2

Given the following scenario, record the relevant facts in the T-accounts for Company A:

a. Company A acquired 15% of Company B on January 1, 19XX for $30,000.
b. Company B earned $15,000 during 19XX.
c. Company B paid total dividends of $4,500.
d. Company A acquires 30 percent of Company C in June 30, 19XX for $60,000.
e. Company C earns $10,000 during 19XX.
f. On September 30, 19XX, Company C paid total dividends of $4,000.

The several ways of accounting for the acquisition of the equity securities of another corporation can be quickly summarized as follows:

Percentage of Investment in Voting Stock	*Method of Accounting*
Over 50%	Consolidation (see Chapter 16)
20% or more but less than or equal to 50%	Equity method
Less than 20%	Cost method (lower of cost or market)

The remaining problems on long-term investments deal with reporting on the bonds of another corporation that are acquired for investment. The related problems involving premiums and discounts are treated in Chapter 13, although accounting for them is now "reversed," since we are considering the problem from the standpoint of the investor rather than that of the borrower. But, since the material is substantially similar, it need not be repeated. If you are having any difficulty, refer to Chapter 13.

Examples of an extensive treatment of long-term investments are found in Figures 15-1 and 15-2. American Express Company invests its funds in earning assets such as common stocks, preferred stocks, and bonds. A careful reading of the footnote to the financial statements (Figure 15-2) does not disclose any long-term investments in which American Express has a 20-percent interest or more. Consequently all investments seem to be valued at cost or the lower of cost or market, where applicable.

American Express Company 44

Consolidated Balance Sheet
(millions)

December 31,	1979	1978
Assets		
Cash	$ 1,051.5	$ 844.4
Time deposits (note 2)	976.0	891.0
Investment securities—at cost (notes 1 and 3):		
U.S. Government obligations	448.9	395.0
U.S. Government agencies' obligations	70.0	40.0
State and municipal obligations	4,104.0	3,808.0
Other bonds and obligations	1,044.4	735.2
Preferred stocks	51.7	47.4
Total (market: 1979, $5,069.8; 1978, $4,685.6)	5,719.0	5,025.6
Investment securities—at lower of aggregate cost or market (note 1):		
Preferred stocks	83.7	99.3
Common stocks	82.8	72.2
Total (cost: 1979, $192.3; 1978, $187.6)	166.5	171.5
Investment securities—at market (note 1):		
Preferred stocks	56.9	49.5
Common stocks	651.7	563.3
Total (cost: 1979, $523.0; 1978, $471.5)	708.6	612.8
Loans and discounts, less reserves: 1979, $81.7; 1978, $74.8	3,368.7	3,320.2
Accounts receivable and accrued interest, less reserves: 1979, $213.1; 1978, $170.8	3,596.6	2,705.5
Land, buildings and equipment—at cost, less accumulated depreciation: 1979, $126.3; 1978, $102.6	347.1	284.8
Prepaid policy acquisition expenses	243.5	206.0
Other assets	930.7	636.4
	$17,108.2	$14,698.2

FIGURE 15-1. A presentation of long-term investments

Reprinted with permission of American Express Company.

American Express Company 48

Notes to Consolidated Financial Statements

1. Summary of Significant Accounting Policies

Principles of Consolidation

The accompanying consolidated financial statements include the accounts of the Company and its subsidiaries. All significant intercompany transactions are eliminated. Certain 1978 amounts have been restated for a change in accounting principle effective January 1, 1979 (see note 12).

Foreign Currency

Foreign assets and liabilities are translated into their U.S. dollar equivalents based on rates of exchange generally prevailing at the end of each respective year except for major fixed assets which are translated at historical rates. Revenue and expense accounts are generally translated at exchange rates prevailing during the year. Aggregate exchange gains and losses arising from the translation of foreign assets and liabilities and from foreign currency transactions are reflected in net income.

Net Income Per Share

Net income per share is determined by dividing the weighted monthly average number of common shares outstanding into net income after deducting dividends on the redeemable series $2.00 convertible preferred shares. The weighted average shares used in the computations were 71,250,783 and 71,244,880 for 1979 and 1978, respectively. The potentially dilutive effect on net income per share of the outstanding stock options, convertible preferred stock, and convertible debentures is not material.

Investment Securities

Investment securities other than stocks are carried at amortized cost, except where there is a permanent impairment of value, in which case they are carried at estimated realizable value. All preferred and common stocks of the insurance subsidiaries are carried at market. All other preferred and common stocks are carried at the lower of aggregate cost or market, except that preferred stocks, which either must be redeemed by the issuer or which are redeemable at the option of the holder, are carried at cost. Net unrealized gains relating to stocks carried at market and carried at the lower of aggregate cost or market are reflected in common shareholders' equity at December 31, 1979 and 1978 as follows (millions):

1979	Gains	Losses	Net
Securities carried at market	$234.2	$(48.6)	$185.6
Securities carried at the lower of aggregate cost or market	21.0	(46.8)	(25.8)
			159.8
Less deferred income taxes			44.9
Net unrealized gains			$114.9
1978			
Securities carried at market	$174.2	$(32.9)	$141.3
Securities carried at the lower of aggregate cost or market	14.8	(30.9)	(16.1)
			125.2
Less deferred income taxes			38.2
Net unrealized gains			$ 87.0

Realized gains and losses result from the sales of investment securities or from a permanent impairment of value. The immaterial net gains for 1979 and 1978 are included in other expenses.

Insurance Premiums

Premium revenues on property-liability policies are reported as earned on a prorata basis over the applicable policy periods. Premium revenues on life insurance policies are reported as earned when due.

Reserve for Property-Liability Losses and Loss Expenses

The reserve for losses and loss expenses of the property-liability insurance subsidiaries includes the accumulation of case estimates for losses reported, estimates of losses incurred but not reported, and estimates of expenses for investigating and adjusting all incurred losses, less amounts estimated for salvage and subrogation recoverable.

FIGURE 15-2. Footnotes on investments

Reprinted by permission of American Express Company.

ADDITIONAL EXERCISES

15-3. On November 30, 19XX, the Ocean Marine Salvage Company purchased 6-percent bonds of Gulf Storm Toilets, Inc., with a face value of $300,000, for a total outlay of $302,000, including accrued interest. The 20-year bonds were originally issued precisely 10 years ago. Interest dates are June 30 and December 31. Assuming the investment is long-term, the bond interest earned during 19XX by the Ocean Marine Salvage Company is:

a. $1,454.55.

b. $1,500.

c. $1,545.45

d. $9,000.

e. $9,272.70.

f. None of the above.

15-4. The current market value of interest is 15 percent. You are interested in purchasing a bond of AT&T, which matures in 1995 at which time it will return $1,000. The coupon rate of interest on the bond is 12 percent. How much would you expect to pay for the bond?

a. More than $1,000

b. Less than $1,000

c. About $1,000

15-5. The outstanding common stock of Wheeler, Inc., is owned 85 percent by the Staubus Company and 15 percent by Cerf, Inc. On Cerf's balance sheet the investment in Wheeler, Inc. should be classified as:

a. a current asset.

b. another asset.

c. a long-term investment.

d. a fixed asset.

15-6. Using the same information as in question 15-5, the investment on Cert's sheet should be recorded using:

a. the cost method.

b. the equity method.

c. the consolidate method.

d. none of the above.

On January 1, 19XX the Freeman-Penman Company, Inc. purchased as a long-term investment 10,000 share of XYZ Co. common stock on the New York Stock Exchange for

$6 per share. XYZ Co. currently has 100,000 common shares authorized and 50,000 outstanding. The following data for XYZ Co. was available at the end of 19XX:

End of 19XX, XYZ Co.:

Reported profits	$30,000
Cash dividends declared and paid	$15,000
Market value per share	$ 9

15.7. Which method of accounting for Freeman-Penman's investment in XYZ Co. should be used? Why?

___

___

___

15.8. What income should be recorded on Freeman-Penman's books from this investment for 19XX?

___

___

___

15-9. At what amount will this investment be shown on Freeman-Penman's books at the end of 19XX? ___

15-10. Suppose Freeman-Penman had purchased 30,000 shares of XYZ Co. What method of accounting would be used?

___

15-11. If Freeman-Penman had bought 5,000 shares of XYZ Co., what would your answers to questions 8 and 9 be?

___

___

SOLUTIONS

15-1. a. b—The equity method of accounting is used.

b. c—It would increase each year because the discount would be amortized.

15-2.

Cash		Investment in B		Investment in C	
(c) $ 675	(a) $30,000	(a) $30,000		(d) $60,000	(f) $1,200
(f) $1,200	(d) $60,000			(e) $ 3,000	

Income from Investment C		Income from Investment B	
	(e) $3,000		(c) $675

15-3. c (accrued interest purchased, $7,500; so the bond discount is $5,500)

15-4. b

15-5. c

15-6. a

15-7. The equity method should be used (20 percent investment).

15-8. $6,000

15-9. $63,000

15-10. The equity method is not appropriate in this case. The financial statements must be *consolidated* to properly reflect the ownership of Freeman-Penmain in XYZ.

15-14. $1,500 for question 8; $30,000 for question 9.

16

Consolidated Financial Statements

Part of the difficulty associated with the presentation of consolidated financial statements arises from the fact that the accountant is attempting to present separate legal entities (two or more corporations) as one economic entity. The other part of the problem stems from the intent of the parties who join in the business combination. If, on the one hand, the parties intend to join hands and go forth together, accountants refer to this as a *pooling of interests.* If, on the other hand, the acquiring corporation's intent is clearly to "purchase" the other corporation, then the accountant would come up with different consolidated financial statements.

THE ENTITY CONCEPT—PURCHASE METHOD

The *entity concept,* as it applies to consolidated financial statements, means simply that all transactions between the parties should be eliminated from the financial statements. In effect, the accounts would reflect only transactions that occur with external entities or persons. For example, the entity concept would tell us that intercompany sales (sales between the parent corporation and its subsidiaries) should be eliminated in presenting the financial statements. Also the investment appearing on the parent's books must be eliminated against the stockholders' equity of the subsidiary's books. One method for accounting for this sort of transaction is called the *purchase method*, which is best explained by way of example.

FIGURE 16-1. Consolidated statements

A Parent Corporation
BALANCE SHEET
December 31, 19XX

Assets		*Liabilities and Stockholders' Equities*		
Current assets	$ 500,000	Current liabilities		$ 100,000
Investment in subsidiary	200,000	Due to subsidiary		150,000
Other assets	300,000	Stockholders' Equity:		
		Capital stock	$400,000	
		Retained earnings	350,000	750,000
	$1,000,000			$1,000,000

A Subsidiary Corporation
BALANCE SHEET
December 31, 19XX

Assets		*Liabilities and Stockholders' Equities*		
Current assets	$175,000	Current liabilities		$125,000
Due from parent	150,000	Long-term debt		100,000
Other assets	75,000	Stockholders' Equity:		
		Capital stock	$ 50,000	
		Retained earnings	125,000	175,000
	$400,000			$400,000

In Figure 16-1, let's assume that the Parent Corporation acquired 100 percent of the capital stock of Subsidiary Corporation for $200,000 in cash, which is reflected in the investment account on Parent's books. As sometimes happens after acquisition, Parent found itself short of cash and immediately borrowed $150,000 from Subsidiary, which is also reflected in the balance sheets of both corporations. Now the formal way of presenting consolidated is to prepare an elaborate worksheet with elegant eliminating entries and proper totals. This completed worksheet would then be used to prepare the consolidated financial statements. But for our purposes, we can reflect all the necessary information by using the following T-accounts:

Current Assets

(P) $500,000	
(S) $175,000	

Due to Subsidiary

(a) $150,000	(P) $150,000

Investment in Subsidiary

(P) $200,000	(b) $200,000

Long-Term Debt

	(S) $100,000

Due from Parent

(S) $150,000	(a) $150,000

Capital Stock—Parent

	(P) $400,000

Other Assets

(P) $300,000	
(S) $ 75,000	
(b) $ 10,000	

Retained Earnings—Parent

	(P) $350,000

Goodwill

(b) $15,000	

Capital Stock—Subsidiary

(b) $50,000	(S) $50,000

Current Liabilities

	(P) $100,000
	(S) $125,000

Retained Earnings—Subsidiary

(b) $125,000	(S) $125,000

*(P) = parent company balance; (S) = subsidiary company amount.

Let's assume further that the fair market value (FMV) of the underlying current and other assets acquired by Parent from Subsidiary was $260,000, while the book value is $175,000 (as given in the financial statements in Figure 16-1). Armed with this information, we can now proceed with the consolidation:

1. Set up the T-accounts as illustrated, combining in one account those items that will simply be added to arrive at the consolidated amounts.
2. Set up separate T-accounts for those accounts requiring some adjustment or separate identification.
3. Eliminate intercompany receivables and payables. Debit the Due to subsidiary account for $150,000; Credit Due from parent the same amount.
4. Compute goodwill purchased by Parent:

Total investment in Subsidiary	$200,000
Less: Equity acquired	175,000
	25,000
Less: FMV increment of assets acquired	10,000
Goodwill purchased	$ 15,000

5. Make the following entry in the accounts (Entry b).

Dr Capital stock—Subsidiary	$ 50,000
Dr Retained earnings—Subsidiary	125,000
Dr Goodwill ($25,000 – $10,000)	15,000
Dr Other assets for increase in fair market value ($260,000 – $250,000) =	10,000
Cr Investment in Subsidiary	$200,000

6. Add up all the T-accounts and prepare the consolidated balance sheet (Figure 16-2). The entries made to arrive at this consolidated balance sheet are as follows:

FIGURE 16-2. Consolidated balance sheet for December 31, 19XX

Assets		*Liabilities and Stockholders' Equities*		
Current assets	**$ 675,000**	**Current liabilities**		**$ 225,000**
Other assets	**385,000**	**Long-term debt**		**100,000**
Goodwill	**15,000**			
		Stockholders' Equity:		
		Capital stock	**$400,000**	
		Retained earnings	**350,000**	**750,000**
	$1,025,000			**$1,025,000**

EXERCISE 16-1

Company P acquired all the outstanding common stock of Company S. At that time Company S had current assets of $60,000 and other assets of $100,000 (book values). Company S also had current liabilities of $25,000, other liabilities of $35,000, and retained earnings of $10,000. Company P paid cash for the 10,000 shares of Company S stock at $11 per share. The fair market value of the assets of Company S at the date of purchase was $163,000. The goodwill purchased by Company P was:

a. $6,000.
b. $7,000.
c. $8,000.
d. $9,000.
e. Some other amount.

THE POOLING METHOD

Compared with the purchase method, the pooling method is really quite simple. The underlying assumption is not that one corporation acquires the other, but rather that the two businesses merge and continue to grow together. So all assets and liabilities are carried at their book values (as opposed to fair market value), and the Investment account on Parent's books is replaced by the assets and liabilities of Subsidiary. In the process, of course, the Capital stock accounts of subsidiary are eliminated, but no goodwill is recorded on the transaction. (See Figure 16-3 for a summary of the major differences between the pooling and purchase methods.)

FIGURE 16-3. Summary of differences between pooling and purchase methods

	Purchase Method	*Pooling Method*
Is purchased goodwill recorded?	Yes	No
Are the assets of Subsidiary reflected at fair market value in the consolidation?	Yes	No
Are intercompany accounts eliminated?	Yes	Yes
Is the Retained earnings account of Subsidiary carried forward?	No	Yes
Are the Net earnings of Subsidiary included for the entire year during which the acquisition occurred?	No	Yes

EXERCISE 16-2

When a parent company applies the pooling-of-interests method of accounting to a business combination effected at midyear, the income statement for the year:

a. must be consolidated and should report the parent's income for the whole year and the subsidiary's income earned since the combination.

b. must be consolidated and report income for both parent and subsidiary for the entire year with footnotes as to certain income statement items of the separate companies for the first half of the year.
c. may be unconsolidated and should report the parent's income for the whole year and the subsidiary's income earned since the combination.
d. may be unconsolidated and should report the parent's income for the whole year and the dividends received from the subsidiary since the combination.

The excerpt shown in Figure 16-4 is taken from the 1980 annual report of BankAmerica Corporation. This footnote summarizes the accounting principles that are used by the Bank of America in presenting their financial statements, and that are discussed in this and the preceding chapter on long-term investments.

ADDITIONAL EXERCISES

For each of the following questions, indicate whether each of the following actions is indicative of a: POT—Pooling transaction, PUT—Purchase transaction, or IT—Indeterminate transactional. Consider each question independently:

16-3.

Item	*Action Taken or Result Observed*	*Answer*
a. Measurement and recording at date of acquisition	The asset accounts are debited for the fair market value of the resources acquired	a. ______
b. Goodwill	Goodwill is never recognized	b. ______
c. Eliminations	Eliminate all intercompany debts, revenues, and expenses	c. ______
d. Usuaul comparative effects on the consolidated statement of income for a company acquired in midyear	Revenues and expenses for year of acquisition as reported by each company are aggregated	d. ______

Financial Statement Presentation

The consolidated financial statements of BankAmerica Corporation and its subsidiaries (the corporation) include the accounts of BankAmerica Corporation (the parent), Bank of America NT&SA (the bank), and their consolidated subsidiaries, that is, companies in which more than 50 percent of the voting stock is owned directly or indirectly. The income, expense, assets, and liabilities of the subsidiaries are included in the respective accounts in the consolidated financial statements, after elimination of all material intercompany accounts and transactions.

Investments in affiliates (20-to-50-percent-owned companies) and joint ventures are accounted for by the equity method and classified in investment securities at values proportionate to the corporation's share in the entities' net worth. Income or loss from affiliates is included in other revenue, and translation gains and losses are reported in profits on foreign exchange activities.

Investments in other entities are carried at the lower of cost or market, and income is reported when dividends are received.

FIGURE 16-4. Financial statement presentation.

e. Measurement and recording at date of acquisition	**The cost principle is not applied**	**e.** ______
f. Method of aggregation to derive balance sheet	**Assets and liabilities of the subsidiary are added, at book value, to those of the parent**	**f.** ______
g. Goodwill	**Goodwill is recognized to the extent that the purchase price exceeds FMV of assets acquired**	**g.** ______
h. Eliminations	**Retained earnings of the subsidiary are not eliminated**	**h.** ______

On October 31, 19X1, the Fair Deal Corporation exchanged 10,000 shares of its $5 par common stock for a 100-percent ownership in Strate & Shute, Inc. At that time Fair Deal stock was selling at a market price of $50 per share; Strate & Shute was a family-owned corporation and there was no market in its shares. Balance sheets drawn up for the two corporations before the

acquisition transaction was consummated showed the following (in summary form):

BALANCE SHEETS
October 31, 19X1

	Fair Deal	*Strate & Shute*
Assets:	$1,000,000	$250,000
Stockholders' equity		
Common stock	$ 200,000	$100,000
Additional paid-in capital	300,000	70,000
Retained earnings	500,000	80,000
	$1,000,000	$250,000

Earnings for the two companies for the fiscal year ended November 30, 19X1 were:

	Fair Deal	*Strate & Shute*
12/1/X0–10/31/X1	$120,000	$40,000
11/1/X1–11/30/X1	20,000	5,000
Total	$140,000	$45,000

No intercompany sales were made during the year. No dividends were declared by either company during the year. A set of consolidated financial statements was prepared as of 11/30/X1. The fair market value of Strate & Shute's assets were $400,000 at 10/31/X1.

Complete the following matrix under both the pooling and purchase assumptions:

	Pooling	*Purchase*
16-4. Consolidated goodwill	____________	____________
16-5. Consolidated retained earnings	____________	____________
16-6. Minority interest	____________	____________
16-7. Consolidated net income	____________	____________

Effective November 30, 19XX, Berk Corporation acquired, in exchange for common stock, all the assets and liabilities of Oak Corporation, after which the latter company distributed the Berk stock to their shareholders in complete liquidation and dissolution. Berk increased its outstanding stock for purposes of this acquisition. The balance sheets for the two corporations immediately prior to merger on November 30, 19XX follow. The assets were deemed to be worth their book values.

	Berk	*Oak*
Current assets	$ 2,000,000	$ 500,000
Fixed assets (net)	10,000,000	4,000,000
Total	$12,000,000	$4,500,000
Current liabilities	1,000,000	300,000
Long-term debt	3,000,000	1,000,000
Capital stock ($10 par)	3,000,000	1,000,000
Retained earnings	5,000,000	2,200,000
Total	$12,000,000	$4,500,000
Other data relative to acquisition:		
Shares outstanding	300,000	100,000
Fair market value per share	$40	$40
Numbers of shares of Berk's Stock to be exchanged for Oaks assets		100,000
Old management to continue?		Yes
Old shareholders to elect Director on Berk's board?		Yes

Based on this information, answer the following three questions referring to the combined balance sheet of Berk and Oak immediately after the merger:

16-8. The transactions should be handled as a

____
(pooling, purchase)

16-9. The amount of contributed capital, in excess of par:

$_____________.

16-10. The amount of retained earnings: $_________________.

SOLUTIONS

16-1. b (purchase price of $110,000 – (163,000 – 60,000) = $7,000.

16-2. b

16-3. a. PUT
b. POT
c. IT

d. POT
e. POT
f. POT
g. PUT
h. POT

	Pooling	*Purchase*
16-4.	0	$100,000
16-5.	$605,000	$525,000
16-6.	0	0
16-7.	$185,000	$145,000

16-8. Pooling

16-9. Zero

16-10. $7,200,000

17
Statement of Changes In Financial Position

The newest addition to the family of financial statements is the statement of changes in financial position. The purpose of this statement is to explain to the financial statement reader the change from one year to the next in working capital, which, you will recall the difference between current assets and current liabilities.

To construct the statement of changes in financial position:

1. Start with the working capital at the beginning of the year and add all the *sources* of working capital during the year.
   a. funds provided by operations,
   b. proceeds of sale of capital stock or bonds,
   c. proceeds of sale of other assets, and
   d. proceeds of bank loans (long-term).
2. Then list all the *uses* of working capital during the year under review, and add them up.
   a. purchase of property, plant, and equipment,
   b. redemption of stock,

   c. repayment of long-term loans, mortgages, or bond issues,
   d. purchase of long-term investments, and
   e. payment of dividends.

3. Now subtract the uses of working capital from the total of all the sources, and you have the working capital at the end of the year.

This exercise makes it easy to explain to readers what the company has done with its "money" (loosely defined to mean working capital) during the year. This statement is so useful to readers of financial statements that it is now required by the Securities and Exchange Commission for all registrants.

EXERCISE 17-1

a. Which of the following items set out in the statement of changes in financial position are also disclosed in other statements?

   a. acquisition of fixed assets
   b. purchases of treasury stock
   c. depreciation expense for the year
   d. payments on long-term debt
   e. proceeds from sale of fixed assets (if material)

b. A basic objective of the statement in financial position is to:

   a. supplant the income statement and balance sheet.
   b. disclose changes during the period in all asset and all liability accounts.
   c. disclose the changes in working capital.
   d. provide essential information for financial statement users in making economic decisions.
   e. none of the above.

How does the accountant prepare the statement of changes in financial position? In many instances a "trial-and-error" method is possible. The procedural steps are as follows:

1. Compute the change in working capital from the Current assets and Liabilities section of two successive balance sheets.
2. Set up the statement of changes in financial position, leaving spaces for the appropriate dollar amounts.
3. Examine the Noncurrent asset and Liability accounts for changes, and enter these changes in the Statement prepared in step 2.
4. Determine the noncash expenses for the period for which the statement is being prepared (such as depreciation, amortization, and depletion).

5. Verify that the total of items added and subtracted from the change in working capital is correct. If it is not, you have made some error in computation, which must be located before a proper statement of changes in financial position is complete.

EXERCISE 17-2

Prepare a statement of changes in financial position from the information given, using the following form:

A Corporation
BALANCE SHEETS

	June 30, 19X1	*June 30, 19X2*
Current assets	$ 100,000	$ 140,000
Property, plant, and equipment	350,000	350,000
Less: Accumulated depreciation	(80,000)	(100,000)
Total assets	$ 370,000	$ 390,000
Current liabilities	35,000	45,000
Long-term debt	110,000	100,000
Stockholders' equity		
Capital stock	125,000	130,000
Retained earnings	100,000	115,000
Total equities	$ 370,000	$ 390,000

Note: Net income for the year was $40,000.

A Corporation
Statement of Changes in Financial Position
Year Ended June 30, 19X2

Funds were obtained from:		
Net income for the year	$________	
Depreciation	________	
Sale of capital stock	________	
Total funds acquired		$________
Funds were used for:		
Payment of long-term debt	$________	
Payment of dividends	________	
Total funds used		$________
Increase in working capital for the year		$________

Let's take an example. A charter airline owns one DC-3 and wants to sell its stock. It is therefore faced with the task of preparing a statement of changes in financial position for the year ended December 31, 19X1.

Fly Low and Slow Airline, Inc.
BALANCE SHEETS

	19X0	*19X1*
Cash	$ 10,000	$ 31,250
Airplane	125,000	147,500
Hangar building	25,000	25,000
Other equipment	5,000	15,000
Accumulated depreciation	40,000	50,000
Total Assets	$125,000	$168,750
Mortgage payable	$ 50,000	$ 65,000
Common stock	50,000	60,000
Retained earnings	25,000	43,750
Total equities	$125,000	$168,750

We are also told that Fly Low and Slow paid a cash dividend of $10,000 during the year. The procedures that you should use in preparing a statement of changes in financial position are as follows:

1. Set up a T-account for each Noncurrent asset, liability, and Equity account, since all Current asset and Liability account changes are represented in the single account, Working capital changes.
2. Set up an additional T-account labeled Working capital changes.
3. Enter differences between beginning and ending balances in each T-account. These represent working capital changes for the year.
4. Summarize the journal entries that must have been made to those T-accounts during the year.
5. The remaining difference in the Retained earnings account, along with the Working capital changes account, represent the funds provided by operations.

Airplane

$22,500	
(1) $22,500	

Retained Earnings

	$18,750
(3) $10,000	(7) $38,750
(6) $10,000	

Hangar Building

No charge during the year

Other Equipment

Debit	Credit
$10,000	
(2) $10,000	

Accumulated Depreciation

Debit	Credit
	$10,000
	(3) $10,000

Mortgage Payable

Debit	Credit
	$15,000
	(4) $15,000

Common Stock

Debit	Credit
	$10,000
	(5) $10,000

Working Capital Changes

	Debit	Credit
	$21,250	
Mortgage	(4) $15,000	(1) $22,500 Airplane improvements
Stock	(5) $10,000	(2) $10,000 Purchase equipment
Funds provided by operations	(7) $38,750	(6) $10,000 Dividends paid

Since 1 through 3 are self-explanatory, we will begin with step 4, the journal entries:

* *Entry 1*: The increase in the Airplane account must be due to the improvements in the DC-3. So the summary entry is a debit to Airplane and a credit to Cash. Since there is no cash account, the effect of this summary entry is reflected in the working Capital changes account.
* *Entry 2*: Similarly the increase in Other equipment must be a purchase.
* *Entry 3*: The increase in Accumulated depreciation must be due to the provision for depreciation—a debit to Depreciation expense (Retained earnings) and a credit to Accumulated depreciation. We must debit Retained earnings rather than Working capital, since net income is reflected in to Retained earnings.
* *Entry 4*: An additional Mortgage payable must have been secured, and this mortgage is a source of funds. This requires a debit to Working capital changes and a credit to mortgage payable.

* *Entry 5*: There must have been a sale of common stock—a debit to Cash (Working capital changes) and a credit to Common stock.
* *Entry 6*: The payment of a dividend is accounted for by debiting Retained earnings and crediting Cash (Working capital changes).
* *Entry 7*: What is left over in Retained Earnings must be the Funds provided by operations. The final entry closes out Retained earnings and credits Working capital changes.

Now all we have to do is prepare the statement, which is shown in Figure 17-1. Figure 17-2 shows an actual statement of changes in financial position.

FIGURE 17-1. The prepared statement

Fly Low and Slow Airlines, Inc.
STATEMENT OF CHANGES IN FINANCIAL POSITION
Year Ending December 31, 19XX

Funds Provided by Operations:			
Net income	$28,750		
Depreciation	10,000	$38,750	
Additional Funds Were Provided by:			
Proceeds of mortgage		$15,000	
Proceeds from sale of stock		10,000	$63,750
Funds Were Used to:			
Improve airplane		$22,500	
Purchase of equipment		10,000	
Payment of dividends		10,000	$42,500
Increase in working capital funds			$21,250

ADDITIONAL EXERCISES

Your cousin, who took Introduction to Financial Accounting last year, has just completed the following set of T-accounts. Unfortunately, he was taken ill (while eating at the company lunchroom) and will be spending the rest of the week in the hospital. In the meantime his superior, the controller of the company, desparately needs the statement of changes in financial position this week. Since the controller has never used the T-account method, she is somewhat confused and has asked you to assist her.

TANDEM COMPUTERS INCORPORATED AND SUBSIDIARIES

CONSOLIDATED STATEMENT OF CHANGES IN FINANCIAL POSITION

For the Years Ended September 30, 1980 and 1979

	(In Thousands)	
	1980	1979
WORKING CAPITAL PROVIDED FROM (USED FOR):		
Net income	$10,687	$ 4,920
Add back items not requiring the use of working capital:		
Depreciation and amortization	2,547	1,365
Deferred income taxes	2,284	737
Working capital provided from operations	15,518	7,022
Acquisition of property and equipment	(10,255)	(5,770)
Net book value of equipment sold or retired	289	337
Increase in capitalized lease obligations, net of current maturities	507	429
Increase in deferred income taxes	—	304
Sale of common stock, net of repurchases	27,271	10,837
Tax benefit of stock options and stock purchase plans	806	235
Net increase in working capital	$34,136	$13,394
WORKING CAPITAL INCREASE REPRESENTED BY:		
Increase in current assets—		
Cash and cash investments	$ 9,487	$ 2,311
Accounts receivable	22,671	11,766
Inventories	9,597	4,985
Prepaid expenses and other	580	766
Increase in current liabilities—		
Current portion of capitalized lease obligations	(101)	(172)
Accounts payable	(5,388)	(1,909)
Accrued expenses	(1,947)	(316)
Accrued income taxes	(763)	(4,037)
Net increase in working capital	$34,136	$13,394

The accompanying notes are an integral part of this statement.

FIGURE 17-2. Statement of changes in financial position—an example
Reprinted by permission of Tandem Computers, Inc.

Working Capital	
$ 52,000	
(1) $343,000	(4) $240,000
(2) $259,000	(5) $200,000
(8) $100,000	(9) $210,000

Bonds Payable—7%	
	$250,000
	(2) $250,000

Common Stock ($10 par)	
	$100,000
	(3) $100,000

Equipment (net)	
$110,000	
(5) $200,000	(6) $90,000

Premium Bonds Payable	
	$9,000
	(2) $9,000

Paid-In Capital—Common Stock	
	$5,000
	(3) $5,000

Goodwill	
	$10,000
	(7) $10,000

Preferred Stock ($100 par)	
$200,000	
(4) $200,000	

Retained Earnings	
	$ 28,000
(3) $105,000	(1) $343,000
(6) $ 90,000	(8) $100,000
(7) $ 10,000	
(9) $210,000	

Paid-In Capital—Preferred Stock	
$40,000	
(4) $40,000	

Respond to the controller's questions:

17-3. The net income was:
- a. $ 28,000.
- b. $443,000.
- c. $100,000.
- d. $343,000.
- e. None of the above.

17-4. The net increase in working capital was:
  a. $702,000.
  b. $ 52,000.
  c. $410,000.
  d. $650,000.
  e. $ 28,000.

17-5. The amount spent for the purchase of fixed assets was:
  a. $110,000.
  b. $ 90,000.
  c. $200,000.
  d. Cannot be determined.

17-6. What caused the increase in the common stock account?
  a. Stock dividend
  b. Purchase of treasury stock
  c. Sale of treasury stock
  d. Stock split
  e. None of the above

17-7. The amount paid in cash dividends during the year was:
  a. $210,000.
  b. $315,000.
  c. $415,000.
  d. $ 90,000.
  e. None of the above.

17-8. The working capital provided by operations was:
  a. $343,000.
  b. $259,000.
  c. $702,000.
  d. $443,000.
  e. None of the above.

17-9. The preferred stock retired at what price per share:
  a. $120.
  b. $100.
  c. $ 10.
  d. $240.
  e. None of the above.

17-10. The depreciation expense for the year was:

a. $110,000.

b. $ 90,000.

c. $200,000.

d. $ 20,000.

e. Cannot be determined.

REVIEW PROBLEM

The December 31, 19X1 and 19X2 statements of financial position of the Cindyr Company carried the following debit and credit amounts:

	December 31	
Debits	*19X2*	*19X1*
Cash	$ 10,200	$ 12,600
Accounts receivable (net)	35,100	32,900
Merchandise inventory	85,200	86,400
Prepaid expenses	1,500	1,800
Office equipment	5,000	5,600
Store equipment	29,800	28,300
Totals	$166,800	$167,600
Credits		
Accumulated depreciation—Office equipment	$ 2,500	$ 2,400
Accumulated depreciation—Store equipment	7,500	6,500
Accounts payable	22,400	23,500
Notes payable, current	10,000	5,000
Common stock, $10 par	110,000	100,000
Premium on common stock	6,500	5,500
Retained earnings	7,900	24,700
Total	$166,800	S167,600

Additional information:

1. The net loss for the year was $1,900.
2. Depeciation expense on office equipment was $500; on store equipment it was $1,700.
3. Office equipment that was carried at its cost of $600 with accumulated depreciation of $400 was sold for $300. The gain was mistakenly carried directly to Retained earnings.
4. Store equipment costing $2,200 was purchased.
5. Fully depreciated store equipment that cost $700 was dis-

carded, and its cost and accumulated depreciation were removed from the accounts.

6. Cash dividends of $4,000 were declared during the year.
7. A 1,000-share stock dividend was declared and issued. On the date of declaration, the common stock of the company had a fair market value of $11 per share.

From this information, prepare the necessary T-accounts for a complete analysis. (Note: You need not prepare a formal statement of changes in the internal content of working capital.)

Cindyr Company
STATEMENT OF CHANGES IN FINANCIAL POSITION
(Working Capital Basis)
For the Year Ended December 31, 19X2

T-Accounts are required only for the solution!

Office Equipment

Retained Earnings

Store Equipment

Working Capital

Accumulated Depreciation—
Office Equipment

Common Stock

Accumulated Depreciation—
Store Equipment

Premium on Common Stock

SOLUTIONS

Additional Exercises

17-1. a. c—Depreciation expense is also disclosed in the income statement.

b. d—Provides information not otherwise available to the reader.

17-2.

Net income for the year	$40,000	
Depreciation	20,000	
Sales of capital stock	5,000	$65,000
Payment of long-term debt	$10,000	
Payment of dividends	25,000	35,000
Increase in working capital		$30,000

17-3. d	17-7. a
17-4. b	17-8. d
17-5. c	17-9. a
17-6. a	17-10. b

Review Problem

Office Equipment

	$600
	(3) $600

Retained Earnings

$16,800	
(1) $ 1,900	(3) $ 100
(2) $ 2,200	(8) $2,200
(6) $ 4,000	
(7) $11,000	

Store Equipment

$1,500	
(4) $2,200	(5) $700

Office Equipment—Accumulated Depreciation

	$100
(3) $400	(2) $500

Store Equipment—Accumulated Depreciation

	$1,000
(5) $700	(2) $1,700

Common Stock

	$10,000
	(7) $10,000

Premium on Common Stock

	$1,000
	(7) $1,000

Working Capital

	$5,600
Sale F/A (3) $ 300	(1) $1,900 Net loss
Dep. (8) $2,200	(4) $2,200 Purchase of Store Equipment
	(6) $4,000 Dividends Paid

18

Analysis of Financial Statements

Even though financial statement analysis utilizes all that we have learned about financial statements and how to interpret them, there is no absolute standard for judging the performance or financial solvency of a business entity. So a great deal of the evaluation is subjective. For example, how do you measure the quality of management, the potential acceptance of a new product, or the estimation of potential liability resulting from a pending antitrust suit? Such evaluations may ultimately be based on the experience and judgment of the financial analyst making the assessment. Even large companies occasionally make mistakes in acquiring other companies. But to lessen this degree of uncertainty, we can follow a number of procedures, most of which are based on accounting numbers. We can at least pose three questions, which can be answered with relative degrees of precision to help us in our task:

* What are the historical trends of sales and earnings, and how might these be extrapolated into the future?

* How does this company compare with other companies in the same industry?
* Is the company financially sound and well-managed, and is it a good buy on today's market?

Accounting numbers can help us come up with answers to all three of these questions.

HISTORICAL TRENDS

Generally, published financial statements include a summary of the relevant balance sheet and income statement information over some period. For example, Figure 18-1 is a 5-year summary of selected financial data for Prentice-Hall, Inc. Taking this information, an analyst could project these amounts into the future, after taking into account economic trends, statements by management, and trends in the industry. This type of analysis is beyond the scope of this book, although you should be aware of the additional potential value to be gained from historical financial information.

COMPARISONS WITHIN THE INDUSTRY

To compare firms within their industry, you must reduce their financial statements to a *common size*. What is a "common size" statement? The income statement that you prepared in Chapter 2 (Exercise 2-3 or 2-8) was prepared on a percentage basis. Using percentages rather than absolute numbers allows you to compare companies of different sizes by comparing their relative strengths and weaknesses. Classification of published statistics by the Standard Industrial Code (SIC) allows you also to compare a company's percentages against industrial averages.

The balance sheet can also be expressed in percentages. Each asset and liability account is simply presented as a percentage of total assets. For example:

$$\frac{\text{Cash}}{\text{Total assets}} = \text{Percentage of cash to total assets}$$

Then we simply ask how this percentage compares to other companies within the same SIC classification.

SELECTED FINANCIAL DATA

(Dollars In Thousands, Except Per Share Data And Current Ratio)

	1980	1979	1978	1977	1976
Sales and Other Revenue	**$353,413**	$281,552	$254,912	$230,637	$208,211
Cost of Operations	**291,466**	231,057	203,002	184,298	168,591
Income from Operations	**61,947**	50,495	51,910	46,339	39,620
Interest Expense	**(7,311)**	(832)	(212)	(161)	(341)
Other Income—Net	**2,369**	1,609	1,030	490	829
Write-Down of Investment and Notes Receivable	**—**	—	—	—	(3,135)
Income Before Income Taxes	**57,005**	51,272	52,728	46,668	36,973
Income Taxes	**26,200**	23,450	26,000	22,950	18,250
Net Income	**$ 30,805**	$ 27,822	$ 26,728	$ 23,718	$ 18,723
Per Share Data:					
Net Income (Based on average shares outstanding)	**$3.11**	$2.80	$2.68	$2.38	$1.88
Cash Dividends	**$1.50**	$1.39	$1.27	$1.15	$1.09
Balance Sheet Data (At December 31):					
Total Assets	**$296,373**	$269,455	$198,905	$178,260	$161,467
Working Capital	**$ 84,487**	$ 82,424	$ 69,172	$ 64,777	$ 56,547
Current Ratio	**1.92**	1.92	2.05	2.08	2.03
Long Term Borrowings	**$ 33,283**	$ 30,813	—	—	—
Stockholders' Equity	**$159,010**	$143,073	$130,293	$116,391	$104,138

A copy of the Company's Form 10-K as filed with the Securities and Exchange Commission will be furnished without charge to stockholders upon written request to:
The Controller's Office, Prentice-Hall, Inc., Old Tappan, N.J. 07675

TRANSFER AGENT

Chemical Bank • Corporate Trust Department • 20 Pine Street • New York, N.Y. 10005

REGISTRAR

The Chase Manhattan Bank • National Association • One New York Plaza • New York, N.Y. 10005

31

FIGURE 18-1. Excerpt from Prentice-Hall, Inc. Annual Report for 1980.
Reprinted by permission of Prentice-Hall, Inc.

FINANCIAL SOLVENCY, MANAGERIAL EFFICIENCY, AND MARKET VALUE

Financial solvency is specifically related to the current financial statements. So in this chapter we will become very specific about financial ratios. We classify ratios according to the following description:

* ratios affecting the balance sheet only,
* ratios affecting the income statements only,
* balance sheet/income statement ratios, and
* ratios affected by the market price of the stock.

Balance Sheet Ratios

The three basic balance sheet ratios are:

* current ratio,
* quick asset ratio, and
* long-term debt to equity ratio.

The *current ratio* measures the proportion of current assets to current liabilities. It is computed from the following formula:

$$\text{Current ratio} = \frac{\text{Current assets}}{\text{Current liabilities}}$$

This ratio sometimes called the working capital ratio, is traditionally supposed to be at least two-to-one. In other words, current assets should be at least twice the current liabilities. But this rule, of course, varies from industry to industry, and like any rule of thumb, should be used only as a very rough guide.

The *quick asset ratio* measures the short-term liquidity position of a business entity and is computed from the following relationship:

$$\text{Quick asset ratio} = \frac{\text{Cash + Temporary investments + Accounts receivable}}{\text{Current liabilities}}$$

Let's suppose that the business entity did not sell any items from inventory. In that case, the amount of cash that it would generate in the short run is the sum of its cash, temporary investments, and accounts receivable. The question to ask, Is the sum of these three items sufficient to pay all the current liabilities? In other words, is the *quick asset ratio* at least one-to-one?

The *long-term debt to equity ratio* represents the amount of long-term investment in the business by creditors as it relates to the long-term investment by shareholders. We can measure this relationship by making the following calculation:

$$\text{Long-term debt to equity ratio} = \frac{\text{Long-term debt}}{\text{Shareholders' equity}}$$

As you might expect, the amounts invested by shareholders should be at least as great as the amount of capital furnished by creditors in the form of bonds or mortgages. Ideally, long-term debt should be somewhat less than 50 percent of shareholders' equity.

EXERCISE 18-1

Calculate the following ratios from the Prentice-Hall, Inc. balance sheet for 1980 in Figure 18-2:

Current ratio: ____________ = ____________

Quick asset ratio: ____________ = ____________

Long-term debt to equity ratio: ____________ = ____________

Income Statement Ratios

Any income statement, once reduced to a common-size (that is, to a series of percentages), can then be compared with the statements of any other businesses, either larger or smaller. The common denominator is net sales. For example, the three most useful comparisons to make are:

$$\frac{\text{Gross margin}}{\text{Net sales}} = \text{Gross margin percentage}$$

$$\frac{\text{Operating expenses}}{\text{Net sales}} = \text{Operating expense ratio}$$

$$\frac{\text{Net income}}{\text{Net sales}} = \text{Net income percentage}$$

These three ratios, all of them with *net sales* as the *denominator,* can be used to compare the performance of a single business entity at successive points in time. Secondly, they can be used to compare several business firms within the same industry. Finally, they can be used to compare a business' performance in one industry with that of businesses in other industries.

PRENTICE-HALL, INC. AND SUBSIDIARIES

CONSOLIDATED BALANCE SHEETS

ASSETS

(Dollars in Thousands)	DECEMBER 31	
	1980	1979
Current Assets:		
Cash	**$ 3,212**	$ 4,802
Marketable securities and certificates of deposit at market (cost: 1980—$1,284; 1979—$4,572) (Note 1)	**1,080**	3,689
Receivables (Notes 1 and 5)	**95,093**	86,664
Finished goods inventories	**50,196**	44,061
Paper, supplies, and other inventories	**10,805**	11,425
Prepaid expenses	**10,394**	11,427
Deferred income tax benefits (Notes 1 and 8)	**5,891**	9,675
Total Current Assets	**176,671**	171,743
Property and Equipment—at cost (less accumulated depreciation: 1980—$54,828; 1979—$44,962) (Notes 1 and 6)	**77,398**	70,055
Other Assets:		
Receivables (Notes 1 and 5)	**25,073**	12,598
Advances to authors (Note 1)	**8,495**	7,818
Excess of cost over net value of assets acquired (Note 1)	**8,524**	6,041
Cash value of life insurance (less insurance policy loans: 1980—$1,416; 1979—$407)	**212**	1,200
Total Other Assets	**42,304**	27,657
TOTAL	**$296,373**	$269,455

FIGURE 18-2. Prentice-Hall, Inc. balance sheet for 1980.
Reprinted by permission of Prentice-Hall, Inc.

Perhaps the most popular term among Wall Street analysts is *earnings per share* (EPS). With this ratio, analysts and accountants compare the net income of a business entity to the number of shares of common stock outstanding. It tells investors how much of the earnings would be allocated to their shares of stock. Besides being useful all by itself, it is also part of the closely watched *price/earnings ratio* (see the section on "Market Ratios" in this chapter). This versatile ratio is computed from the following ratio:

$$\text{Earnings per share (EPS)} = \frac{\text{Net income}}{\text{Shares of common stock outstanding}}$$

LIABILITIES AND STOCKHOLDERS' EQUITY

(Dollars in Thousands)	DECEMBER 31	
	1980	1979
Current Liabilities:		
Notes payable—banks (Note 4)	**$ 1,000**	$ 7,500
Accounts payable	**8,145**	12,161
Accrued royalties	**17,257**	15,560
Other accrued expenses (Note 7)	**27,592**	21,496
Federal and foreign income taxes	**14,309**	10,689
Unexpired subscriptions	**7,910**	7,005
Advance subscription payments (Note 1)	**15,971**	14,908
Total Current Liabilities	**92,184**	89,319
Long-Term Liabilities:		
Long-term borrowings (Note 3)	**33,283**	30,813
Future service costs of rental contracts (Note 1)	**5,826**	2,742
Deferred gain on sales of land	**1,392**	2,046
Deferred income taxes payable (Note 1)	**4,678**	1,462
Total Long-Term Liabilities	**45,179**	37,063
Stockholders' Equity (Notes 2 and 10)**:**		
Common stock—authorized 15,000,000 shares of $.33-1/3 par value; issued, 10,429,888 shares	**3,477**	3,477
Capital surplus	**21,447**	21,447
Retained earnings	**146,507**	130,570
Total	**171,431**	155,494
Less treasury stock at cost, 518,100 shares	**12,421**	12,421
Stockholders' Equity	**159,010**	143,073
TOTAL	**$296,373**	$269,455

FIGURE 18-2. (cont.)

EXERCISE 18-2

Calculate the following ratios from the income statement for Prentice-Hall, Inc. for 1980 in Figure 18-3.

Gross margin percentage: ____________ = ____________

Operating expense ratio: ____________ = ____________

Net income percentage: ____________ = ____________

Earnings per share (EPS): ____________ = ____________

Balance Sheet/Income Statement Ratios

So far, the ratios discussed related only to one statement. Balance sheet/income statement ratios, on the other hand, deal with such questions as, "How effective is the performance of the company, based on the amount of funds invested?" Such questions relate to managerial efficiency. The ratios we will cover are as follows:

* return on stockholders' equity,
* return on total assets,
* inventory turnover ratio, and
* accounts receivable turnover.

Return on Stockholders' Equity

This ratio provides a standard of comparison with other (alternative) forms of investment:

$$\text{Return on stockholders' equity} = \frac{\text{Net income}}{\text{Stockholders' equity}}$$

Return on Total Assets

A variant of the first ratio, this one says nothing about how the business is financed. But it serves as an excellent standard of comparison by assuming that management is given a bundle of assets and then asking the question, "How well did they do?" It can be calculated as follows:

$$\text{Return on total assets} = \frac{\text{Net income}}{\text{Total assets}}$$

Other more specific measures of managerial efficiency can be calculated. For example, how well is management using the funds invested in inventory?

$$\text{Inventory turnover ratio} = \frac{\text{Cost of goods sold}}{\text{Average inventory}}$$

To calculate such a ratio from published financial statements, simply take the beginning and ending inventories, add them together, and then divide by two to obtain the average.

Accounts Receivable Turnover Ratio

This computation asks, "How efficient is management's credit policy?"

$$\text{Accounts receivable turnover ratio} = \frac{\text{Net credit sales}}{\text{Average accounts receivable}}$$

To determine the average accounts receivable, use the same method as for determining average inventory. Credit managers sometimes refer to *total day's sales outstanding,* which they calculate by taking the accounts receivable turnover and dividing it by 365 (days in a year).

EXERCISE 18-3

Calculate the following ratios from the information given in Figures 18-2 and 18-3:

Return on stockholders' equity: ________ = __________

Return on total assets: ________ = __________

Inventory turnover ratio: ________ = __________

Accounts receivable turnover ratio: ________ = __________

Market Ratios

Two ratios use the market price of the stock as one of their components:

* price/earnings ratio, and
* dividend payout (yield) ratio.

The more widely used is the *price/earnings ratio* (usually referred to as the *P/E ratio*):

$$\text{P/E ratio} = \frac{\text{Market price of stock (per share)}}{\text{Earnings per share (EPS)}}$$

This ratio can also be used not only as an indicator of one company's performance, but also as a standard of comparison among several possible investments.

At the present writing, the average P/E ratio for the so-called "Blue Chip" companies is around seven times earnings. In other words, for each share of stock that you purchase, you would pay

PRENTICE-HALL, INC. AND SUBSIDIARIES

STATEMENTS OF CONSOLIDATED INCOME AND RETAINED EARNINGS

(Dollars in Thousands, Except Per Share Data)	YEAR ENDED DECEMBER 31		
	1980	1979	1978
Sales and other revenue	**$353,413**	$281,552	$254,912
Cost of operations:			
Cost of sales	**130,739**	104,838	94,353
Selling, general, and administrative expenses	**160,727**	126,219	108,649
Total cost of operations	**291,466**	231,057	203,002
Income from operations	**61,947**	50,495	51,910
Other:			
Interest expense	**(7,311)**	(832)	(212)
Gain on sales of land—installment basis	**1,168**	545	238
Other income—net	**1,201**	1,064	792
Total other	**(4,942)**	777	818
Income before income taxes	**57,005**	51,272	52,728
Income taxes (Notes 1 and 8):			
Federal and foreign	**15,300**	20,875	23,370
State and local	**3,900**	3,600	3,600
Deferred	**7,000**	(1,025)	(970)
Total income taxes	**26,200**	23,450	26,000
Net income	**30,805**	27,822	26,728
Retained earnings at beginning of year (Note 2)	**130,570**	116,543	102,467
Cash dividends—per share, $1.50 in 1980; $1.39 in 1979; $1.27 in 1978	**(14,868)**	(13,795)	(12,652)
Retained earnings at end of year	**$146,507**	$130,570	$116,543
Net income per share of common stock	**$3.11**	$2.80	$2.68

FIGURE 18-3. Prentice-Hall, Inc. Income Statement for 1980.
Reprinted by permission of Prentice-Hall, Inc.

about seven times that stock's earnings per share. "Glamour stocks" are defined as those stocks whose P/E ratios are at least one and a half times the average of the more prosaic Blue-Chips. In other words, if the market is anticipating increased earnings, this expectation would drive the market price up and simultaneously increase the P/E ratio.

The *dividend payout (yield)* ratio involves the actual yield, which of course is the dividend rate. This ratio also takes the market price of the stock into account: The dividend payout ratio is included by the *Wall Street Journal* in its daily listing of stocks on the American and New York Stock Exchange.

$$\text{Dividend payout (yield) ratio} = \frac{\text{Dividend (annual basis)}}{\text{Market price (per share)}}$$

Let's say an investor must choose between, say, a savings and loan association and a common stock. In such a case, a simple calculation of the two dividend payout ratios would produce two sets of numbers for comparison. Note that the excerpt from the *Wall Street Journal* in Figure 18-4 lists not only the dividend per share but also the yield "%," as well as the P/E ratio. Other figures quoted for the stock relate to the market value at various points of time. All quotations are pre-share quotations. Note the listing for Prentice-Hall stock in Figure 18-4.

EXERCISE 18-4

Calculate the following market ratios from the information given in Figures 18-2 and 18-3. Assume that the current market price of Prentice-Hall stock is $25 per share.

Price/earnings (P/E) ratio: ________________ = ____________

Dividend payout ratio: ________________ = ____________

Reminder: Chapters 19 and 20 are optional. So after completing the Additional Exercises for this chapter, you may either proceed directly to the Third Progress Test (which follows Chapter 20) or go on to the next two chapters before taking that examination. Our recommendation is that the material on constant dollar accounting, which is found in the next two chapters, is invaluable and should be covered.

ADDITIONAL EXERCISE

18-5. Prepare a balance sheet on the form provided from the information that follows:

1. **Working capital is $200,000, and the current ratio is 2.6 to 1.**
2. **Net credit sales are $1,200,000, and the accounts receivable turnover is 12 times per year (assume a constant accounts receivable balance).**
3. **The quick asset ratio is one to one.**
4. **Cost of goods sold for the year is $600,000, and the inventory turns over three times per year on the average.**

Amex-Composite Transactions

Tuesday, November 24, 1981

Quotations include trades on the New York, Midwest, Pacific, Philadelphia, Boston and Cincinnati stock exchanges and reported by the National Association of Securities Dealers and Instinet.

52 Weeks High	52 Weeks Low	Stock	Div.	Yld %	P-E Ratio	Sales 100s	High	low	Close	Net Chg.
15	9⅜	Ollaind	.40	3.2	6	x3	12⅝	12½	12½	.....
59¼	35⅛	OOkiep	.28l	..	..	z100	35½	35½	35½	.....
24⅜	10	OrioleH	1b	7.4	5	37	13½	13½	13½	− ¼
9⅜	4½	Ormand		..	10	10	5¼	5¼	5¼	.....
20	6½	Orrox		..	..	307	8⅞	8	8⅞	.....
8⅞	3½	OxfrdFt	.61t	14.	6	5	4¼	4¼	4¼	.....
13⅜	5¼	OzarkA	.15e	1.6	4	93	9¼	9	9¼	+ ¼
		— P–Q —								
12⅜	10	PGEpfA	1.50	15.	..	37	11	10⅛	10⅛	− ½
10⅞	8¾	PGEpfB	1.37	14.	..	5	9½	9⅛	9½	+ ⅜
11⅛	7¾	PGEpfC	1.25	14.	..	3	9	8¾	9	+ ⅝
10½	7⅝	PGEpfD	1.25	15.	..	145	8⅞	8½	8½	.....
10¾	7⅝	PGEpfE	1.25	15.	..	141	8⅝	8¼	8¼	− ⅜
9⅞	7⅜	PGEpfG	1.20	15.	..	107	8¼	7½	8¼	+ ⅛
29⅜	24¾	PGEpfZ	4.06	15.	..	325	27½	27	27	− ¾
24⅝	19⅜	PGEpfY	3.20	15.	..	88	22¾	21¾	21⅞	− ⅛
22¼	15⅝	PGEpfW	2.57	15.	..	55	17½	16⅝	17½	+ ⅜
17½	14	PGEpfV	2.32	15.	..	16	15¼	15	15¼	.....
19⅜	15	PGEpfT	2.54	15.	..	23	17⅜	17	17¼	.....
20⅛	15¾	PGEpfS	2.62	15.	..	16	17¾	17½	17½	− ¼
9¼	7	PGEpfH	1.12	14.	..	103	7⅞	7¾	7¾	.....
18¼	14⅛	PGEpfR	2.37	15.	..	18	16¾	16	16¼	+ ¼
15⅝	12½	PGEpfP	2.05	15.	..	22	14⅜	13⅜	13½	− ¼
16⅛	12	PGEpfO	2	14.	..	2	14⅛	14⅛	14⅛	− ¼
16¾	12	PGEpfM	1.96	14.	..	50	13⅝	13¼	13⅝	+ ⅜
17¼	13⅝	PGEpfL	2.25	15.	..	12	15	14⅛	15	+ ⅞
16¼	12⅜	PGEpfK	2.04	15.	..	15	14	13⅞	14	− ⅛
17⅝	14	PGEpfJ	2.32	15.	..	3	15⅞	15⅝	15⅞	+ ⅜
8½	6⅞	PGEpfI	1.09	14.	..	2	7⅞	7⅞	7⅞	+ ⅜
37	17¼	PGTrn	.72	2.7	13	63	27	26¼	26½	− ⅛
32½	27½	PacLt	pf4.40	14.	..	z50	32	31½	31½	− ½
34½	28¼	PacLt	pf4.50	15.	..	z250	31	30⅞	30⅞	+ ⅛
46	28¾	PacPLpf	5	14.	..	z50	35½	35½	35½	+ ½
35¾	23	PacTrst	1.60	4.6	14	37	35¼	34¾	34⅞	+ ½
24⅝	10⅞	Page g		..	..	139	13⅜	12¾	13¼	+ ⅜
39⅞	26½	PallCp	.36	1.1	20	169	32⅜	31¼	32⅜	+ 1⅜
2½	1¼	PalmrF		..	..	4	1½	1½	1½	.....
6¼	2⅞	Pantast	.05r	1.4	6	14	3⅝	3½	3½	+ ⅛
23⅛	11¾	ParkEl		.	9	2	13⅛	13⅛	13⅛	− ⅛
18	9½	PatFsh	.15e	.9	4	3	16¾	16⅝	16⅝	− ⅛
6⅝	5⅜	PUMG		..	55	2	6	6	6	.....
19⅜	9	PenRs n		..	20	267	10¼	9¾	10	− ⅛
38	16⅞	PenEM	.80a	3 7	11	10	21½	21½	21½	− ⅛
19¼	12½	PenTr	1.20	9 3	5	7	13	12⅞	12⅞	− ⅛
3⅞	2	PECp	.29t	13.	6	36	2¼	2⅛	2¼	+ ⅛
13⅝	7¼	PenobS	.40a	5.4	5	1	7⅜	7⅜	7⅜	+ ⅛
16⅞	8	Penril	.17	1.5	10	10	11⅛	11	11	.....
1⅝	⅞	Pentron		..	..	4	⅞	⅞	⅞	− 1-16
33	17⅝	Perini	.60	2.0	8	76	31	29¾	30½	+ 1⅜
13	6⅛	PeryD s	.24	2.2	9	22	11⅛	10⅝	10⅞	− ⅛
40¾	13⅝	PetLew	2.23t	12.	13	382	18¾	18⅜	18½	− ¼
12¼	10	PetLe	pf1.65	14.	..	19	12	11¾	11⅞	+ ⅛
5⅞	4	PhilLD	.65r	15.	3	7	4⅜	4¼	4⅜	.....
3⅜	1⅞	Phoenix		..	..	46	2	1⅞	1⅞	− ⅛
6⅞	4	PionrSy		..	14	44	5¾	5⅝	5¾	+ ⅛
6⅞	4	PitWVa	.56a	9.5	3	33	6	5¾	5⅞	.....
60	22	PitDM	.92	3.7	9	45	24⅝	23⅝	24⅝	+ 1¼
58¾	36⅝	Pittway	1.65	3.0	8	73	55½	55⅜	55⅜	− ⅜
11½	3⅞	Pizzaln		..	11	7	6⅞	6¾	6¾	− ⅛
25½	11¾	PlcrD g	.30	2.2	..	2	13⅜	13⅛	13⅜	+ ¼
8	3¼	Plantin		..	13	27	3¾	3⅝	3¾	+ ⅛
8½	5¾	PlyGm	.40	4.8	7	51	8⅜	7¾	8⅜	+ ½
26⅜	15¾	PneuSc	1	6.1	409	2	16⅜	16⅜	16⅜	− ¼
14¾	8⅛	PopeE s		..	9	56	10¼	10	10	− ⅛
23⅞	14½	PortSy n		..	40	43	23½	23	23¼	+ ⅛
31⅞	15⅞	PostCp	.50	1.9	16	7	26⅞	26¾	26¾	+ ⅛
15¼	11½	PostIP n	.20	1.7	12	12	11¾	11½	11¾	+ ¼
16⅜	10	PowrT n	.30b	2.5	28	11	12⅛	12	12	+ ⅛
21⅜	11	PrairO g		..	..	19	14⅝	14½	14⅝	− ⅛
20⅞	15½	PratLm	1.22	7.0	6	13	17½	17⅜	17⅜	− ⅞
6⅞	4⅝	PrattRd	.30	5.1	8	7	5⅞	5⅞	5⅞	.....
26	12½	PrecMt	1.65e	13.	8	96	13	12⅝	13	+ ⅛
5⅜	3¾	PremR n		..	20	88	4⅜	4¼	4¼	+ ⅛
26⅝	19¼	PrenHa	1.64	6.6	8	62	24⅞	24⅜	24⅞	+ ⅛
4¼	2⅝	PresR A	.20	5.2	19	5	3¼	3⅛	3¼	+ ⅛
8	6	Presid n		..	81	37	6½	6⅛	6½	+ ⅜
27⅝	20⅛	PrpCT	2.10e	7.8	13	21	27¼	26¾	27	− ½
16⅛	12⅜	ProvEn	1.44	11.	4	1	12¾	12¾	12¾	+ ¼
6	3¾	PrudBld	.24	5.3	9	10	4½	4½	4½	+ ⅛
17¼	14	PgSP	pfC2.34	14.	..	3	16¼	16¼	16¼	.....
17¾	14¾	PgSP	pfD2.34	14.	..	4	16½	16½	16½	+ ⅛
17⅜	10¼	PulteH	.20	1.5	8	5	13¾	13¾	13¾	− ¼
16⅛	7⅜	PuntaG		..	7	1	9¼	9¼	9¼	− ⅛
19½	10⅜	Punta	pf1.10	8.7	..	3	12⅝	12⅝	12⅝	.....
19	8½	Quebcr	g.40	4.3	..	340	9¼	9¼	9¼ −	
		— R–R–R —								
[illegible]	7	REDM		..	6	33	8⅛	[illegible]		
	[illegible]½	RMS El		..	14	40	[illegible]			
		[illegible]SC	.10	[illegible]3	..					
		— T–T–T —								
10⅞	6½	TriaCp	.25	3.8	10	2	6⅝	6⅝	6⅝	.....
34	12¾	TritOil	.10	.6	19	83	17⅞	17¼	17½	− ⅜
6⅜	2⅝	TubMx s		..	5	660	3⅛	3	3	.....
14¼	6⅞	Tultex	.52	5.2	4	4	10⅛	10	10	.....
33⅝	18	TurnrC	1.60	5.6	7	5	28¾	28½	28½	− ⅛
8⅞	3¾	TwinFr		..	..	26	6	5¾	5¾	− ⅛
		— U–U–U —								
16⅜	7¾	U&I		..	..	10	8⅝	8¼	8¼	− ¼
5⅛	3⅝	UNA	.28	7.7	10	9	3⅝	3⅝	3⅝	.....
18	10½	URS	.40b	2.9	17	18	14	13⅝	13⅞	+ ¼
3⅝	1⅝	USR Ind		..	..	7	2	1⅞	1⅞	− ⅛
12¼	7⅛	Ultmte n		..	30	16	10⅛	9⅞	9⅞	− ¼
16¼	10½	Unicorp	.40	3.3	30	7	12⅜	12⅛	12⅛	− ½
5⅞	3½	Unimax		..	68	2	4¾	4¾	4¾	+ ⅛
23⅛	11⅝	UAirPd	.64	4.3	20	17	14⅞	14⅛	14⅞	+ 1
11¼	4⅞	UnAbst		..	4	93	6⅝	6⅜	6⅜	− ⅛
24⅝	12⅞	UnCosF	.84b	3.8	9	11	22⅜	22⅜	22⅜	− ¼
3½	1⅞	UnFood	.20	8.4	10	16	2⅝	2⅜	2⅜	− ⅛
8¾	7⅛	UtMed n		..	12	51	7½	7⅜	7⅜	.....
21	12⅛	UNatCp		..	26	1	19¾	19¾	19¾	− ⅛
15½	10¼	UnRitIn	1.11e	10.	10	8	11⅜	11⅛	11⅛	− ⅛
15⅝	4⅜	USAir wt		..	..	17	5⅞	5⅞	5⅞	.....
17⅛	8½	UnvCm n		..	19	24	10⅞	10⅝	10⅞	+ ⅛
32⅞	15¼	UnvRs s	.20	1.0	14	85	20½	20	20¼	.....
		— V–V–V —								
7⅜	4¼	Valles		..	625	49	6½	6¼	6¼	+ ¼
16⅜	8	Valspar	.52	3.5	6	28	14¾	14½	14¾	.....
43⅞	21¼	Vrbtm n		..	33	91	39¾	39⅜	39⅜	− ¼
3⅜	1½	Verit		..	29	9	2	1⅞	2	.....
20¼	14	VtAmC	.36b	2.1	7	3	17	16¾	17	+ ¼
32¾	9⅛	VtRsh	.15e	1.0	11	6	14¾	14¾	14¾	.....
19	12	Verna		..	6	10	15	14¾	14⅞	.....
21½	10⅜	Vernit s	.10	.8	9	121	12	11½	12	+ ½
6¼	3⅝	Vertiple	.15	3.1	5	16	4⅞	4¾	4⅞	.....
4¾	2¾	Viatech		..	4	17	4⅜	4	4⅛	− ⅛
18	8¼	Vicon s		..	10	34	9	8¾	8¾	.....
6	2½	Vintge		..	8	12	4⅜	4⅜	4⅜	.....
15⅝	6½	Vishay	.60t	6.2	16	23	9⅝	9⅝	9⅝	.....
9⅝	4½	VisualG	.24	4.9	7	20	5	4⅞	4⅞	.....
7⅜	3⅞	VolMer	.12e	1.9	4	2	6⅜	6⅜	6⅜	− ⅛
17¼	9¼	Voplex	.52	5.8	15	10	9⅛	d 9	9	− ¼
15⅞	7⅛	VulcCp	.28a	2.5	5	15	11½	11⅛	11⅛	− ⅜
		— W–W–W —								
9½	4¼	WTC		..	..	24	6	5¾	6	+ ¼
7	2⅞	Wadell		..	17	2	4	4	4	.....
54	30⅝	Walbar	.40	1.0	11	18	41¼	40½	40½	− ¼
30	20½	Walco	.80b	3.4	6	7	24	23½	23½	− ⅝
11¼	4½	WallcS	.32	6.1	9	7	5¼	5	5¼	+ ⅛
45⅝	24	Wang B	.12	.4	21	844	30⅝	29⅜	30⅝	+ 1⅛
42⅛	22¼	Wang C	.02	.1	18	33	26¾	26⅛	26¾	+ ¼
13¼	6	Wards s	.12	1.6	5	13	7⅜	7	7⅜	.....
25½	7¾	WrnC wt		..	..	10[illegible]	20¾	20¼	20½	+ ¼
2⅛	1¼	WshHm		..	..	[illegible]	1¼	1¼	1¼	− ⅛
33	19⅜	WshPst	.50	1.6	15	30[illegible]	31⅛	30⅞	31	− ¼
19⅝	11	WRIT s	1	7.1	16	16	14	14	14	− ⅛
13⅜	7½	Watsco	.30	2.5	9	14	12⅛	11⅞	12	+ ⅛
38¾	13⅞	Wthfrd s	.32	1.8	7	17[illegible]	17¾	17¼	17⅝	+ ⅛
4⅜	2⅝	Weiman	.08e	3.0	..	[illegible]	2⅝	2⅝	2⅝	.....
22½	10½	WeldT s	.30	1.8	8	3	16⅝	16⅜	16⅝	+ ⅛
42⅛	40¾	WlGrd n	.40	1.0	15	152	40¾	d39¾	40⅜	− ⅝
35¼	26⅜	WTex	pf4.40	14.	..	z30	31½	31½	31½	+ ¼
28½	18	Wstbrn	g.70	..	..	124	21	20⅝	21	+ ⅜
20⅝	8	WstFin	.26l	..	..	29	11⅛	10⅞	11⅛	+ ⅜
4	2½	WhitCbl		..	6	5	3½	3½	3½	+ ⅛
51	16¾	Whitehal		..	17	65	44½	43⅝	44¼	+ ½
23⅝	9⅛	Wichit s		..	56	45	10	9½	10	.....
4	1⅝	WillcxG		..	4	42	2	2	2	+ ⅛
23¼	15	Wmhou s	.60	2.9	8	x15	20⅜	20	20⅜	+ ⅝
1½	1	WilsnB		..	..	15	1	1	1	.....
20¾	15½	Wincorp	.40	2.4	33	1	17	17	17	.....
2⅞	1⅞	WolfHB		..	..	120	2¼	2¼	2¼	+ ⅛
9	6	Wdstrm	.60	8.6	7	5	7	7	7	.....
13⅞	8¼	WkWear	.48	5.3	7	4	9¼	9⅛	9⅛	.....
15⅞	5¼	WwEn s		..	..	120	8	7¾	7¾	− ¼
33⅝	18⅝	Wrathr	.05	.2	..	4	22½	22½	22½	+ ¼
7⅝	2⅛	WrghtH g		..	..	77	2⅜	2¼	2 5-16	.....
		— X–Y–Z —								
18½	12⅝	Xoil n		..	90	2	15⅜	15¼	15¼	− ¼
15¼	7	YankO s		..	20	51	14¼	13⅝	13⅝	− ⅞
20⅞	7¼	Zimmer	.3[illegible]	1.9	9	[illegible]5	19[illegible]	19⅛	19[illegible]	

FIGURE 18-4. Stock quotations from the *Wall Street Journal.*

The Maxe Company
BALANCE SHEET
October 31, 19X1

		Assets	
Current Assets:			
Cash		$ 25,000	
Accounts receivable	$______		
Less allowance for doubtful accounts	5,000	______	
Inventories		______	$______
Property, Plant, and Equipment:			
Land		$ 50,000	
Building, machinery, and equipment	$______		
Less: Accumulated depreciation	$20,000	150,000	______
Total assets			$______
	Liabilities and Stockholders' Equity		
Current Liabilities:			
Accounts		$______	
Accrued liabilities		$25,000	$______
Long-Term Liabilities:			
8% bonds due October 31, 19X3		200,000	
Stockholders' Equity:		______	______
Capital stock		$100,000	
Retained earnings			
Total liabilities and stockholders' equity			$______

SOLUTIONS

18-1. Current asset ratio: $176,671 ÷ $92,184 = 1.92 to 1
Quick asset ratio: $99,385 ÷ $92,184 = 1.08 to 1
Long-term debt to equity: $45,179 ÷ $159,010 = 0.28 to 1

18-2. Gross margin percentage: $222,674 ÷ $353,413 = 63%
Operating expense ratio: $160,727 ÷ $353,413 = 45%
Net income percentage: $30,805 ÷ $353,4913 = 9%
EPS: $30,805 ÷ [$10,430 – 518 (treasury stock)] = 3.11 per share

18-3. Return on shareholders' equity: $30,805 ÷ $159,010 = 19%
Return on total assets: $30,805 ÷ $296,373 = 10%
Inventory turnover ratio: Avg. invent. = ($50,196 + $44,061) ÷ 2 = $47,129;
$130,739 ÷ $47,129 = 2.77 times per year
Accounts receivable turnover ratio: Average AR: $95,093 + $86,664 ÷ 2 = $90,879
$353,413 ÷ $90,879 = 3.89 times per year

18-4. Price/earnings ratio: $25 ÷ $3.11 = 8 to 1
Dividend payout ratio: $1.50 ÷ 25 = 6%

18-5.

Accounts receivable	$105,000
Inventories	$200,000
Buildings et al	$170,000
Accounts payable	$100,000
Retained earnings	$100,000

19

Changing Price Levels And Financial Statements

Chapters 19 and 20 are not fundamental to the understanding of financial statements, as these statements appear at the present time. Why not? As recently as September, 1979, the Financial Accounting Standards Board (FASB) affirmed the primary financial statements should continue to incorporate measurements based mainly on historical prices. But the FASB also concluded that an urgent need existed for enterprises to provide information about the effects of general inflation and other price changes. on their activities. General inflation adjustments to financial statements are referred to as *constant dollar accounting,* which is defined in FASB #33 (page 9) as:

> A method of reporting financial statement elements in dollars each of which has the same (i.e.) constant general purchasing power. This method of accounting is often described as accounting in units of general purchasing power or as accounting in units of current purchasing power.

Publicly held corporations were required to present *constant dollar accounting* information for the first time in 1979. Figure

19-1 shows an excerpt from the annual report of Safeway Stores, Inc. for 1979. The reported earnings per share of Safeway amounted to $5.49 per share, when based conventional accounting principles. But when these figures are adjusted for inflation, that $5.49 turns into a loss of 8¢ per share! A study of almost 700 companies, recently completed by Ernst & Whinney, concluded that the effects of inflation on traditional financial statements for 1979 resulted in an average decline of 40 percent in net income, along with a decline of 50 percent in return on equity.

Note N—Supplementary Financial Data Adjusted for the Effects of Changing Prices (Unaudited).

The Company's primary financial statements are prepared based mainly on historical prices, that is, the prices that were in effect when the transactions occurred. The supplementary financial information discloses the effects of general inflation on the Company's merchandise inventories and property. These disclosures are made in accordance with Financial Accounting Standards Board Statement No. 33, which requires certain "constant dollar" accounting disclosures in 1979 annual reports to stockholders.

Amounts restated for the effect of general inflation shown in the supplementary financial data are stated in dollars of average purchasing power for the year 1979, using the Consumer Price Index for All Urban Consumers (CPI-U) as the basis for restating amounts recorded in dollars of purchasing power at the time of the original transactions (historical costs).

The effect on net income of general inflation in cost of sales and depreciation and amortization expense is shown below:

Net income as reported in the consolidated statement of income	$ 143,323,000
Adjustments to restate costs for the effect of general inflation:	
Cost of sales, excluding depreciation and amortization	(69,443,000)
Depreciation and amortization in:	
Cost of sales	(21,784,000)
Operating and administrative expenses	(54,284,000)
Net loss adjusted for the effect of general inflation	$(2,188,000)

The provision for income taxes as stated in the primary financial statements has not been modified to give effect to the restated amounts of cost of sales and depreciation and amortization expense.

Another supplemental disclosure is the "gain from the decline in purchasing power of net monetary liabilities," which is a component of the total increase in the Company's purchasing power during the year. Net monetary liabilities represent all monetary liabilities less all monetary assets. Monetary assets are essentially cash and claims to cash (receivables) and monetary liabilities are obligations to pay fixed amounts of cash. In a period of inflation the purchasing power of cash declines; thus, a debt incurred at the beginning of a period provides dollars of greater purchasing power than the dollars needed to repay the debt at a later point in time. The Company holds a debt position with regard to monetary items, that is, monetary liabilities exceed monetary assets, and this results in a gain in the Company's overall purchasing power during periods of inflation. The gain from the decline in purchasing power of net monetary liabilities was $202,723,000 in 1979.

Following is a comparison of selected financial data for five years, adjusted for the effect of general inflation, in dollars of 1979 average purchasing power. Amounts shown for "net assets" include restated amounts only for merchandise inventories and property (including property under capital leases). Such amounts do not purport to represent selling price, replacement cost, or any other measure of the current value of those assets.

	1979	1978	1977	1976	1975
Financial Statement Information:					
Sales	$13,717,861	$13,963,632	$13,474,486	$13,314,993	$13,104,539
Net income (loss)	(2,188)	46,681	25,826	48,180	112,438
Net income (loss) per share of common stock	(.08)	1.79	.99	1.86	4.34
Net assets at year-end	1,716,096	1,676,061	1,614,965	1,574,756	1,578,667
Other Information:					
Gain from the decline in purchasing power of net monetary liabilities	202,723	138,545	105,666	73,679	110,070
Cash dividends per share of common stock	2.60	2.56	2.64	2.61	2.56
Market price per share of common stock at year-end	32.62	43.13	48.33	62.52	59.32
Average Consumer Price Index	217.4	195.4	181.5	170.5	161.2

Note: Dollars are in thousands except per share figures.

FIGURE 19-1. Excerpt from Safeway Stores, Inc. annual report for 1979

Reprinted by permission of Safeway Stores, Inc.

ISSUES IN CONSTANT DOLLAR ACCOUNTING

The accountant runs into four major problems when attempting to present historical financial information in constant dollars:

* the choice of an index,
* the computation of purchasing power gain or loss on net monetary items,
* the presentation of nonmonetary items in the financial statements, and
* the presentation of revenue and expense items in the income statement.

Index

With respect to the choice of an index, FASB #33 (paragraph 39, page 14) states:

> The index used to compute information on a constant dollar basis shall be the Consumer Price Index for All Urban Consumers, published by the Bureau of Labor Statistics of the U.S. Department of Labor.

The statement goes on to say that an enterprise that is using constant dollar accounting may measure the components of those statements either in average-for-the-year constant dollars or in end-of-year constant dollars. Most companies likely opt for the average-for-the-year approach, since it will allow all revenue and expense accounts (with the exception of cost of goods sold, depreciation, and amortization expense items) to be reported without change on the income statement. They base this expectation on the assumption that the average inflation component does not differ markedly from the flow of revenue and expenses during the year being restated in constant dollars. We will come back to the latter point a bit later.

Computation of Gain or Loss

Before computing a gain or loss on holding monetary items, we must first define *monetary.* A relatively simpling working definition is: an asset (or liability) that remains fixed in dollar amount regardless of fluctuations in either general or specific price levels. Examples of monetary assets would include: cash, accounts receivable, bonds or preferred stock held for investment. Examples of monetary liabilities would include: accounts and notes payable, bonds payable, and deferred income taxes.

Now obviously, holding cash in a period of rising prices results in a loss, and incurring a debt that can be paid in future years with cheaper dollars results in a gain to the debtor. So, to determine the net monetary position, you add up all the monetary assets and liabilities. Either the monetary assets will exceed the monetary liabilities, or vice versa. For example, in computing the amount of net monetary items at the beginning of 1980, the changes in the net monetary items during the year and the amount at the end of the year are translated into average current year (1980) dollars.

The format for this computation is shown in Figure 19-2. If the company in this figure had a net monetary liability position, this purchasing power adjustment would be a gain.

FIGURE 19-2. Excerpt from FASB #33

	Historical Cost		*Conversion Factor*		*Constant Dollars*
Balance, 12/31/79	**$75,000**	X	**220 (Average 1980) / 210 (12/31/79)**	=	**$78,570**
Increase in net monetary assets during 1980	**10,000**		**(note)**		**10,000**
					$88,570
Balance, 12/31/80	**$85,000**	X	**220 (Average 1980) / 240 (12/31/80)**	=	**77,900**
Purchasing power loss on holding net monetary assets					**C$10,570***

The "C" is used as a convention by the FASB to designate constant dollars.** ***Note: **Changes in the net monetary asset position during the year are assumed to be at average-for-the-year 1980 dollars. So no conversion factor is requires.**

Presentation of Nonmonetary Items

Any item on the balance sheet that is not a monetary item is by definition a nonmonetary item. In general this category comprises all assets included in Property, plant, and equipment, as well as all items included in Inventories. If you were preparing a constant dollar balance sheet, all monetary items would appear at their historical values (with the gain or loss on holding these items reflected in the income statement). Also, all nonmonetary items would be restated at their constant dollar values according to the following formula:

$$\text{Historical cost of Item} \times \frac{\text{Average CPI (current year)}}{\text{Average CPI (year of acquisition)}}$$

Suppose, for example, you have land that was purchased for $5,000 when the CPI was 100. If the current CPI is 120, the formula would give you the constant dollar value of the land:

$$\text{Constant dollar value} = \$5{,}000 \times \frac{120}{100} = \text{C}\$6{,}000$$

Presenting Revenues and Expenses

This problem is conceptually much simplier if the average-for-the-year consumer price index (CPI) is used, since sales and operating expenses need not be restated for constant dollar financial statements. Two items must be restated, namely depreciation and cost of goods sold. Depreciation is restated because it is computed on an increased base—constant dollar valuation of property, plant, and equipment. Cost of goods sold must be restated since both beginning and ending inventories are affected by the conversion to constant dollars. Treating this subject in any great depth is beyond the scope of this book, although the appendix at the end of this chapter follows through with a comprehensive example of conversion to constant dollar accounting.

CURRENT COSTS

The FASB #33 (page 9) defines current costs as:

> A method of measuring and reporting assets and expenses associated with the use or sale of assets, at their current cost or lower recoverable amount at the balance sheet date or at the date of use or sale.

A conversion from constant dollars to current costs affects mainly inventories on the one hand (with consequent changes in the cost of goods sold) and property, plant, and equipment on the other hand (with corresponding changes in the income statement resulting from the restatement of depreciation expense). In addition, you need an account entitled "Excess of increase in specific prices over increase in the General price level." Such an account represents changes in the balance sheet accounts (Inventories and Property, plant, and equipment) resulting from changes in specific price levels of these items during the current year. These changes are called holding gains or losses.

APPENDIX

Here is simplified illustration of a comprehensive restatement of the balance sheet and income statement to constant dollars. Let's take the accounting information, which is based on historical cost, shown in Figure 19-3. For purposes of this example, assume that the CPI for various dates was as follows:

January 1, 19X1	100
Average CPI for 19X1	110
December 31, 19X1	120
Average CPI for 19X2	125
December 31, 19X2	130

FIGURE 19-3. Illustrative balance sheets

Valley Pumps, Inc.
BALANCE SHEETS
December 31, 19X1 and 19X2

	December 31	
Assets	*19X1*	*19X2*
Monetary assets	$110,000	$170,000
Land (nonmonetary)	20,000	20,000
Property, plant, and equipment (nonmonetary)	70,000	60,000
	$200,000	$250,000
Liabilities and Stockholders' Equities		
Monetary liabilities	$ 50,000	$ 50,000
Stockholders' Equity:		
Capital stock	100,000	100,000
Retained earnings	50,000	100,000
	$200,000	$250,000

Valley Pumps, Inc.
INCOME STATEMENTS
For the Years Ended
December 31, 19X1 and 19X2

	December 31	
	19X1	*19X2*
Revenues from services rendered	$150,000	$150,000
Operating expenses	90,000	90,000
Net income (before depreciation)	60,000	60,000
Depreciation expense	10,000	10,000
Net income	$ 50,000	$ 50,000

Note: Assume that this company began operations on January 1, 19X1.

Our original structure for a company in its first year:

(1) $$A - L = CS + R - E_C - E_D$$

is divided into monetary (M) and nonmonetary (N) items (everything that is not monetary, by definition is considered to be nonmonetary):

(2) $$(A_M - L_M) + A_N = CS_N + R - E_C - E_D$$

Converting to constant dollars, we have (use "Δ" as the measure of change):

(3) $$(A_M - L_M) + \Delta(A_M - L_M) + A_N + \Delta A_N = CS_N + \Delta CS_N + R + \Delta R - (E_C + \Delta E_C) - (E_D - \Delta E_D)$$

If we use the CPI for the average-for-the-year instead of year-end, we can simplify the problem. Equation (3) then becomes:*

(3A) $$(A_M - L_M) + \Delta(A_M - L_M) + A_N + \Delta A_N = CS_N + \Delta CS_N + R - E_C - (E_D - \Delta E_D)$$

Let's assume that the monetary assets and liabilities were acquired when the CPI was 110 and that the nonmonetary assets and liabilities where acquired when the CPI was 100 that is, at the inception of the business. Then:

$$(110{,}000 - \$50{,}000) + \$20{,}000 + \$70{,}000 + (2{,}000 + \$7{,}000) = \$10{,}000 + \$10{,}000 + \$150{,}000 - \$90{,}000 - (\$10{,}000 + \$1{,}000)$$

This computation requires a bit of explanation. The net monetary assets are $110,000 − $50,000 = $60,000. Since they were acquired when the CPI was 110, no adjustment is required since 110/110 = 1. Land and the net book value of property, plant, and equipment are adjusted by the fraction 110/100. Since the historical cost is $90,000 ($20,000 + $70,000), the adjustment for 1979 amounts to $9,000. Total assets are therefore $159,000. On the equity side of the balance sheet, capital stock (a nonmonetary item) must be adjusted by the fraction 110/100. Since the historical cost is $100,000, the account becomes $110,000. For the first year of operation, Retained earnings, is simply the net income for the year on the historical basis of $50,000, but adjusted downward for the increase in depreciation by the same fraction, namely 110/100. This adjustment makes the equity side of the balance sheet total $159,000, which, of course, equals the asset side computed independently.

E_C refers to expenses requiring an outlay of cash.
E_D refers to expenses of a noncash nature such as depreciation and amortization.

If the company is in its second year (or in any year other than the first), you must modify the equation as follows:*

(4) $$A_M - L_M + A_N = CS + RE_b + R - E_C - E_D$$

(5) $$(A_M - L_M) + \Delta(A_M - L_M) + A_N + \Delta A_N = CS_N + \Delta CS_N + RE_b + \Delta RE_b + R - E_C - (E_D + \Delta E_D)$$

$$(\$170{,}000 - \$50{,}000) + (\$15{,}000 - \$6{,}818) + \$80{,}000 + \$20{,}000 = \$100{,}000 + \$25{,}000 + \$49{,}000 + \$6{,}682 + \$150{,}000 - \$90{,}000 - \$12{,}500$$

An interpretation of the changes in retained earnings since the inception of Valley Pumps, Inc. is as follows:

Retained earnings, beginning of 19X1		0
Historical earnings, 19X1	$50,000	
Reduction in earnings from indexing depreciation [$10,000 × 125/100 – $10,000]	1,000	
Net income, year ended 12/31/X1	$49,000	
Restatement of 19X1 income in 19X2 [$49,000 × (125/110)]		C$55,682
Historical earnings, 19X2	$50,000	
Reduction in earnings from indexing depreciation [$10,000 × 125/100 – $10,000]	2,500	
Net Income, year ended 12/31/X2	C$47,500	
Less: Loss from holding net monetary assets	8,182	39,318
Retained earnings, 12/31/X2		C$95,000

Valley Pumps, Inc.
BALANCE SHEET
(in constant dollars)
December 31, 19X2

Assets		*Liabilities and Stockholders' Equity*	
Current Assets:		Current Liabilities:	
Monetary assets	C$170,000	Monetary liabilities	C$ 50,000
Property, Plant, and Equipment (net of depreciation):	C$100,000	Stockholders' Equity:	
		Capital stock	C$125,000
		Retained earnings	C$ 95,000
	C$270,000		C$270,000

*Note: RE_b = retained earnings at end of year one restated in constant dollar of year two.

20
Time and Money

The time value of money is of vital importance to the investor. In fact, it is one of the most important variables of the investment decision. To the accountant, it is somewhat less important, although bond yield calculations, investment opportunities, and capital budgeting decisions depend to a large measure on the understanding of its impact. So we include Chapter 20 as an optional portion.

The basic concept seems trivial and simple, but the subject rapidly becomes more complex as the examples become more difficult. If you deposit \$100 in a savings account paying 6-percent interest compounded annually, then one year from today you'll have earned \$6. You will have \$106 in the bank. Since interest is compounded annually for the succeeding year, you will earn interest on \$106. The interest for year 2 becomes \$6.36, and you will have \$112.36 in the savings account. These computations are depicted in Figure 20-1, which represents this information by a time line. By supplying the information that you already know—the original investment, the interest rate, and the number of periods—you can indicate the unknown quantity—the amount earned—by an arrow.

These computations can also be extended over ten periods in Table 20-1. To use such a table effectively, you must know the number of periods (2, in this instance) and the interest rate (6-percent rate). Looking down the "Period" column to 2 and then across to the "6%" column, we find the factor of 1.1236. Multiplying that factor by the investment, $100, we obtain $112.36. That's how much you'll have in the bank after two years.

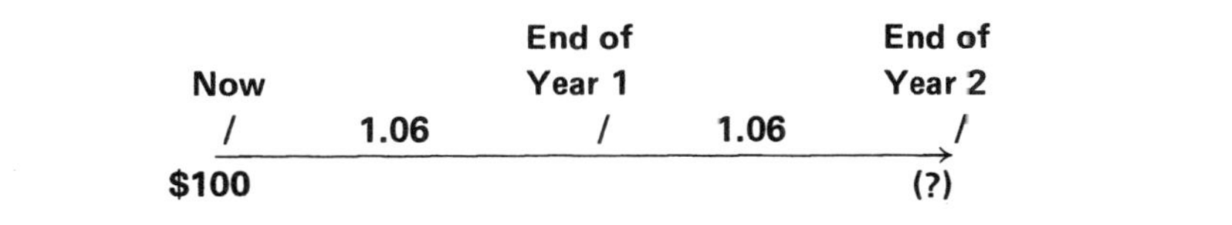

FIGURE 20-1. Compound amount of 1

Table 20-2 may be used the same way. It is based on the notion of what S1 payable at some future date is worth today. It is the mirror image of the problem just discussed. If you know the future amount, S112.36, what amount would you have to deposit today to be able to withdraw exactly $112.36 in two years. (The diagram (or time line) is sketched in Figure 20-2.)

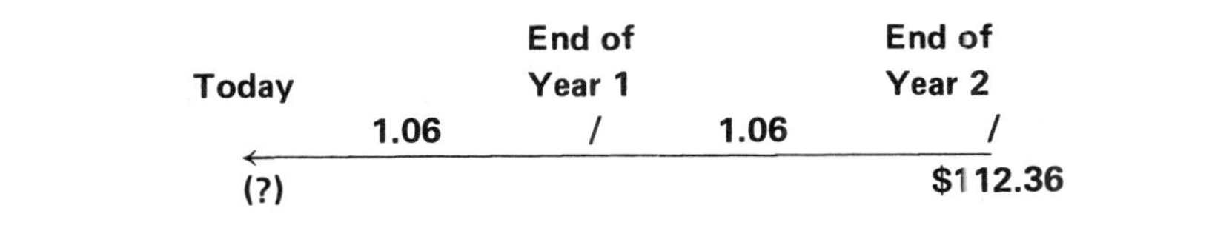

FIGURE 20-2. Present value of 1

Once again, read down the left-hand column to period 2, and then across to the 6-percent column. At that point you find the entry, 0.8900. Multiply it by $112.36, and you obtain exactly $100. Also note that the reciprocal of 0.89 is 1/0.89 = 1.1236, which is the factor used in the previous example.

Table 20-3 is a convenient way of handling multiple payments of identical amounts. If you deposit $100 today, you already know that (at 6-percent interest, compounded annually) it will be worth $112.36 in two years. You also know that, if you deposit $100 one year from today, in two years it will be worth $106. Adding those two investments gives us $218.36. But we had to do two separate calculations and look up two entries in the tables to find the answer.

Table 20-3 gives us the answer in one step. Looking up three (not two) periods at 6 percent, you find the entry, 3.1836—which is not quite 2.1836 (218.36). Why not? Well, you have to subtract 1.000 from the entries found in this table. And, in fact, 3.1836 − 1.0000 = 2.1836.

Do you see how Table 20-3 is constructed. The time line is shown in Figure 20-3.

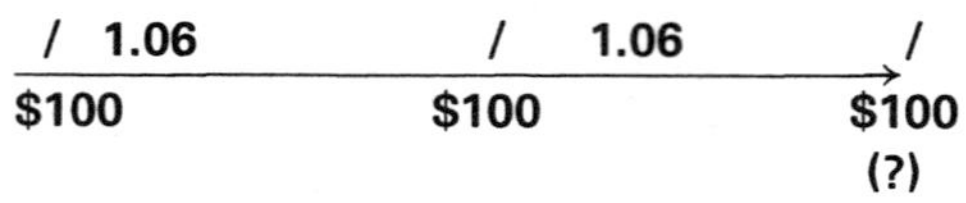

FIGURE 20-3. Amount of 1 per annum at compound interest

In that figure, you might see for yourself, you have to look up three periods and subtract 1.0000. The table assumes that you have made the third payment, while in our case you made only payments.

> *Example:* Your grandmother is giving you $1,000 per year over the next four years, beginning today, to finance your graduation trip to Europe. How much will you have (at a 5-1/2-percent interest rate) immediately after you receive the fourth and final payment. The time line is shown in Figure 20-4). In this case, the last (fourth) payment is made. So you enter Table 20-3 at four periods and at 5-1/2-percent. You find the entry 4.3423 and multiply it by $1,000, to obtain $4,342.30.

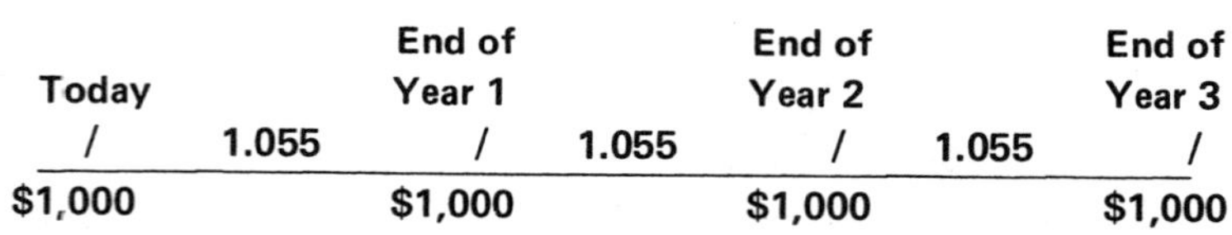

FIGURE 20-4. Example of the amount of 1 at compound interest

In any future value problem, be sensitive to whether that last payment is made immediately before withdrawal. Read any such problem carefully and diagram it in detail before attempting the solution.

Finally, we come to Table 20-4, the present value of 1 per annum at compound interest. Unlike the present value of $1 table, which deals with only one amount received sometime in the future, this table considers *numerous, equal payments* received at *equally spaced intervals* in the *future.*

> *Example:* Your brother-in-law agrees to give you $1,000 per year, starting one year from now, for four years to cover the costs of his living with you. Your bank pays 6-1/2-percent interest, compounded annually. How much is the contract worth to you today.

FIGURE 20-5.

Today	End of Year 1	End of Year 2	End of Year 3	End of Year 4
/ 1.065	/ 1.065	/ 1.065	/ 1.065	/
(?)	$1,000	$1,000	$1,000	$1,000

With Table 20-4, you can arrive at the present value of that $4,000 while saving yourself some work. Table 20-4 does it all in one easy step. Just enter the table at four periods and 6-1/2-percent. The entry there is 3.4258.

Alternatively, you could enter Table 20-2 for each of the $1,000 payments and discount them back to the present, but this approach would require four separage calculations:

Periods	*Interest Rate*	*Factor*
1	6 1/2%	0.9390
2	6 1/2%	0.8817
3	6 1/2%	0.8278
4	6 1/2%	0.7773
Total		3.4258

EXAMPLE

Leslie has to pay off her $1,000 student loan in five years. The money market fund's rate of interest is 12 percent compounded *semiannually.* Leslie will put $80 in the money market fund account every six months, starting in six months. She suspects she will not have to make a full final $80 payment on the loan's due date since she will have earned interest on her previous payments. But she doesn't know what the payment will be, and she has asked you to help her. How much of a last payment will she need to make up the differenc for a $1,000?

The 12-percent annual interest rate corresponds to 6-percent every six months for semiannual compounding. Since the missing payment's value is due in five years, we're going to need a future value table. Finally, since Leslie will be making nine equal $80 payments, we know Table 20-3 will be used. The factor at the intersection of 9 periods and 6 percent is 11.4913. Once we have that, the rest is a simple calculation:

$$\$80 \times 11.4913 = \$919.30$$

4-1/2 Years	5 Years
/ 1.06	/
$919.30	(1)

Now it is a simple matter to compute from Table 20-1:

$$\$919.30 \times 1.06 = \$974.46$$

So Leslie need pay only $25.54 for her last payment at the end of five years.

Fortunately, most hand held calculator manufacturers offer a financial calculator for under $50 which provides quick answers to present value problems. For example, if you enter present value, periodic interest rate, number of payments (term of loan), at the flick of a button, you obtain the monthly payment required to amortize the loan according to the given terms. It is still instructive, however, to understand the theory behind the numbers. Hence the value of this chapter.

TABLE 20-1. Compound amount of 1

Periods	*5%*	*5 1/2%*	*6%*	*6 1/2%*
1	1.0500	1.0550	1.0600	1.0650
2	1.1025	1.1130	1.1236	1.1342
3	1.1576	1.1742	1.1910	1.2079
4	1.2155	1.2388	1.2625	1.2865
5	1.2763	1.3070	1.3382	1.3701
6	1.3401	1.3788	1.4185	1.4591
7	1.4071	1.4546	1.5036	1.5540
8	1.4775	1.5347	1.5938	1.6550
9	1.5513	1.6191	1.6895	1.7626
10	1.6289	1.7081	1.7908	1.8771

TABLE 20-2. Present value of 1

Periods	*5%*	*5 1/2%*	*6%*	*6 1/2%*
1	0.9524	0.9479	0.9434	0.9390
2	0.9070	0.8985	0.8900	0.8817
3	0.8638	0.8516	0.8396	0.8278
4	0.8227	0.8072	0.7921	0.7773
5	0.7835	0.7651	0.7473	0.7299
6	0.7462	0.7252	0.7050	0.6853
7	0.7107	0.6874	0.6651	0.6435
8	0.6768	0.6516	0.6274	0.6042
9	0.6446	0.6176	0.5919	0.5674
10	0.6139	0.5854	0.5584	0.5327

Periods	5%	5 1/2%	6%	6 1/2%
1	1.0000	1.0000	1.0000	1.0000
2	2.0500	2.0550	2.0600	2.0650
3	3.1525	3.1680	3.1836	3.1996
4	4.3101	4.3423	4.3746	4.4072
5	5.5256	5.5811	5.6371	5.6936
6	6.8019	6.8881	6.9753	7.0637
7	8.1420	8.2669	8.3938	8.5229
8	9.5491	9.7216	9.8975	10.0769
9	11.0266	11.2563	11.4913	11.7319
10	12.5779	12.8754	13.1808	13.4944

TABLE 20-3. Amount of 1 per annum at compound interest

Periods	5%	5 1/2%	6%	6 1/2%
1	0.9524	0.9479	0.9434	0.9390
2	1.8594	1.8463	1.8334	1.8206
3	2.7232	2.6979	2.6730	2.6485
4	3.5460	3.5052	3.4651	3.4258
5	4.3295	4.2723	4.2124	4.1557
6	5.0757	4.9955	4.9173	4.8410
7	5.7864	5.6830	5.5824	5.4845
8	6.4632	6.3346	6.2098	6.0888
9	7.1078	6.9522	6.8017	6.6561
10	7.7217	7.5376	7.3601	7.1888

TABLE 20-4. Present value of 1 per annum at compound interest

ADDITIONAL EXERCISES

20-1. For each of the following diagrams, indicate whether you would use Table 20-1, 20-2, 20-3, or 20-4:

a. ______________

Today Year 1 Year 2 Year 3 Year 4 Year 5

/ 1.05 / 1.05 / 1.05 /1.05 / 1.05 /

←

(?) $100 $100 $100 $100 $100

b. ______________

Today Year 1 Year 2 Year 3 Year 4 Year 5

/ / / / 1.06 / 1.06 /

→

$500 (?)

c. ______________

Today Year 1 Year 2 Year 3 Year 4

1.05 /1.05/1.05/ 1.05/ 1.05/1.05 /1.05 /1.05/

←

(?) $1,000 $2,000

d. ___________

Today	Year 1	Year 2	Year 3	Year 4	Year 5
/ 1.06	/ 1.06	/ 1.06	/ 1.06	/	/
$500	$500	$500	$500	$500 (?)	

20-2. Refer to Exercise 20-1, and complete the following table with respect to each time line:

Problem	Periods	Interest Rate	Factor
a.	___________	___________	___________
b.	___________	___________	___________
c. $2,000	___________	___________	___________
$1,000	___________	___________	___________
d.	___________	___________	___________

20-3. Analyze each of the following four situations independently by diagramming the relevant variables on a time line. Indicate which table (20-1, 20-2, 20-3, 20-4) you would use to solve the case:

a. George Smith deposits $2,500 in an investment account that earns 11-percent interest per year, compounded semi-annually. What is the value of this investment at the end of 2-1/2 years? ___________

b. Five years ago Northfield Company invested some money at 12-percent interest compounded semiannually. The investment has grown to a total of $35,816. What was the original investment? ___________

c. The year is 19X1. Camden Corp. needs $500,000 on March 1, 19X5 to pay off a maturing bond issue. The corporation will make seven equal payments semiannually beginning March 1, 19X2 to raise the funds. If the corporation can earn 13 percent compounded semiannually in a trust fund, how much must be deposited in each payment? ___________

d. Wheeler Corp. negotiated a new pension agreement that will require it to deposit $10,000 in the employees' pension fund each year for three consecutive years. The first payment is due one year from today. Given that the pension fund earns 6 percent compounded annually, if Wheeler decides instead to deposit enough today to cover its entire three-year obligation, how much must Wheeler deposit? __________

20-4. For each of the four separate cases in Exercise 20-3, complete the following table:

Problem	*Periods*	*Interest Rate*	*Factor*
a.	________	________	________
b.	________	________	________
c.	________	________	________
d.	________	________	________

20-5. Your brainy adolescent daughter found your savings account passbook (on which interest is compounded annually) and noted that you deposited $5,000 on January 1, 1970, made no deposits or withdrawals, and had $8,954 on January 1, 1980. You have no entries since that date. Since she read Chapter 20 of this book, she sat down and calculated what interest rate you had to be earning on the account. What figure did she come up with? __________

20-6. Hans collects rare coins. He just spotted a rare Dutch guilder that he can purchase for $10,000. Knowing the numismatics market, he figures he can resell the coin in three years for $15,000. Of course, he could always invest his money in a money-market fund earning 10 percent compounded semiannually. Should he:

a. buy the coin, or

b. invest the money?

20-7. BCD, Inc. just bought an ore crusher for $71,888. BCD will make annual installments of $10,000 starting one year from today to pay for the equipment. Each $10,000 payment is calculated to include 6-1/2 percent annual interest on the unpaid balance at the beginning of each payment year. How many installments are required to pay for the ore crusher?

20-8. Under its new $50,000 bonus agreement with its president, Carillon Corp. is required to invest $10,000 annually in a trust fund paying 6-percent interest compounded annually. The payments begin July 1, 19X0. The president will begin making four equal annual withdrawals from the accumulated funds upon his retirement on July 1, 19X5. How much should he withdraw each time to totally exhaust the fund by the fourth withdrawal? ____________

20-9. Kim deposits $300 in a savings account paying 11-percent interest compounded semiannually. She makes seven more deposits like this every six months. How much money will be in her account three years after the last deposit?

SOLUTIONS

20-1. a. 20-4

b. 20-1

c. 20-2

d. 20-3

20-2.

a.		5	5%	4.3295
b.		2	6%	1.1236
c.	$2,000	6	5%	0.7462
	$1,000	2	5%	0.9070
d.		5	6%	5.6371

20-.3. a. Today 6 mo. 1 yr. 1-1/2 yrs. 2 yrs. 2-1/2 yrs.

/ 1.055 / 1.055 / 1.055 /1.055 /1.055 /

———————————————————→

$2,500 (?)

Use Table 20-1.

b. (Total 10 periods)

Today 1/2 yr. 1 yr. 1-1/2 yrs. 2 yrs. 2-1/2 yrs. . . . 5 yrs.

1.06 / 1.06 / 1.06 / 1.06 / 1.06 / . . . /

←——————————————————— —

(?) $35,816

Note: To save time, all periods need not be spelled out.

Use Table 20-2.

c. Today 6 mo. 1 yr. 1-1/2 yrs. 2 yrs. 2-1/2 yrs. 3 yrs.

/1.065 /1.065 /1.065 /1.065 /1.065 /1.065 /

———————————————————→

(?) (?) (?) (?) (?) (?) (?)

$500,000

Use Table 20-3.

d.
```
    Today       1 yr.      2 yrs.     3 yrs.
     / 1.06      / 1.06     / 1.06     /
    <-------------------------------------
    (?)         $10,000    $10,000    $10,000
```

Use Table 20-4.

20-4. For each of the four separate cases in Exercise 20-3, complete the following table:

Problem	Periods	Interest Rate	Factor	Answer
a.	5	5 1/2%	1.3070	$ 3,267.50
b.	10	6%	0.5584	$20,000.00
c.	7	6 1/2%	8.5229	$58,665.48
d.	3	6%	2.6730	$26,730.00

20-5. $8,954/$5,000 = 1.7908: From Table 20-1, for ten periods, we find the answer in the "6%" column.

20-6. a—If Hans invests $10,000 at 10 percent (5 percent for six periods), then:

$$\$10{,}000 \times 1.3401 = \$13{,}401$$

Since this is less than $15,000, he should buy the coin today.

20-7.
```
    Today     1 yr.     2 yrs.    3 yrs. . . . (?)
      /1.065   / 1.065   / 1.065 /
  $71,888   10,000    10,000    10,000
```

$$\frac{\$71{,}888}{10{,}000} = 7{,}1888$$ (from Table 20-4, 6-1/2%, we find a match at ten periods.)

20-8.
```
Now 1 yr.  2 yrs.  3 yrs.  4 yrs.  5 yrs.  6 yrs.  7 yrs.  8 yrs.
 /1.06/1.06  /1.06   /1.06   /1.06   /1.06   /1.06   /1.06   /
 *     *      *       *       *      (?)     (?)     (?)     (?)
                                   $59,753
```

*indicates a $10,000 investment.

After five years of investing $10,000 at 6 percent from Table 20-3, we find (for six periods): 6.9753 × $10,000 = $69,753. But we did not make the sixth payment. So ($69,753 − $10,000) = $59,753. The second part of the problem is to compute the amount of four equal payments that can be made from this fund. You will recall that Table 20-4 assumes that the first payment will be made one year hence. So our factor for periods must be 3. But then we must add the first payment, which earns no interest (1.000). We obtain 1.0000 + 2.6730 = 3.6730. Dividing that into $59,753, we get:

$$\frac{59753}{3.6730} = \$16,268 \text{ the annual withdrawal}$$

Proof:	*End of Year*	*Beginning Fund Balance*	*Withdrawal*	*Earned*
	5	$59,753	$16,268	$2,609
	6	46,094	16,268	1,790
	7	31,616	16,268	920
	8	16,268	16,268	0

20-9.

Rate	1	2	3	4	5	6	7	8	9	10	11	12	13	14
5.5%	/	/	/	/	/	/	/	/	/	/	/	/	/	/
	300	300	300	300	300	300	300	300						
								$291.48						(?)

From Table 20-3, 8 periods at 5.5 percent, the factor is 9.7216:

$$\$300 \times 9.7216 = \$2916.48$$

The second half of the problem is simple: Use Table 20-1 to find that:

$$\$2916.48 \times 1.3788 = \$4021.24$$

Third Progress Test

The Third (and final) Progress Test covers all the material covered to this point:

* The first five questions (1 through 5) deal with the problem of errors and how they might affect financial statements.
* The next five questions (6 through 10) deal with the theory behind consolidated financial statements.
* Questions 11 through 15 are related to *constant dollar accounting,* and you should attempt to answer these questions only if you have studied Chapter 19 of the book (which was designated as optional). We strongly recommend that if you have not studied this chapter that you do so now before taking this test.
* The remainder of the questions relate to the financial statements of PSA, Inc. a regional airline on the West Coast. These questions give you a chance to apply your knowledge of financial statement analysis (Chapter 18). In a very real sense, these questions are the culmination of all the time and effort you have spent on this course. When you have calculated all

the required ratios, you begin to have an understanding of the liquidity, equity position, and market performance of PSA. These ratios reflect what financial analysts call the "fundamentals" of a company. A wise investor would make them all before considering a purchase of the stock.

A friend of yours, who is presently taking intermediate financial accounting, has asked you to review his solution to the problem that he has prepared and that is due tomorrow. In reviewing his solution to the problem, you find the following errors in his solution:

* Your friend has understated the inventory at the beginning of the year by $5,000.
* The friend has failed to grasp the notion of the lower of cost or market as it relates to marketable securities. Accordingly the entire portfolio of marketable securities is overvalued at the year-end by $15,000.
* Although the ending inventory is correctly stated on the balance sheet, the purchase on credit of $10,000 worth of merchandise on credit was omitted from the T-accounts.
* Depreciation was overstated by $3,000 because your friend depreciated some equipment below salvage value.
* Dividends paid during the year of $7,000 have been incorrectly deducted from net income as an expense.

When you point these errors out, your friend asks you the following questions (to which you are to respond with the appropriate alternative):

1. Current assets are:

   a. overstated by $5,000.
   b. overstated by $15,000.
   c. understated by $25,000.
   d. overstated by $25,000.
   e. none of the above.

2. Net income is:

   a. understated by $10,000.
   b. overstated by $20,000.
   c. overstated by $8,000.
   d. understated by $27,000.
   e. none of the above.

3. Inventory at year-end is:

   a. understated by $5,000.
   b. overstated by $5,000.

c. neither understated nor overstated.
d. overstated by $15,000.
e. correct answer is not given.

4. Retained earnings at year-end are:

a. understated by $8,000.
b. overstated by $30,000.
c. overstated by $22,000.
d. understated by $7,000.
e. neither overstated nor understated.

5. Liabilities are:

a. overstated by $10,000.
b. understated by $27,000.
c. understated by $7,000.
d. overstated by $14,000.
e. none of the above.

Answer questions 6-10 regarding the following T-accounts:

*Accounts Receivable—B**	
$12,000	

Capital Stock—A	
	$2,500,000

Dividend Revenues	
(2) $13,000	$13,000 (A)

Investment in B	
$850,000	(1) $850,000

Retained Earnings—A	
$50,000	$236,000

Cost of Goods Sold	
(A) $440,000 (B) $ 80,000	

Goodwill	
(1) $80,000	

Capital Stock—B	
(1) $500,000	$500,000

Depreciation Expense	
(A) $120,000 (B) $ 50,000	

Other Assets	
(A) $2,138,000 (B) $1,000,000 (1) $ 100,000	

Retained Earnings—B	
$ 13,000 (1) $170,000	$170,000 (2) $ 13,000

Administrative Expense	
(A) $80,000 (B) $40,000	

*A refers to Company A.
B refers to Company B.

Accounts Payable—A	
	$12,000

Sales	
	$900,000 (A) $250,000 (B)

Income Taxes	
(A) $104,000 (B) $ 32,000	

Other Liabilities	
	$145,000 (A) $283,000 (B)

6. The foregoing T-accounts are used in lieu of a worksheet in order to:
   a. develop a set of financial statements from a single company after taking certain year-end adjustments into account.
   b. substitute for a worksheet in the preparation of the statement of changes in financial position.
   c. develop consolidated financial statements using the purchase assumption.
   d. develop consolidated financial statements using the pooling assumption.
   e. The use of the T-accounts cannot be determined with certainty from the information given.

7. The net income of Company A is:
   a. $16,900.
   b. $169,000.
   c. $182,000.
   d. $191,000.
   e. cannot be determined from the information given.

8. The consolidated net income of Company A and Company B, prior to amortization of goodwill and depreciation on the fair market value increment of fixed assets, if any, is:

   a. $169,000.
   b. $154,000.
   c. $217,000.
   d. $204,000.
   e. some other amount.

9. If goodwill is amortized over a 20-year life, the correct consolidated retained earnings would be (ignore depreciation on the fair market value increment of fixed assets, if any):

   a. $406,000.
   b. $390,000.
   c. $402,000.
   d. $351,000.
   e. $386,000.

10. Assume that the excess of fair market value of Company B, if any, over the book value of the assets of Company B is not subject to depreciation and that goodwill is amortized over 20 years. The correct total for the consolidated shareholders' equity of Company A and Company B is then:

    a. $2,572,000.
    b. $2,810,000.
    c. $2,890,000.
    d. $2,886,000.
    e. some other amount.

The following data refers to questions 11-15. Adjust all answers to reflect constant dollars determined by the average-for-the-year CPI (all urban consumers):

Historical Cost/Nominal Dollar Financial Statements and Other Background Information

Balance Sheets as at December 31, 1980 and 1979

(000s)

	1980	*1979*
Current assets:		
Cash	$ 1,000	$ 2,000
Accounts receivable	36,000	30,000
Inventories, at FIFO cost	63,000	56,000
Total current assets	100,000	88,000
Property, plant, and equipment, at cost	100,000	85,000
Less accumulated depreciation	56,000	46,000
	44,000	39,000
	$144,000	$127,000

	1980	*1979*
Current liabilities:		
Bank indebtedness	$ 35,000	$ 22,000
Accounts payable and accrued expenses	12,000	10,000
Income taxes payable	6,000	6,000
Current portion of long-term debt	5,000	5,000
Total current liabilities	58,000	43,000
Deferred income taxes	6,000	5,000
Long-term debt	34,000	39,000
Total liabilities	98,000	87,000
Shareholders' equity	46,000	40,000
	$144,000	$127,000

Statement of Earnings and Shareholders' Equity

For The Years Ended December 31, 1980 and 1979

(000s)

1980

	1980	*1979*
Sales	$253,000	$220,000
Cost of goods sold, exclusive of depreciation	197,000	170,600
Selling, general, and administrative expenses	20,835	25,500
Depreciation	10,000	8,500
Interest	7,165	3,400
	235,000	208,000
Earnings before taxes	18,000	12,000
Income taxes	9,000	6,000
Net income	9,000	6,000
Shareholders' equity at beginning of the year	40,000	37,000
	49,000	43,000
Dividends	3,000	3,000
Shareholders' equity at end of the year	$ 46,000	$ 40,000
Net income per share	$ 6.00	$ 4.00

Average	1973	133.1
"	1974	147.7
"	1975	161.2
"	1976	170.5
"	1977	181.5
"	1978	195.4
"	1979	205.0*
"	1980	220.9‡

Average 4th Qtr.	1979†	210.0
Average 4th Qtr.	1980†	237.8
December	1979	212.9*
December	1980	243.5*

*Estimated for illustrative purposes.
†Calculated by averaging the estimated monthly indexes for each quarter.
‡Calculated by averaging the estimated monthly indexes for 1980. The index for the last month of the year may not be available at the time of preparing the supplemental disclosures and may be estimated by extrapolating the rate of change for the previous month.

Example taken from FASB #33, (AICPA, 1979).

11. Assuming that the inventory turns over four times a year, the inventory for December 31, 1980 would be valued for a constant dollar basis at:

a. C$63,000.
b. C$58,523.
c. C$57,271.
d. C$65,367.
e. some other amount.

12. Assuming that the Property, plant, and equipment assets were all acquired when the CPI (all urban consumers) was 170, the net amount for Property, plant, and equipment, as stated in constant dollars, at December 31, 1980 would be:

a. $72,767.
b. $76,968.
c. $44,000.
d. $48,502.
e. some other amount.

13. Using the same data as for question 12, the depreciation expense on the income statement for 1980 restated in constant dollars would be the following expression divided by the useful economic life:

a. $\$100,000 \times \frac{170}{220.9}$
b. $\$100,000 \times \frac{220.9}{170}$
c. $\$100,000 \times \frac{243.5}{170}$
d. $\$44,000 \times \frac{170}{220.9}$
e. none of the above.

14. The net monetary position of the company for the year ended December 31, 1980 would result in:

a. a realized gain.
b. an unrealized loss.
c. a realized loss.
d. an unrealized gain.
e. can not be determined from the data.

15. The net gain (or loss) for the year resulting from the net monetary positions at December 31, 1980 and December 31, 1979 would be:

a. $2,067.
b. $5,662.
c. $7,729.
d. ($2,067).
e. some other amount.

On the following pages we present the balance sheet and the income statements of PSA, INC. for the years ended December 31, 1980 and 1979. Use this information in answering questions 16-30. For the questions relating to market ratios, assume that the market price of PSA's common stock is $40 per share in 1980 and $30 in 1979. Calculate the following ratios for the dates indicated:

	1980	*1979*
16. Current asset ratio:	______	______
17. Quick asset ratio:	______	______
18. Long-term debt to equity ratio:	______	______
19. Operating expense percentage	______	______
20. Net income percentage:	______	______
21. Earnings per share (EPS):	______	______
22. Return on shareholders' equity:	______	______
23. Return on total assets:	______	______
24. Supplies inventory turnover:	______	______
25. Price/earnings ratios:	______	______
26. What was the largest source of funds (in dollars)?	______	______
27. What was the principal use of funds (in dollars)?	______	______
28. How much working capital was generated from operations?	______	______
29. What was the working capital at the end of:	______	______

30. Would PSA be a good "buy" at $40 per share in your opinion? Why?

____

____

PSA, Inc.
CONSOLIDATED BALANCE SHEETS
(In thousands)

ASSETS	December 31, 1980	1979
Current assets:		
Cash	$ 4,141	$ 5,274
Temporary investments at cost, which approximates market	13,738	29,782
Accounts receivable, less allowance for doubtful accounts: 1980, $667 and 1979, $447	23,455	30,260
Maintenance and operating supplies, at average cost less allowance for obsolescence: 1980, $6,805 and 1979, $6,324 (Note 1)	21,054	17,965
Refundable deposits on flight equipment purchase contracts	4,952	
Refundable income taxes	2,761	
Prepaid expenses	4,983	3,138
Total current assets	75,084	86,419
Funds held in interest bearing escrow account for purchase of flight equipment, pledged (Note 2)	46,350	
Property and equipment at cost (Note 1):		
Flight equipment, partially pledged (Note 2)	242,213	241,795
Deposits on flight equipment purchase contracts (Note 7)	70,412	47,540
Other property and equipment	47,480	42,828
	360,105	332,163
Less accumulated depreciation	121,249	128,183
	238,856	203,980
Property and equipment under capital leases (Notes 1 and 3):		
Flight equipment	37,549	37,549
Other property	3,540	3,540
	41,089	41,089
Less accumulated amortization	18,753	16,148
	22,336	24,941
Other assets	10,973	10,344
	$393,599	$325,684

See accompanying Notes to Consolidated Financial Statements.

20

LIABILITIES AND STOCKHOLDERS' EQUITY	December 31, 1980	1979
Current liabilities:		
Accounts payable and other accrued liabilities	$ 25,300	$ 25,712
Salaries, wages and vacation benefits payable	11,457	9,725
Air traffic liability (Note 1)	7,399	8,270
Accrued interest	5,136	3,961
Income taxes payable (Note 6)	2	3,017
Accrued taxes other than income taxes	2,481	2,486
Current portion of long-term obligations (Note 2)	43,062	20,659
Total current liabilities	94,837	73,830
Long-term obligations (Notes 2 and 3):		
Senior debt	114,660	56,982
Subordinated debt	38,605	43,594
Capital leases	27,030	29,422
	180,295	129,998
Deferred credits and other long-term liabilities:		
Deferred federal income tax (Note 6)	14,446	13,651
Other, principally deferred credits	9,992	7,982
	24,438	21,633
Commitments (Notes 3 and 7)		
Stockholders' equity:		
Preferred stock, par value $1 per share; 500 shares authorized, none issued		
Common stock, par value $1 per share; 9,500 shares authorized, 3,491 shares issued and outstanding (3,426 in 1979) (Note 8)	3,491	3,426
Additional paid-in capital	37,668	36,840
Retained earnings (Note 2)	52,870	59,957
Total stockholders' equity	94,029	100,223
	$393,599	$325,684

PSA, Inc.
CONSOLIDATED STATEMENTS OF INCOME
(In thousands except per share amounts)

	Years ended December 31, 1980*	1979	1978
Continuing operations:			
Operating revenues:			
Passenger transportation (Note 1)	$280,143	$276,510	$199,162
Other flight revenue	15,773	11,510	8,686
Aircraft lease revenue	11,214	6,085	311
Maintenance and other revenues	63,074	41,733	21,726
	370,204	335,838	229,885
Operating expenses (Note 1):			
Operations	196,427	163,790	120,402
Maintenance	36,311	31,432	24,970
Costs and expenses of maintenance and other revenues	51,518	33,763	18,579
Reservations, sales and advertising	29,600	29,463	18,905
General and administrative	24,122	18,270	16,588
Depreciation and amortization	20,113	19,055	16,239
	358,091	295,773	215,683
Operating income	12,113	40,065	14,202
Non-operating income (expense) (Note 1):			
Interest expense	(17,231)	(14,129)	(9,250)
Interest capitalized	6,676	3,448	740
Gains on disposition of equipment (Note 5)	6,880	1,587	6,283
Interest income and other	5,184	2,409	1,107
	1,509	(6,685)	(1,120)
Income before taxes based on income	13,622	33,380	13,082
Provision for taxes based on income (Notes 1 and 6)	969	11,274	3,464
Income from continuing operations	12,653	22,106	9,618
Discontinued operations (Note 4)		991	
Income before extraordinary item and cumulative effect of changes in accounting	12,653	23,097	9,618
Extraordinary item (Note 4)			(936)
Cumulative effect on prior years of changes in accounting (Note 1)			2,905
Net Income	$ 12,653	$ 23,097	$ 11,587
Net income per common share (Note 1):			
Primary:			
Income from continuing operations	$ 3.58	$ 6.32	$ 2.79
Discontinued operations		.28	
Extraordinary item			(.27)
Cumulative effect on prior years of changes in accounting			.84
Net Income	$ 3.58	$ 6.60	$ 3.36
Fully diluted:			
Income from continuing operations	$ 3.20	$ 5.83	$ 2.79
Discontinued operations		.25	
Extraordinary item			(.27)
Cumulative effect on prior years of changes in accounting			.84
Net Income	$ 3.20	$ 6.08	$ 3.36
Pro forma amounts assuming that the changes in accounting made in 1978 were applied retroactively:			
Income before extraordinary item			$ 9,618
Per share (primary and fully diluted)			$ 2.79
Net income			$ 8,682
Per share (primary and fully diluted)			$ 2.52

See accompanying Notes to Consolidated Financial Statements.

* 1980 results were adversely affected by a 52-day strike by PSA's pilots.

22

PSA, Inc.
CONSOLIDATED STATEMENTS OF CHANGES IN FINANCIAL POSITION
(In thousands)

	Years ended December 31, 1980	1979	1978
Working capital was provided by:			
Continuing operations:			
Income	$ 12,653	$ 22,106	$ 9,618
Charges (credits) to income not involving working capital:			
Depreciation and amortization	20,113	19,055	16,239
Gain recognized on exchange of subsidiary for treasury shares (Note 5)	(7,644)		
Deferred federal income tax and other	(4,319)	5,182	2,404
Working capital from continuing operations	20,803	46,343	28,261
Discontinued operations - working capital effect		(445)	
Working capital provided from operations before extraordinary item and cumulative effect of changes in accounting	20,803	45,898	28,261
Extraordinary item - working capital effect			(1,800)
Cumulative effect on prior years of changes in accounting - working capital effect			(3,653)
Working capital provided from operations	20,803	45,898	22,808
Additions to long-term obligations	98,676	99,161	27,448
Stock of subsidiary exchanged to acquire treasury shares (carrying value of subsidiary stock - $8,284) (Note 5)	18,200		
Disposal of property and equipment	4,202	9,265	6,655
Refundable deposits on flight equipment purchase contracts	6,186		
Employee stock options exercised	364	528	276
Common stock issued on conversion of debentures	606		
Additions to deferred credits and other	4,451	1,269	5,254
Total working capital provided	153,488	156,121	62,441
Working capital was used for:			
Additions to property and equipment	64,988	84,792	46,664
Funds held in escrow for purchase of flight equipment	46,350		
Reductions in long-term obligations	48,482	67,211	14,640
Treasury shares acquired in exchange for subsidiary stock (substantially redistributed) (Note 5)	18,200		
Reduction in deferred credits and other	6,193	3,405	156
Dividends paid	1,617		
Payment of federal income tax (Note 6)		181	8,793
Total working capital used	185,830	155,589	70,253
Increase (decrease) in working capital	$(32,342)	$ 532	$ (7,812)
Working capital (deficit) at end of year	$(19,753)	$ 12,589	$ 12,057
Analysis of increase (decrease) in working capital:			
Cash and temporary investments	$(17,177)	$ 16,748	$ (797)
Accounts receivable and refundable income taxes	(4,044)	7,331	3,311
Maintenance and operating supplies, refundable deposits and prepaid expenses	9,886	8,462	583
Accounts payable and other accrued liabilities	(758)	(9,709)	(6,086)
Salaries, wages and vacation benefits payable	(1,732)	(1,949)	(5,784)
Air traffic liability	871	(5,826)	763
Income taxes payable	3,015	(3,017)	
Current portion of long-term obligations	(22,403)	(11,508)	198
	$(32,342)	$ 532	$ (7,812)

See accompanying Notes to Consolidated Financial Statements.

23

PSA, Inc.
CONSOLIDATED STATEMENTS OF STOCKHOLDERS' EQUITY
(In thousands)

	Common Stock	Additional Paid-in Capital	Retained Earnings	Treasury Stock	Total
Balance at December 31, 1977	$3,292	$36,170	$25,273		$ 64,735
Net income			11,587		11,587
Employee stock options exercised	54	222			276
Balance at December 31, 1978	3,346	36,392	36,860		76,598
Net income			23,097		23,097
Employee stock options exercised	80	448			528
Balance at December 31, 1979	3,426	36,840	59,957		100,223
Net income			12,653		12,653
Debt converted to stock (Note 2)	20	586			606
Stock redemption (Note 5)				$(18,200)	(18,200)
Stock dividend (Note 5)			(17,895)	17,842	(53)
Employee stock options exercised	45	242	(281)	358	364
Cash dividends			(1,564)		(1,564)
Balance at December 31, 1980	$3,491	$37,668	$52,870		$ 94,029

See accompanying Notes to Consolidated Financial Statements.

ARTHUR YOUNG

ARTHUR YOUNG & COMPANY
110 WEST A STREET, SUITE 1400
SAN DIEGO, CALIFORNIA 92101

The Board of Directors and Stockholders
PSA, Inc.

We have examined the accompanying consolidated balance sheets of PSA, Inc. at December 31, 1980 and 1979 and the related consolidated statements of income, stockholders' equity and changes in financial position for each of the three years in the period ended December 31, 1980. Our examinations were made in accordance with generally accepted auditing standards and, accordingly, included such tests of the accounting records and such other auditing procedures as we considered necessary in the circumstances.

In our opinion, the statements mentioned above present fairly the consolidated financial position of PSA, Inc. at December 31, 1980 and 1979 and the results of operations and changes in financial position for each of the three years in the period ended December 31, 1980, in conformity with generally accepted accounting principles consistently applied during the period subsequent to the changes, with which we concur, made as of January 1, 1978 in the method of accounting for vacation pay and investment tax credits as described in Note 1.

Arthur Young & Company

February 16, 1981

24

Reprinted by permission of PSA, Inc.

NOTES TO CONSOLIDATED FINANCIAL STATEMENTS

1. SUMMARY OF SIGNIFICANT ACCOUNTING POLICIES

Consolidation: The consolidated financial statements include the accounts of PSA, Inc. and its subsidiaries (PSA).

Depreciation and Amortization: Depreciation and amortization to estimated residual value is computed on the straight-line basis over the estimated useful lives of the related assets, which are up to 16 years for flight equipment and generally up to 10 years for other property and equipment.

Interest Capitalized: PSA capitalizes interest on deposits for flight equipment.

Retirement Plans: PSA maintains defined benefit retirement plans for many of its employees. In addition, a number of employees are included in a union-sponsored plan toward which PSA makes contributions. The cost of PSA's sponsored plans charged to operating expense was $5,782,000 in 1980, $4,630,000 in 1979 and $4,068,000 in 1978. The cost of future retirement benefits under PSA's plans is spread over the aggregate future service lives of the participants. It is PSA's policy to fund retirement costs accrued.

The actuarial present value of the vested and non-vested accumulated plan benefits at December 31, 1979 (the most recent benefit information date) was $20,407,000 and $6,324,000 respectively. The assumed rate of return used in determining these values was 6%. Net assets of the plans available for benefits were $44,856,000 at December 31, 1980.

Investment Tax Credit: Investment tax credit is accounted for using the flow-through method as a reduction of federal income tax expense.

Passenger Revenue: Passenger ticket sales are recognized as revenue when the transportation is used. The value of unused tickets is included in current liabilities until the transportation provided by PSA is used or until PSA is billed by other carriers for PSA tickets used for transportation provided by them.

Net Income Per Common Share: Primary net income per share is based on the weighted average number of shares outstanding during the period plus the number of shares issuable upon the exercise of stock options using the treasury stock method. Shares used in this per share calculation were 3,537,000 in 1980, 3,499,000 in 1979 and 3,453,000 in 1978.

Fully diluted net income per share for 1980 and 1979 is based on shares used in the primary calculation plus shares assumed issued on conversion of the convertible debentures which were issued in 1979. Net income is adjusted to eliminate the interest on the convertible debentures, net of the tax effect. Shares used in this calculation were 4,521,000 in 1980 and 3,921,000 in 1979.

Cumulative Effect of Accounting Changes Made In 1978: In 1978, PSA changed its method of accounting for vacation pay and investment tax credits to those used predominantly by the airline industry; the cumulative effect of these changes was to increase net income by $2,905,000.

2. LONG-TERM DEBT

Long-term debt consists of the following at December 31:

	1980	1979
	(in thousands)	
Senior debt:		
Equipment trust certificates, 90% guaranteed by U.S. Government bearing interest at 9-3/4% to prime plus 5/8%, due 1995	$ 61,693	
Equipment trust certificates bearing interest at 10.6%, due 1995	26,688	$ 28,594
Notes to aircraft manufacturer bearing interest at prime, due on delivery of DC-9-80 aircraft	5,388	15,347
Bank revolving credit agreement bearing interest at prime, due 1984	15,000	
Bank note bearing interest at 1/4% over prime, due 1981		6,000
Other	5,891	7,041
	$114,660	$ 56,982
Subordinated debt:		
11-1/8% convertible debentures, due 2004....	$ 29,393	$ 30,000
6% debentures, due 1987 (face amount: 1980, $9,812 and 1979, $14,341) less unamortized balance of original discount - effective interest rate 7-1/2%	9,212	13,594
	$ 38,605	$ 43,594

The equipment trust certificates guaranteed by the U.S. Government are secured by the funds held in escrow, one DC-9-80 aircraft and three spare engines. The carrying value of the one aircraft and three spare engines used as security is $22,810,000. The U.S. Government guarantees the payment of 90% of the unpaid principal on the notes and 100% of the unpaid interest on the notes.

The equipment trust certificates bearing interest at 10.6% are secured by three Boeing 727-200 aircraft and two spare engines (carrying value $36,954,000).

In March 1980, PSA entered into a revolving credit agreement for borrowings up to $30,000,000 as needed through December 31, 1984. $15,000,000 has been borrowed as of December 31, 1980; an additional $5,000,000 is currently available and another $10,000,000 will become available in March 1981.

The subordinated convertible debentures are convertible at $30 per share, subject to adjustment in certain events; sinking fund payments of $1,500,000 are due annually commencing August 1, 1989. The debentures are redeemable at 110.383% of par plus accrued interest before August 1, 1981, declining annually to par on August 1, 1994.

As of December 31, 1980, PSA had purchased and retired $5,268,000 face amount of the 6% subordinated debentures in excess of sinking fund requirements. This amount will be applied against future sinking fund requirements of $1,560,000 due annually on October 1.

Principal payments and sinking fund requirements on long-term debt in each of the four years after 1981 are as follows: $13,658,000 in 1982; $7,426,000 in 1983; $22,546,000 in 1984; and $8,147,000 in 1985. 1981 and 1982 principal payments include manufacturer's notes of $22,867,000 and $5,388,000 respectively, which PSA intends to refinance at maturity.

All of the $52,870,000 of retained earnings are represented by undistributed earnings of subsidiaries. Under the most restrictive terms of PSA's various loan agreements, $3,807,000 of these undistributed retained earnings at December 31, 1980 are not restricted as to the payment of cash dividends.

3. LEASES

The following is a schedule by year of future minimum lease payments (before applying minimum future non-cancellable sublease rentals) together with the present value of minimum lease payments under capital leases as of December 31, 1980:

	Capital leases	Operating leases
	(in thousands)	
1981	$ 5,146	$ 3,126
1982	4,785	2,958
1983	4,424	2,896
1984	4,424	1,455
1985	4,424	1,278
Later years	23,332	10,300
Total minimum lease payments	46,535	$22,013
Less: Amount representing interest	17,113	
Present value of minimum lease payments	$29,422	

PSA's capital leases are for three aircraft, including two L-1011's which are subleased through September 1982, and a jet engine maintenance facility. Operating leases are principally for aircraft and airport and maintenance facilities.

PSA's operating leases generally require PSA to maintain the facilities or equipment, carry insurance and pay certain taxes which may be levied on the leased property. There are no material rent escalation provisions in PSA's leases. Rental expense under operating leases aggregated $4,504,000 in 1980, $3,756,000 in 1979 and $2,961,000 in 1978.

27

4. EXTRAORDINARY ITEM AND DISCONTINUED OPERATIONS

In 1978 all pending antitrust litigation between PSA, another airline and its parent company was settled. The settlement, net of previously accrued legal fees and expenses, resulted in an extraordinary charge of $1,800,000 ($936,000 net of the deferred income tax effect) in 1978.

In 1975, a program was adopted for the disposition of PSA's hotel and radio broadcasting operations. Prior to 1979 all operations had been disposed of except for two hotels. PSA's interest in one of these hotels was terminated during 1979, and the remaining unused loss provision was eliminated in 1979 because the unsold hotel was operating profitably. During 1980 PSA's interest in the remaining hotel was sold.

5. STOCK REDEMPTION AND REDISTRIBUTION

In 1980, PSA redeemed 700,000 shares of its common stock owned by Valhi, Inc. The redemption was a tax-free exchange of the 700,000 shares for all of the outstanding shares of PSA's subsidiary, Jetair Leasing, Inc., the sole assets of which were four Boeing 727-200 aircraft. The redeemed shares were redistributed in the form of a 25% stock dividend declared on February 26, 1980. Commencing on the closing of the transaction Pacific Southwest Airlines leased the four aircraft through April 30, 1981 for a total rental of $8,712,000. The following table reflects the components and net effects of the exchange and share distribution:

	Income effect of transaction	Effect on stockholders' equity - increase (decrease)
	(in thousands)	
Shares redeemed (redistributed via 25% stock dividend):		
700,000 shares of PSA, Inc. valued at $26 per share - market value	$18,200	$(18,200)
Less:		
Net book value of the four Jetair aircraft	10,052	
Deferred tax on depreciation timing differences	(1,768)	
	8,284	
Gain on exchange before effect of future rentals (not subject to tax)	9,916	
Less rent expense (net of tax)	4,281	
Net gain from exchange	$ 5,635	5,635
Cumulative effect on stockholders' equity through April 30, 1981		$(12,565)

The net gain recorded from this transaction during 1980 was $4,587,000 ($1.30 per share primary and $1.01 per share fully diluted).

Because the common stock dividend was planned coincidently with the common stock redemption from Valhi, Inc., and the number of outstanding shares of common stock remained the same after the common stock dividend as before the common stock redemption, no retroactive adjustments have been made for the stock dividend to previously published per-share amounts. The effect of such retroactive adjustment, if it had been made, would have been to reduce earnings per share prior to the stock dividend by approximately 20%; i.e., primary income from continuing operations per common share would have been $3.46, in 1980, $5.27 in 1979 and $2.32 in 1978, and $3.11, $4.95 and $2.32 fully diluted.

6. PROVISION FOR TAXES BASED ON INCOME

Provision for taxes based on income consists of the following:

	1980	1979	1978
		(in thousands)	
Current:			
Federal, before investment tax credit	$(1,536)	$ 8,588	$ 7,969
Investment tax credit		(4,748)	(2,886)
Cumulative effect of change in accounting for investment tax credit			(4,805)
Excess of tax over book investment tax credit		(1,676)	(124)
Net current - federal	(1,536)	2,164	154
State	1,665	757	644
Deferred	2,608	9,268	(4,756)
Tax savings resulting from stock redemption (Note 5)	(1,768)		
	$ 969	$ 12,189	$ (3,958)

Included in the accompanying consolidated statements of income as:

	1980	1979	1978
Provision for taxes - continuing operations	$ 969	$ 11,274	$ 3,464
Provision for taxes - discontinued operations		915	
Extraordinary item			(864)
Cumulative effect of changes in accounting			(6,558)
	$ 969	$ 12,189	$ (3,958)

Deferred taxes result from timing differences in the recognition of revenue and expense for tax and financial statement purposes. The source of these differences and the tax effect of each were as follows:

	1980	1979	1978
		(in thousands)	
Depreciation	$ 2,390	$ 3,224	$ 621
L-1011 loss settlement	9,859		
Discontinued operations		2,194	
Capitalized interest	2,990	1,861	(598)
Investment tax credit:			
Arising from current year investments	(3,370)		
Available due to tax loss carryback	(11,375)		
Carryforward		1,676	124
Accrued insurance premium	583	470	(1,280)
Gains on disposition of flight equipment		(426)	(2,456)
Accrued vacation expense	466	434	(2,291)
Interest on tax payment	961	169	926
Deferred revenue	(707)		(374)
Rent expense	763	(445)	
Other	48	111	572
	$ 2,608	$ 9,268	$(4,756)

A reconciliation between the amount computed by multiplying income before taxes by the statutory federal rate, and the amount of reported taxes on income is as follows:

	Percent of income before taxes		
	1980	1979	1978
Statutory federal rate	46%	46%	48%
Increase (reductions) in taxes resulting from:			
Investment credits, net of recapture	(25)	(14)	(22)
State income taxes, net of federal income tax benefit	14	1	3
Capital gains tax rate on disposition of flight equipment			(5)
Non-taxable gain on exchange for common stock (Note 5)	(33)		
Other	5	1	2
	7%	34%	26%

PSA has received statutory notices of deficiency from the Internal Revenue Service (IRS) proposing additional federal income taxes in the amount of $6.8 million for the years 1971-1974. PSA has paid the proposed tax deficiencies, and has contested all the major issues raised by the IRS in the notices of deficiency by filing claims for refund. In the opinion of management, adequate provision has been made for the tax deficiencies plus related interest, and the resolution of this matter will not have a material adverse effect on PSA's financial condition or results of operations. The amount of unused investment tax credit for tax return purposes at December 31, 1980 will depend on the ultimate resolution of this matter.

7. COMMITMENTS

At December 31, 1980, PSA had an agreement for the purchase of 19 DC-9-80 aircraft, twelve of which are scheduled for delivery in 1981 and seven in 1982. In addition, PSA has on order two spare engines, a DC-9-80 simulator and other spare parts related to the above aircraft. Future expenditures for the aircraft and spare equipment will approximate $293,000,000 during the years 1981 and 1982.

PSA has an option exercisable through May 1, 1981 to purchase six additional DC-9-80 aircraft for 1983 delivery.

8. STOCK OPTIONS

Under PSA's stock option plan, options for 117,000 shares of common stock were outstanding at December 31, 1980 at prices from $3.19 to $19.98 per share (all of which were exercisable). During 1980, options for 105,000 shares were exercised at prices ranging from $3.19 to $13.77 per share. Options granted in 1980, 1979 and 1978 were 49,000, 4,000 and 67,000 respectively and options exercised were 105,000, 80,000 and 54,000 respectively.

Options for 118,000 shares are available for grant at prices not less than 85% of the market value on date of grant and expire ten years after grant. Options become exercisable six months after date of grant.

At December 31, 1980, options for 19,000 shares are outstanding which provide an alternative settlement of issuance of cash or stock equivalent in value to the difference between the aggregate stock option price and market value on the date of exercise, subject to certain approvals and limitations.

9. BUSINESS SEGMENTS

PSA operates two principal business segments consisting of the airlines, which provides primarily passenger service, and a jet engine overhaul facility, which provides maintenance and overhaul services for airlines and other customers. Intersegment sales are made at prevailing market prices.

	Airlines	Jet engine maintenance	Other operations	Intersegment sales	Consolidated
			(In thousands)		
Revenues:					
1980	$322,267	$43,865	$10,758	$(6,686)	$370,204
1979	292,906	40,337	8,733	(6,138)	335,838
1978	206,138	24,040	4,948	(5,241)	229,885
Operating income:					
1980	6,236	5,297	580		12,113
1979	35,696	4,098	271		40,065
1978	13,707	866	(371)		14,202
Identifiable assets at December 31:					
1980	362,619	21,575	9,405		393,599
1979	281,938	24,657	19,089		325,684
1978	195,935	18,880	13,537		228,352
Depreciation and amortization:					
1980	18,843	437	833		20,113
1979	17,930	398	727		19,055
1978	15,508	375	356		16,239
Capital expenditures:					
1980	63,206	459	1,323		64,988
1979	82,847	379	1,566		84,792
1978	45,155	77	1,432		46,664

SOLUTIONS

1. b	6. c	11. b
2. b	7. b	12. e ($57,174)
3. c	8. d	13. b
4. c	9. e	14. a (There is theoretical support for d also.)
5. b	10. d	15. c

	1980	*1979*			
16.	0.79/1	1.17/1	20.	3.4%	6.9%
17.	0.44/1	0.88/1	21.	$3.58	$6.60
18.	1.92/1	1.30/1	22.	13.5%	23%
19.	97%	88%	23.	3.2%	7.1%

24. Can't be determined from the data given. You might divide inventories by maintenance expense, but the result would be relatively meaningless.

25. 11.17/1 4.55/1

26. Additions to long-term obligations, in 1980, $98,676,000 in 1979, $99,161,000.

27. Additions to property and equipment, in 1980, $64,988,000; in 1979, $84,792,000.

28. In 1980, $20,803,000; in 1979, $45,898,000.

29. In 1980, a deficit in working capital of $19,753,000; in 1979, working capital was $12,589,000.

30. This is a tough question since a 52-day strike by the pilots of PSA materially affected operations. In 1979, at a price of $30 per share, PSA appears to be a good buy. But in 1980, at a price of $40 per share, with decreased liquidity, a substantial drop in EPS, and a long-term debt ratio of 2/1, investors should be cautious in the short-term. For the longer term, based on past performance, the stock is a good candidate for growth.

Glossary/Index

Note: Most of the items included in the glossary are referenced to specific pages in the text. Some additional definitions are included for general reader interest in other terms used in accounting.

accelerated depreciation (p. 161 et seq.)
A depreciation method that charges off more of the original basis of the asset in the earlier years of the economic life of the assets (such as sum-of-the-years'-digits method, double-declining balance method).
account (p. 45, 60)
A subdivision of a ledger in which the changes for a single balance sheet account or income statement account are recorded.
account payable (p. 81)
An amount owed by the business entity, usually to one of its creditors.
account receivable (p. 80, 126)
An amount owed to the business entity, usually by one of its customers.
accounting cycle (p. 32)
The basic steps in the processing of accounting data, including capturing original transaction data, journalizing, posting, and preparing financial statements.
accounting period (p. 17)
The time between the scheduled closing of the accounting records and the preparation of financial statements, usually one year. Sometimes referred to as an annual accounting period as distinguished from an interim accounting period.
accounting principles
All the concepts, standards, conventions, rules, procedures, and codification of practices that make up accepted accounting practice.
accounting system (p. 32)
The procedures that proscribe the capture, conver-

sion, and retention of accounting data from source documents to financial statements.

accounts receivable turnover (p. 251)
A financial analysis ratio that is calculated from the formula:

$$\frac{\text{Net credit sales}}{\text{Average accounts receivable}} = \text{Accounts receivable turnover ration}$$

accrual basis (p. 79)
The matching process whereby expenses are matched with realized revenues irrespective of when cash is received or disbursed.

accrued expense (p. 89)
An expense that has been incurred but that is not yet due and payable.

accrued revenue (p. 91)
Revenue earned but not yet billed to a customer.

accumulated depreciation (p. 99, 160 et seq.)
The cumulative sum of all depreciation recognized since the date of acquisition of a particular asset or group of assets. This account, called a "contra asset" account, is ordinarily deducted from the related fixed asset accounts in the financial statements.

additional paid-in capital (p. 186)
Capital contributed by the shareholders in excess of the par or stated value of issued capital stock (contained in the stockholders' equity section of the balance sheet).

adjusting entry
A journal entry made for the purpose of correcting or adjusting one or more general ledger accounts. A surrogate for a journal entry, which is illustrated in this text by using T-accounts.

affiliated company
A company that has 20 to 50 percent of its voting shares owned by another company or two companies that have a common ownership.

allowance for doubtful accounts (p. 126)
An account that represents management's best estimate of the total amount of accounts receivable that will ultimately become uncollectible. This account, a "contra asset" account, is ordinarily deducted from the related accounts receivable account in the financial statements.

amortization (p. 166)
A method of allocating the cost of an intangible asset to the appropriate accounting period.

asset (p. 2, 4)
An economic resource of a business entity that is expected to benefit future activities and that is measurable.

audit
An examination made by Certified Public Accountants in accordance with generally accepted auditing standards. The audit is usually performed on an annual basis, and the auditor's certificate is contained in the annual report of the business entity.

bad debt (p. 126)
An account receivable that becomes uncollectible.

balance sheet (p. 2 et seq.)
A "snapshot" of a business entity listing assets and equities as they appear at a given moment of time.

bank reconciliation (p. 148 et seq.)
A computation that explains the differences between the balance shown by the current bank statement and the balance shown by the corresponding account on the books of the business entity.

bond (p. 176, 187)
A certificate that evidences a written promise of the business entity to repay a stipulated amount (usually in denominations of $1,000) at a specified time and that bears interest at a specified rate.

bond discount (*see* **discount on bonds**)

book value (p. 192)
A shortened expression for book value per share, which is computed by the following formula:

$$\frac{\text{Shareholder's equity} - \text{Claims of preferred stock}}{\text{Common stock shares outstanding}}$$

capital stock (p. 185)
A shareholder's equity account setting forth the par or stated value of stock when originally issued. When there is more than one class of stock, the designations "common stock" and "preferred stock" are usually employed.

cash basis (p. 78)
A method of accounting that takes into account only the cash actually received by the business entity and the cash actually disbursed, as opposed to accrual basis.

cash discounts
A reduction in the invoice price granted to customers or suppliers for prompt payment.

certified public accountant (CPA)
An accountant who has passed a rigorous examination, who has met the experience requirements of state law, and who is therefore entitled to conduct audits of business entities and to express an opinion thereon.

charts of accounts
A comprehensive listing of all accounts utilized by a business entity in its ledgers, together with a corresponding identification or coding reference.

check register
A cash disbursements journal; a book of original entry used in connection with a voucher system.

common-size financial statements (p. 19, 245)
A methodology that permits comparison of business entities of different sizes by expressing balance sheet

items as a percentage of total assets and income statement items as a percentage of net sales.

common stock (p. 189)
That portion of the capital stock of a corporation that comprises the "residual" ownership of a corporation.

conservatism
A basic tenet of accounting that requires the accountant to state the value of an asset at the lower of two acceptable amounts as, for example, the lower of cost or market.

consistency
A basic principle of accounting that requires accounting transactions to be recorded using the same methodology in consecutive accounting periods to facilitate comparative analysis of financial statements.

consolidated statements (p. 209)
Financial statements of two or more separate legal entities that have a parent subsidiary relationship, presented as one economic entity.

constant dollar accounting (p. 260 et seq.)
A method of reporting financial statement elements in dollars, each of which has the same, general purchasing power. This method of accounting is often described as accounting in units of general purchasing power or as accounting in units of current purchasing power [FASB #33, p. 9].

contra account (p. 53)
An account used to value another account as, for example, Allowance for doubtful accounts and accumulated depreciation.

contributed capital (p. 21)
The total amount originally invested by shareholders of a corporation. Contributed capital is distinguished in the shareholder's equity section of the balance sheet from Retained earnings.

convertible bonds
Bonds that may, at the holder's option, be exchanged for other securities as, for example, preferred or common stock.

corporation (p. 21)
One of the three forms that business entities may have (the other two being individual proprietorships and partnerships). A corporation is an "artificial person" created by state law and thus enabled to sell shares of stock and to transact business as if it were a natural person.

cost of goods sold (p. 17, 101 et seq., 138)
An expense that summarizes (and matches) the cost of merchandise sold with the revenue realized from the sale. Calculated from the formula:

$$\text{Beginnings inventory} + \text{Purchases (net)} - \text{Ending inventory} = \text{Cost of goods sold}$$

$$I_b + P - I_e = CGS$$

credit (p. 47 et seq.)
The right-hand side of a ledger account.

creditor
One who extends credit or who loans money to a business entity.

cumulative preferred stock
Stock that, by contract, accumulates dividends which, if not declared, must be paid before a dividend can be declared on the common stock.

current asset (p. 8)
An asset that will be converted into cash during the normal operating cycle of a business entity, usually one year.

current cost accounting (p. 264 et seq.)
A method of measuring and reporting assets and expenses associated with the use or sale of assets, at their current cost or lower recoverable amount at the balance sheet date or at the date of use or sale [FASB #33, p. 91].

current liability (p. 8, 172 et seq.)
A liability that will require the expenditure of cash during the normal operating cycle of a business entity, usually one year.

current ratio (p. 173, 174, 247)
The most frequently used ratio in assessing short-term liquidity of a business entity, computed by the following formula:

$$\frac{\text{Current assets}}{\text{Current liabilities}} = \text{Current ratio}$$

debenture
An unsecured long-term bond.

debit (p. 47 et seq.)
The left-hand side of a ledger account.

deferred income taxes (p. 175, 263)
Additional income taxes that would have been due had the corporation not taken advantage of additional deductions allowable for income tax purposes (a noncurrent liability).

deferred revenue (p. 91, 175)
Unearned revenue.

deficit
The accumulated net losses of a corporation.

depletion (p. 168)
A method of allocating the cost of a wasting asset to the appropriate accounting period.

depreciation (p. 98 et seq., 158 et seq.)
A method of allocating the cost of Property, plant and equipment to the appropriate accounting period.

disbursement (p. 149 et seq.)
Payment.

discount on bonds (p. 76)
The excess of the face value of the bond over the proceeds from the sale of that bond.

dividends (p. 21, 190)
Funds generated by the corporation that are paid out to the shareholders.

dividend/yield ratio
A financial measure of cash received by shareholders that is calculated by the following formula:

$$\frac{\text{Common stock dividends/share}}{\text{Market price/share}}$$

double-declining balance depreciation (DDB) (p. 161, 163)
An accelerated depreciation method that is calculated from the following formula:

$$\frac{2 \times \begin{matrix}\text{Original} \\ \text{cost of asset}\end{matrix} - \begin{matrix}\text{Accumulated} \\ \text{depreciation}\end{matrix}}{\text{Years of useful life}}$$

double-entry accounting (p. 33 et seq.)
The method of accounting usually employed today whereby each transaction can be analyzed and recorded within the following conceptual framework:

$$A + E = L + R + SE$$

earnings per share (EPS) (p. 21, 249)
A financial measure of the share of earnings allocable to each common share of stock. The calculation is as follows:

$$\frac{\text{Net income (after preferred stock requirements)}}{\text{Common stock shares outstanding}}$$

effective interest rate (p. 177)
The market rate on the day of issuance of a bond. Subsequent differences between this rate and the rate printed on the bond causes the bond to sell at a premium or at a discount on the issue date.
equities (p. 4, 184 et seq.)
Claims against the assets of a business entity that can be divided into two general classes—liabilities and shareholder's (owner's) equity.
equity capital (p. 185 et seq.)
The capital raised from shareholders.
ex dividend (p. 190)
Refers to the day that the purchaser would not be entitled to the dividend; the date of record.
expense (p. 17, 124)
A decrease in shareholders' (owners') equity resulting from operations of the business entity.
extraordinary item
An unusual and infrequent material expense or revenue that, together with its tax effects, is shown separately from income on continuing operations in the income statement.
fair market value (FMV) (p. 140-142)
Replacement cost of an inventoriable asset but not in excess of its net realizable value (NRV), nor less than its net realizable value reduced by a normal profit margin.

financial accounting
A branch of accounting concerned with external reporting and therefore centered around financial statements, their preparation, and interpretation.
financial accounting standards board (FASB) (p. 260, 262, 263)
An independent board that functions as the primary regulatory body over accounting principles. It is composed of members from all segments of the private sector of our economy. It issues pronouncements such as FASB #33 on inflation accounting.
first-in/first-out (FIFO) (p. 137)
A method of accounting for inventory that assumes that the first item purchased is the first one sold.
fiscal year (p. 1)
The accounting year of a business entity, which may or may not coincide with the calendar year.
fixed assets (p. 158 et seq.)
The category of long-lived, tangible assets used in the conduct of its operations by a business entity. In this book, this class of assets is referred to simply as Property, plant, and equipment.
franchise
A privilege granted by a government, manufacturer, or distributor to sell a product or service in accordance with specified conditions.
freight-in (p. 131)
Freight charges paid by the business entity on purchased merchandise.
freight-out
Freight charges paid by the business entity on merchandise sold to customers.
GAAP
Generally accepted accounting principle.
general journal (p. 33)
A book of original entry in which all transactions are entered that do not fit into well-defined categories encompassed by the special journals maintained as an integral part of the accounting system.
general ledger (p. 33)
A summary by account classification of all the accounts used by the business entity including assets, liabilities, shareholders' equity, revenue, and expense accounts.
going concern assumption
The accounting concept underlying financial statements that the business entity will continue operations into the indefinite future.
goodwill (p. 221)
The excess of the fair market value of an acquired business entity over the fair market value of its individual, identifiable assets.
gross margin (p. 19)

$$\text{Net sales} - \begin{matrix}\text{Cost} \\ \text{of goods sold}\end{matrix} = \text{Gross margin.}$$

(Synonymous with Gross profit.)

gross margin percentage (p. 19, 125, 248)

$$\frac{\text{Gross margin}}{\text{Net sales}} = \text{Gross margin percentage}$$

holding gains (p. 264)
Increases in the measure of current value of the assets held during the current accounting period.
income (earnings) (p. 16 et seq., 124)
A shorthand expression for Net income, which is the difference between Revenues and Expenses for the current accounting period.
income statement (p. 16 et seq., 124)
One of the main financial statements that shows the calculation of Net income in some detail for the current accounting period.
intangible asset
An asset that grants rights to the owner but that has no physical existence in and of itself (such as patents, trademarks, goodwill).
interim statements (p. 17)
Financial statements prepared between annual accounting periods, usually quarterly although sometimes on a monthly basis.
internal control
The portion of the accounting system concerned primarily with the prevention of errors and irregularities in the operations of the business entity.
inventories (p. 101, 130A)
Merchandise held for sale in the normal course of business.
inventory turnover (p. 132, 251)
A financial analysis ratio calculated from the following formula:

$$\frac{\text{Cost of goods sold}}{\text{Average inventory}} = \text{Inventory turnover ratio}$$

invoice
A document that provides the details of a transaction between a buyer and seller. Can be either a sales invoice or a purchase invoice.
journal (p. 33)
A book of original entry that provides a chronological record of business transactions. Special journals are devoted to particular kinds of business transactions, such as the sales journal, the purchase journal, or the cash receipts journal.
last-in/first-out (LIFO) (p. 137)
A method of accounting for inventory that assumes that the last item purchased is the first one sold.
lease
A contract between the rentor of an asset and its owner specifying the terms of the agreement.
leasehold improvements
Tangible assets acquired by a rentor affixed to the rental property which cannot be removed at the expiration of the lease.
ledger (p. 33)
A book of final entry that summarizes transactions by type of account.
leverage (p. 187 et seq.)
If the shareholders of a business can borrow money to finance new business ventures, they are able to control a larger amount of assets with a given capital structure. This ability is therefore called "leveraging."
liabilities (p. 2, 172 et seq.)
Claims by creditors on the assets of a business entity.
long-term debt (p. 8)
Liabilities that are due more than one year from the balance sheet date. Mortgages and bonds payable are typical examples of these long-term liabilities.
lower of cost or market (LCM) (p. 140)
An example of the conservative approach that underlies the preparation of financial statements and that requires, for example, marketable securities to be stated at the lower of cost or market on the balance sheet.
management accounting
Concerned mainly with how accounting can serve internal decision makers [Horngren, *Fin. Acc.*, p. 724].
marketable securities (p. 151)
Temporary investments that have a well-defined market value and that can be converted into cash within a short period of time—a current asset.
matching concept (p. 81)
The underlying principle of the accrual basis of accounting that requires realized revenue to be matched with related expenses. The timing of payments and receipts is not relevant to matching.
monetary asset (liability) (p. 262)
An asset (or liability) that remains fixed in dollar amount regardless of fluctuations in either general or specific price levels.
mortgage (p. 176)
A liability to repay to a creditor a specific sum at a specific interest rate over a long period of time. This promise to pay is secured by a lien on real property.
net income (p. 17, 248)
The excess of all revenues and gains for a period over all expenses and losses. [Horngren, *Fin. Acc.*, p. 725].
net monetary position (p. 263)
The excess of monetary assets over monetary liabilities or the reverse.
net realizable value (NRV) (p. 140)
The net amount that an item can be sold for, calculated by taking the selling price of the item and deducting the costs of completing and selling the item. It can be expressed by the following formula:

$$\text{NRV} = \text{Selling price} - \text{Costs to complete and sell}$$

next-in/first-out (NIFO)
A method of accounting for inventory that assumes

that the next item to be purchased is the first one sold; the replacement cost method of inventory valuation.

nominal dollars (p. 260 et seq.)
The opposite of constant dollars; historical cost; dollars that are not restated for changes in the purchasing power of the dollar.

nominal interest rate (p. 176)
A contractual rate of interest paid on bonds. Sometimes called the coupon rate [Horngren, *Fin. Acc.*, p. 725].

nonmonetary items (p. 263)
Those items in financial statements not classified as monetary; principally inventories, property, plant, and equipment.

no-par stock
Stock without par value.

note payable (p. 174)
Debt of a business entity evidenced by a written promise to pay, together with the terms applying to the transaction. As opposed to Account payable, which is simply an "open account."

note receivable
Asset of a business entity evidenced by a written promise to pay, together with the terms applying to the transaction. As opposed to Account receivable, which is simply an "open account."

open account
Buying or selling by a business entity on credit, resulting in an account payable or an account receivable, based on mutual trust between the parties.

operating cycle
The conversion of inventory into accounts receivable and eventually into cash, which is then used to pay trade creditors so that more inventory can be purchased. The normal operations of a business entity.

operating expenses (p. 17, 126, 248)
Expenses that include administrative, selling, and warehousing activities and that are deducted from Gross margin in arriving at Operating income on the income statement.

organization expense
Costs incurred in forming a corporation, including attorney's fees, state charter fees, and the like, which become an asset of the corporation subject to amortization.

owner's equity (p. 2, 3, 4)
The equity claim of an owner in a business; applied specifically to proprietorships and partnerships. Called "shareholders' or Stockholders' equity" in the case of a corporation.

Owner's equity = Assets − Liabilities

paid-in capital
The amount paid in by shareholders at the inception of the business and upon any subsequent sales of stock by the corporation in excess of the par or stated value of capital stock.

parent company (p. 219 et seq.)
A company owning more than 50 percent of another company.

partnership
An unincorporated business that has two or more owners.

par value
The value printed on the face of the stock certificate.

patents
Grants by the federal government to inventors, giving them the exclusive right to produce and to sell their inventions for seventeen years.

periodic inventory
The method of accounting used in this text that assumes that physical inventories will be taken at the end of each accounting period. See Physical inventory.

perpetual inventory
A method of accounting for inventory so that each purchase and sale is automatically entered into the account as it occurs, thus enabling management to know the balance in the inventory without taking a physical inventory.

petty cash
A small fund of money held by a business entity to pay small bills.

physical inventory
The counting of each item on hand, usually at the end of the accounting period, to compute the cost of goods sold and to establish a value for the ending inventory on the balance sheet. It is called the "periodic inventory system" as opposed to the perpetual inventory system.

pooling-of-interests method (p. 218)
A methodology for business combinations that assumes both businesses continue in operation as before the combination, that assets therefore retain their precombination values, and that equities are merely added to obtain the combined value of the merged business.

posting (p. 33)
The act of transferring amounts from the journal to the ledger.

preemptive rights
The rights of an existing shareholder to acquire a pro rata share of any new issue of capital stock.

preferred stock (p. 189)
Capital stock that is preferred with respect to payment of dividends and to repayment upon liquidation.

premium on bonds
The excess of the proceeds of the bond over the face value of the bond.

prepaid expense (p. 88)
An expense paid for in advance and usually including

such items as insurance, rent, and interest. Classified as a current asset on the balance sheet.

pretax income
Net income before deduction for income taxes.

price-earnings (P/E) ratio
The financial ratio most closely watched by investment analysts, it is calculated from the following formula:

$$\frac{\text{Market value per share}}{\text{Earnings per share}} = \text{P/E ratio}$$

primary earnings per share (p. 21)
Net income (applicable to common shareholders) divided by the number of common shares of stock outstanding.

proprietorship (p. 4, 184)
A business entity with a single owner (not incorporated).

purchase method (p. 219)
A method of accounting used in consolidated financial statement whereby one corporation purchases another financial statement.

quick asset ratio (also called acid-test ratio) (p. 173, 174, 247)
A short-term liquidity measurement ratio:

$$\text{Quick asset ratio} = \frac{\text{Quick assets}}{\text{Current liabilities}}$$

quick assets (p. 247)
Cash and near-cash items on a balance sheet—usually Cash + Temporary investments + Accounts receivable = Quick assets.

realization
The accounting principle that recognizes revenue at the time the delivery is made, regardless of the terms of payment or the contract to purchase.

receiving report
An original source document evidencing the receipt of goods at the buyer's receiving dock.

retained earnings (p. 21)
The accumulated net earnings of a business less any distributions made to shareholders over the life span of the corporation. If Net losses exceed Net income over time, the word "deficit" is used.

return on stockholders' equity (p. 251)
A profitability ratio that measures management's efficiency with respect to the use of the shareholder's capital investment. The formula is:

$$\text{ROI} = \frac{\text{Net earnings (applicable to common stock)}}{\text{Stockholders' equity}}$$

revenue (p. 17, 124)
An increase in shareholders' (owners') equity resulting from operations of the business entity.

sales (p. 19, 33, 124)
Revenues arising from tangible goods delivered to a customer.

salvage value
The estimated amount that Property, plant, and equipment items can be sold for the end of their useful life.

shareholders (p. 184 et seq.)
Stockholders, the owners of shares of a corporation.

source documents (p. 32)
Original evidence of the occurrence of a business event, such as a canceled check, sales invoice, receiving report, and the like.

statement of changes in contributed capital (p. 192, 193)
A financial statement that explains the changes in the capital stock and related accounts during the current accounting period.

statement of changes in financial position
A required financial statement that explains the change in noncurrent assets, liabilities, and owners' equity during the current accounting period.

statement of retained earnings (p. 192, 193)
The financial statement that explains the changes in Retained earnings during the current account period. The basic calculation is:

$$\begin{array}{c}\text{Retained}\\\text{earnings}\\\text{(ending)}\end{array} = \begin{array}{c}\text{Retained}\\\text{earnings}\\\text{(beginning)}\end{array} + \begin{array}{c}\text{Net}\\\text{income}\end{array} - \text{Dividends}$$

stock dividend (p. 191)
A dividend paid in capital stock of the corporation rather than in cash as happens more frequently.

stockholders (p. 184 et seq.)
Shareholders, the owners of shares of a corporation.

stock split (p. 191)
An increase in the issued stock of a corporation without affecting the dollar value of shareholders' equity. As, for example, a 2-to-1 stock split for which no accounting entry is required.

straight-line depreciation (p. 161)
A method of depreciation that provides a constant write-off during the life of the tangible asset. The formula is:

$$\text{Annual depreciation} = \frac{\text{Original cost} - \text{Salvage value}}{= \text{Economic life (in years)}}$$

subsidiary (p. 219)
A firm that is owned or controlled (more than 50 percent) by another firm.

subsidiary ledger
A ledger that gives the detail of an account in the general ledger. Examples include Accounts receivable, Accounts payable, and Property, plant and equipment ledgers.

sum-of-the-years'-digits depreciation (p. 161 et seq.)
An accelerated depreciation method that is calculated from the following formula:

$$\frac{\text{Original cost of assets} - \text{Salvage value}}{\text{Sum-of-years-of useful life}} \times R$$

where R is the remaining life of the asset in years.
supplier
A creditor, someone who sells merchandise to a business entity for resale.
T-account (p. 47 et seq.)
The method employed in this book to teach accounting concepts. The "T" is suggestive of a ledger account and can be used as a problem-solving device, as well as a means of preparing rather simple financial statements. This method is not used in practice because it is too informal.
tangible asset
Property, plant, equipment, and inventories, as opposed to Intangible assets such as accounts receivable.
trade discount
A method of printing catalogs with list prices from which trade discounts are deducted in figuring selling prices. A change in price requires only a change in the trade discount and the catalog need not be reprinted.
transaction (p. 32)
A business event that is entered in the accounting records of the business entity.
treasury stock (p. 186)
Previously issued stock that has been repurchased by the corporation and is held for reissuance.
trial balance
A test to see whether debits equal credits in order to insure the arithmetic accuracy of the accounts. Note that such a test does not guarantee that the posting was made to the proper account.
unbilled revenue
Work that has been done or services rendered and for which no bill has been rendered. A current asset.
underwriter
A firm that purchases bonds or stock from an issuing firm and resells these securities to the general public.
unearned revenue (p. 175)
Cash that has been received for which the service has not yet been performed. Examples include magazine subscriptions and airline tickets.
working capital (p. 173, 230)
Current assets − Current liabilities = Working capital
working capital ratio (p. 247)
See Current ratio.